Pro Entity Framework 4.0

Scott Klein

Apress®

Pro Entity Framework 4.0

ISBN-13 (pbk): 978-1-59059-990-7

ISBN-13 (electronic): 978-1-4302-0648-4

Printed and bound in the United States of America 9 8 7 6 5 4 3 2 1

Publisher and President: Paul Manning
Lead Editor: Jonathan Gennick
Technical Reviewer: Vidya Vrat Agarwal
Editorial Board: Clay Andres, Steve Anglin, Mark Beckner, Ewan Buckingham, Gary
    Cornell, Jonathan Gennick, Jonathan Hassell, Michelle Lowman, Matthew Moodie,
    Duncan Parkes, Jeffrey Pepper, Frank Pohlmann, Douglas Pundick, Ben Renow-Clarke,
    Dominic Shakeshaft, Matt Wade, Tom Welsh
Project Manager: Anita Castro
Copy Editor: Tiffany Taylor and Mary Ann Fugate
Compositor: Bob Cooper
Indexer: BIM Indexing & Proofreading Services
Artist: April Milne
Cover Designer: Anna Ishchenko

Distributed to the book trade worldwide by Springer-Verlag New York, Inc., 233 Spring Street, 6th Floor, New York, NY 10013. Phone 1-800-SPRINGER, fax 201-348-4505, e-mail orders-ny@springer-sbm.com, or visit www.springeronline.com.

For information on translations, please e-mail rights@apress.com, or visit www.apress.com.

Apress and friends of ED books may be purchased in bulk for academic, corporate, or promotional use. eBook versions and licenses are also available for most titles. For more information, reference our Special Bulk Sales–eBook Licensing web page at www.apress.com/info/bulksales.

To my parents, Richard and Carolyn.

Contents at a Glance

Contents

About the Author

 **Scott Klein** is a Microsoft SQL Server MVP and independent consultant specializing in SQL Server performance and business intelligence. Scott is the author of several books including *Professional SQL Server 2005 XML, Professional LINQ,* and *Professional Windows Communication Foundation,* and was a contributing author on *Pro SQL Server 2008 Relational Database Design and Implementation* as well as *Microsoft SQL Server 2008 Bible.* Scott has also written many articles for *SQL Server Standard* magazine. Scott holds the MCDBA, MCSD, and MCSE certifications and is heavily involved in the South Florida community, running two SQL Server user groups and South Florida SQL Saturday events. He frequently speaks at user groups across South Florida. Scott has nearly 20 years' experience with SQL Server, working and consulting in small to enterprise-size environments.

About the Technical Reviewer

■ **Vidya Vrat Agarwal**, is a Microsoft .NET Purist and an MCT, MCPD, MCTS, MCSD.NET, MCAD.NET, and MCSD and a lifetime member of the Computer Society of India (CSI). Vidya started working on Microsoft .NET with its 1ˢᵗ beta release and has been involved in software development, evangelism, consultation, corporate training, and T3 programs on Microsoft .NET for various employers and corporate clients. He is a published author for Apress titles *Beginning C# 2008 Databases: From Novice to Professional, Beginning VB 2008 Databases: From Novice to Professional and Pro ASP.NET 3.5 in VB 2008 : Includes Silverlight 2Pro* as well as a technical reviewer of many books published by Apress.

Vidya lives with his beloved wife, Rupali, and lovely daughter, Vamika ("Pearly") and believes that nothing will turn into a reality without them. He is the follower of the concept No Pain, No Gain and believes that his wife is his greatest strength. He is a bibliophile and blogs at http://dotnetpassion.blogspot.com. You can reach him via email at Vidya_mct@yahoo.com.

Acknowledgments

Anyone who has written a book knows that it isn't the work of a single individual. Although the author (or authors) are at the forefront, a myriad of individuals behind the scenes actually make the book a reality, making sure all the pieces come together smoothly (or as smoothly as possible). It is these behind-the-scenes individuals whom I want to thank profoundly.

First and foremost, the people at Apress. Jonathan Gennick, the person who has stuck by me while getting this project off the ground and through a period when we thought it would never get done: my hat is off to you. Thank you for your support.

Anita Castro, the coordinating editor who kept me honest and on schedule as best she could. I hope I didn't put you through too much stress.

Greg and Keith, what can I say? Great times.

In addition to those already mentioned, you are reading this book because of the support of many friends and family. Herve and Jared, you guys rock, and your friendship is unmeasurable. Joe Healy, what would South Florida do without you?

To my contacts at Microsoft who allowed me to ask a thousand questions: Elisa Flasko, Noam Ben-Ami, Diego Vega, Alex James, Daniel Simmons, and Tim Mallalieu. Thank you for your time and help in this great endeavor.

Nothing, however, compares to the support and love that you receive from those at home. To my wife and children (Lynelle, Sadie, Forrest, Allara, and Shayna), thank you for the love, support, and wonderful home. You make it all worth while.

CHAPTER 1

Introducing the ADO.NET 4.0 Entity Framework

In July 2008 Microsoft released the first version of the ADO.NET Entity Framework as part of the Visual Studio 2008 Service Pack 1 as well as the .NET Framework 3.5 Service Pack 1. At the time, Microsoft LINQ (Language Integrated Query) and LINQ to SQL had been out for a while and were gaining a lot of attention. Both the Entity Framework and LINQ to SQL showed that Microsoft was very serious about improving developer productivity, by providing an infrastructure for managing relational data as objects and programming against a conceptual model instead of directly against a storage schema. While Microsoft did its best to tout the Entity Framework, it went somewhat unnoticed out of the gate, primarily due to the rise in popularity of LINQ to SQL and the misunderstanding from the public of what the Entity Framework really was.

By the time this book hits the shelves, Visual Studio 2010 with the .NET Framework 4.0 and ADO.NET Entity Framework will have just been released or will be very shortly. Yet, I still get questions from people wondering what the Entity Framework is or how it differs from LINQ to SQL.

Thus, the reason for this book is twofold; first, it will answer the question of what the Entity Framework is and why Microsoft is dedicating a lot of resources and energy to its development, advancement, and developer acceptance. Second, it will discuss all the new features and enhancements that will be available in ADO.NET 4.0, which will be released with Visual Studio 2010.

This book is intended to address two types of developers: those who have never worked with the Entity Framework before, and those who have but are looking at what the ADO.NET 4.0 Entity Framework has to offer. As such, it will cover all aspects of the Entity Framework and, where appropriate, point out the new features and enhancements found in the EF 4.0.

The Entity Framework does not, nor is intended to, replace existing ADO.NET data access technologies; rather, it is an enhancement to ADO.NET, providing developers an augmented approach to accessing data, letting them work with a conceptual model, and thus enabling developers to deal with data as objects and properties, a concept already familiar to them.

The Need for an Entity Framework

To really understand what the Entity Framework is and why it is so important, we need to take a step back and look at some of the existing data access technologies. Microsoft has put a lot of time and effort into ADO.NET over the past many years. Prior to that, it was RDO, and prior to that it was DAO. Heaven forbid we look prior to DAO. With ADO.NET, developers were finally sensing that Microsoft had settled on a data access strategy and technology. With the improvements and enhancements that were being made to ADO.NET with each .NET release, it was the "go-to" technology for data access.

Developers' data access technologies of choice have primarily been the DataReader and the DataSet, and these have been serving developers well for many years. Yet with all of the improvements being made to ADO.NET, there was still a disconnect between the application and the back-end database.

Developers were spending far too much time trying to keep up with changes being made to the database. Any schema change to a table or stored procedure, for example, could potentially break an application.

Take the following code snippet, for example, which runs against Microsoft's standard AdventureWorks example database. Take a good look at this code sample and then ask yourself two questions:

1. Will it compile?

2. Assuming it compiles, when it runs, will you get the "yep, we have rows" message?

```
try
{
    string connectionString = Class1.GetConnectionString();

    using (SqlConnection conn = new SqlConnection(connectionString))
    {
        conn.Open();
        using (SqlCommand cmd = new SqlCommand())
        {
            cmd.Connection = conn;
            cmd.CommandText = "SELECT FirstName, MidleName, LastName FROM Person.Contact↩
WHERE ContactID = @ContactID";
            SqlParameter param = new SqlParameter("@ContactID", SqlDbType.Int, 50,↩
"ContactID");
            param.Value = 8;
            cmd.Parameters.Add(param);

            SqlDataReader rdr = cmd.ExecuteReader();
            while (rdr.Read())
            {
                Console.WriteLine(String.Format("{0}, {1}",
                    rdr[0], rdr[1]));
            }
        }
    }

}
catch (Exception ex)
{
    MessageBox.Show(ex.Message);
}
```

If you want to try it out, open up a new instance of Visual Studio 2010 (or 2008—this example is not specific to 2010) and create a new C# Windows Forms application. On the form, place a button on the form and in the click event of that button enter the code as you see it above. Prior to running the project, change the connection string username and password for your environment and add the following using statement:

```
using System.Data.SqlClient;
```

If you don't feel like typing, you can download the code from the Apress web site for this book. In any case, run the project and click the button. When the project runs and the form displays, it should be obvious at that point that the code did compile successfully. Now click the button. Did you get the "yep, we have rows" message?

If you typed in the code just as you see it above, you didn't get the message indicating a successful run. Instead you received a message that the column MidName is an invalid column name. The column containing the middle name is actually called MiddleName. The problem is you had to run the application to find that out. Now imagine if yours had been a larger production application and you received a similar error. A larger application makes it much more difficult to find the offending line of code, plus you have the greater overhead of tracking down the actual spelling of the column name.

The point is that developers spend far too much time worrying about things they shouldn't need to when it comes to the database side of things. Developers need to focus only on developing applications and should not be concerned if a table, stored procedure, relationship, or some other database object changes.

In the code example above, the error that you get illustrates an example of a table change being made without informing the developers. When the table was originally created, it possibly could have had a column named MidName, but someone decided to change that column's name to MiddleName to be consistent with the other name columns in the table. Unless that schema change is disseminated to the appropriate people (the developers in this case), no one is going to find out about the change until run time. Think of what could happen if for some reason the change was not picked up and somehow slipped through QA and into the production release. Oops.

What was needed was a model where the database, application, and data move together. This is exactly what the Entity Framework provides. The Entity Framework is a conceptual model that works with databases and applications, eliminating the gap between data and applications (and application languages) that developers normally have to work with when working with the DataReader object and other data access technologies.

This Has Been Tried Before

Modeling applications exist in abundance, but each application has a specific focus such as process data flow or describing objects. The following lists some of the modeling application types and their primary focus.

- *ERM (Entity Relationship Model)*: Used with databases, it is a way to represent logical relationships of entities (objects) in order to create a database.

- *UML (Unified Modeling Language)*: A standard modeling language that is used to describe objects.

- *ORM (Object-Relational Mapping)*: Method of mapping relational databases and object-oriented programming languages.

- *DFD (Data Flow Diagram)*: A graphical representation of the flow of data between processes and between systems.

The problem is that each of these modeling applications is limited in scope. For example, ERM products do logical data models really well, but struggle at UML tasks. UML excels at describing objects, but falls short at performing ERM tasks.

And lest we forget, there are other ERM-like products in the market that have been around for a bit and provide Entity Framework-like capabilities, such as the following:

- *NHibernate*: Ported from Hibernate Core for Java for the .NET Framework, NHibernate for .NET persists plain .NET objects to and from an underlying relational database.

- *SPRINT.net*: An open-source application framework, and based on the Java version of Spring Framework, allowing you to build components that can be integrated into multiple tiers of your application.

While this list is by no means complete, it is provided to illustrate the necessity and need for good ERM application development products that remove many of the complexities of working with databases to help improve productivity.

The ADO.NET Entity Framework does not have the same limitations of other modeling products. This is because the Entity Framework works at a conceptual level that is based on the ERM and, as such, provides a depth and richness of functionality that many of the stand-alone ERMs and UMLs cannot provide.

As the name suggests, the Entity Framework allows you to work directly with Entities that represent your own schema without having to deal with the nuances of `DataReader` and `DataSet` objects. Some developers who have worked with or have some knowledge about Entity Framework compare it to other relational mappers and try to classify it as an object relational mapper. This comparison or thought process is not entirely correct. The Entity Framework does have relational mapping capabilities. But the Entity Framework is much more than just a relational mapper, and the ORM capabilities it does have are implemented much differently than that of other ORM products.

So, What Is the Entity Framework?

The Entity Framework is a set of technologies in ADO.NET that helps fill in the space between object-oriented development (objects) and databases. This gap is commonly known as an "impedance mismatch" and it exists because the mapping and organization of classes does not quite match up to the organization of relational objects. Many mapping solutions have tried to solve this problem by mapping OO (object-oriented) classes and properties straight to tables and columns.

For example, let's use the case of customers and products. First, in a simple mapping scenario, you may have a product class that contains a property that references an instance of a customer class. Second, a customer class might contain a property containing a collection of instances of the product class. While this might seem fine, how do you represent the foreign keys between customer and product in the first case (while in the second case you have a reference of an object-oriented collection of product instances that has no comparable column in the customer table in the database)?

A scenario such as this one is known as the conceptual space and is accomplished by raising the abstraction level to a point that lets developers query entities and relationships in the conceptual model, all while letting the Entity Framework translate the query operations to data source–specific commands. It allows applications to be written against conceptual models and not directly against the database. By doing so, the gap between object-oriented programming and databases has been closed, letting developers focus on the task of developing applications, without concerning themselves about the database (structure or otherwise) or data access.

You should start to see where the gap comes into play, simply because there is no one-to-one mapping. Relationships between relational objects are represented much differently from class relationships. And this is where the Entity Framework takes a much different approach. The EF maps relational objects to conceptual models. Conceptual mapping provides a number of huge benefits. For example, it provides the needed improved flexibility in creating (defining) and enhancing the logical model.

■ **Note** The Entity Framework divides the data model into three separate models: conceptual, logical, and physical. Each of these will be discussed in detail in Chapter 3.

By putting the focus on the conceptual model, the Entity Framework lets you query entities and relationships, letting the EF do the work of translating the query operations into commands specific to the data source, such as Microsoft SQL Server.

Developers can also work in an object-oriented environment that is familiar to them, all while gaining the benefits of operating in such an environment, such as IntelliSense and compile-time checking. For example, had the example a few pages ago been done using the Entity Framework, the error discussed earlier would have been caught during application compilation.

Keep in mind there are many more benefits to Entity Framework than what I've discussed so far. They will be discussed throughout this chapter and the rest of this book.

Database vs. Model

You now have two data access choices. On one hand are the tried and true `DataReader` and `DataSet` objects. On the other is the Entity Framework. Which should a developer choose? Since this book is about the Entity Framework, obviously the book is going to steer you in that direction. However, the next two sections are going to point out the differences between both options.

Database-Driven

Developers familiar with `DataReaders` and `DataSets` know that the majority of the time and code is making a connection to the database, getting data from the database, and then performing some action on the results as the results are assigned to classes. At the very minimum, the code to open a connection and execute a query would look something like the following (modified from the example above):

```
using (SqlConnection conn = new SqlConnection(@"Data Source=(local);Initial↵
 Catalog=AdventureWorks;UID=sa;PWD=pwd"))
{
    conn.Open();
    using (SqlCommand cmd = new SqlCommand())
    {
        cmd.Connection = conn;
        cmd.CommandType = CommandType.Text;
        cmd.CommandText = "SELECT FirstName, MiddleName, LastName FROM Person.Contact↵
WHERE LastName = @LastName";
        cmd.Parameters.Add(new SqlParameter("@LastName",↵
System.Data.SqlDbType.char)).Value = "Smith";
        using (SqlDataReader rdr = cmd.ExecuteReader())
        {
        if (rdr.HasRows)
            {
                Rdr.Read();
                //
            }
        }
    }
}
```

While this type of coding has served developers well in the past, it leaves developers with a mixed model where the application code and data (i.e., schema) are all mixed together; the application implicitly contains the model. In the system I have just described, the application is tied to a specific set of database features and neither the application nor the database makes sense without each other.

Model-Driven

With the Entity Framework, you do not have to worry about the database. Rather, you simply code and query against a set of objects (entities) that reflects the business model. Results are returned as objects, and unlike other data access options, the developer does not have to spend time (code) figuring out rows and columns in the returned results just to bind them to objects. Since results are returned as objects, this work is automatically done.

A term or concept that that you should familiarize yourself with is an Entity Data Model (EDM). The EDM is the foundation of the Entity Framework and is comprised of the three models mentioned earlier: the conceptual model, the logical model, and the storage model. Think of the EDM as an "enhanced" version of an ERM. The EDM is the component that describes the overall structure of your business objects. The Entity Framework does not map your database objects in a simple 1:1 (one-to-one) mapping. While it can do that, it can do much more than that. Consider, for example, the following figure from the AdventureWorks database.

In Figure 1-1 there are three tables: Contact, Employee, and AdditionalContactInfo. Person provides information about a person, while the Employee table provides additional data regarding that person as an employee. The Business Entity table is the source of the ID that connects many of the tables such as people (persons), employees, and other information.

For most, if not all, developers this structure looks very familiar. Developers who write applications that access data are extremely familiar with working with tabular data. The past few pages, however, have highlighted many of the pitfalls when working in that environment.

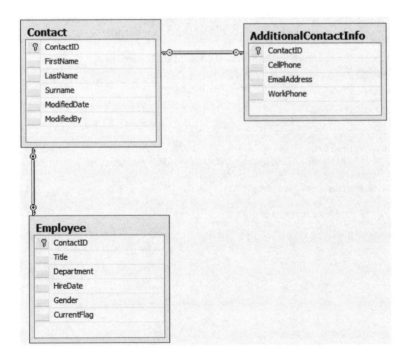

Figure 1-1. Database Model

A developer might need to write a query that pulls information from all of these tables. For example, the application might require that a form that displays the employee's first name, last name, job title, hire date, and possibly some other information. A SQL Server query to pull data might look something like the following:

```
SELECT c.FirstName, c.LastName, e.Title, e.HireDate, aci.CellPhone, aci.EmailAddress
FROM Contact c
INNER JOIN AdditionalContactInfo aci ON c.ContactID = aci.ContactID
INNER JOIN Employee e ON c.ContactID = e.ContactID
```

The)Entity Data Model of the Entity Framework is not the same as the database model, and it is important that a distinction between the two be made. The EDM describes the structure of your business objects; the database model describes the database schema. The two are distinct and separate, but the goal of the EF is to reform or reorganize the database objects in such a way that your EDM matches the goal of your business layer instead of an exact match of your database schema.

For example, using the Entity Framework and the EDM, a developer can take the above three tables and reshape them using inheritance as follows:

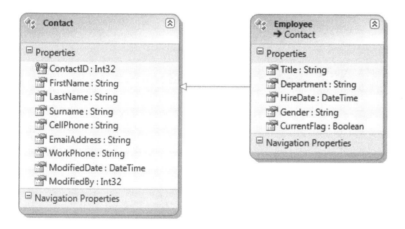

Figure 1-2. Reshaped schema using inheritance

With LINQ the pervious query can now be written much more clearly and cleanly, as follows:

```
From c in Contact.TypeOf<Employee> select c;
```

Remember that with the Entity Framework developers now work at the object level, not at the tabular level. No more tabular translation or the need to manually map results to objects. The next chapter, Chapter 2, will discuss the EDM in great detail.

Working with Entities

A key term any Entity Framework developer needs to know is the term *entity*. The objects in Figure 1-2 are called entities. Chapter 4 will discuss entities in much greater detail, but they are introduced here since they are vital in understanding how to work with the EDM.

In some ways, entities are like objects, for example:

- Entities have a known type.

- Entities have properties, and these properties can hold scalar values.

- Entity properties can hold references to other entities.

- Each entity has a distinct identity.

Even though entities have properties, entities have very little behavior. What behavior they do have is strictly limited to the methods that enable change tracking.

Entities also differ from objects, for example:

- Entities live within a collection.

- Each entity has associations with other entities.

- Entities have primary keys that uniquely identify the entity.

Equally important, entities also have some similarities to relational data:

- Entities live within an entity set.

- Entities have relationships to other entities.

- They have a primary key.

On the flip side, they differ from relational data:

- Entities support complex types.

- Entities support inheritance.

- Entities do not have physical storage knowledge.

Entities are extremely flexible, meaning that they can be reshaped as you saw a few pages ago when models were discussed. Entities can have relationships between them, and those relationships can be defined directly in the EDM Designer.

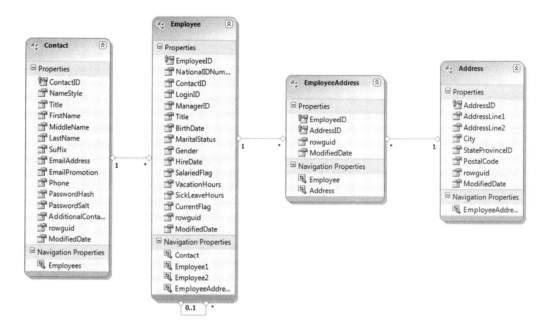

Figure 1-3. Entities and relationships

You saw earlier how easy it is to query against this type of model. The model provides all the appropriate and necessary navigation between the entities, and you will see a lot more of this in Chapter 4. The EDM makes it extremely simple to visually see how the entities are linked. In Figure 1-3, each entity has a navigation property. This property visually illustrates how a developer can easily "navigate" between the entities.

One of the many nice features of the Entity Framework is the ability to retrieve what is called a graph. This does not refer to the pie/bar chart type of graph. An Entity Framework graph is the ability to return shaped data. For example, in a single result I can return data such as a salesperson and all of that person's contact details along with it.

Entity Framework 4.0 Features

Lastly, this chapter is going to briefly cover some of the new features in version 4.0 of the Entity Framework. There are a lot of new features and enhancements, but these next few pages will highlight some of the most requested and needed features.

Following are some of the more important features and enhancements to be aware of. Some saw the lack of some of these features in the first version of the Entity Framework as a notable shortcoming.

- Plain Old CLR Objects (POCO) Support

- Model-First Support

- Deferred Loading of Related Objects

- Functions in LINQ to Entities Queries

- Plurality Naming Support
- Complex Type Support
- Customized Object Layer Code Generation
- Model Browser Improvements

The following sections will briefly discuss each item. A more detailed discussion of each item is included throughout the book.

POCO Support

One of the more powerful new features of the Entity Framework is the ability to add and use your own custom data classes in conjunction with your data model. This is accomplished by using CLR objects, commonly known as "POCO" (Plain Old CLR Objects). The added benefit comes in the form of not needing to make additional modifications to the data classes. This is also called persistence-ignorance.

The flexibility of extending these partial classes means more control over the core entity object functionality. This is a huge advantage as developers can now leverage and preserve valuable customizations and business logic, which they might not have been able to do previously.

Model-First Support

In the first version of the Entity Framework, developers could create a conceptual model using the Create Database Wizard, but that model could not be persisted (created) based on that model. This changes with the ADO.NET 4.0 Entity Framework.

When creating your initial conceptual model via the Create Database Wizard you can now create the database based on the conceptual model. This is a huge plus for developers who like to create the object model first and generate the database based on the model. This functionality supports the data-driven design that the EDM is purely based on.

Related Object–Deferred Loading

Deferred loading is also known as lazy loading, and in the first version of the Entity Framework, related objects were not automatically loaded from the data source as navigation properties were accessed.

In ADO.NET 4.0 Entity Framework, query results can be shaped by composing queries that explicitly navigate the relationships via the navigation properties.

LINQ-to-Entities Function Support

Function support in the first version of the Entity Framework was limited. A *function* represented either a stored procedure or a UDF in the database.

Two new classes have been added to the Entity Framework for this release to address this issue, the `EntityFunctions` and `SqlFunctions` classes. These classes provide developers the ability to access canonical and database functions via LINQ to Entities queries.

Additionally, a new attribute called `EdmFunctionAttribute` gives the Entity Framework the ability to use a CLR method to serve as a proxy for a function defined in the conceptual model.

More on function support is discussed in Chapter 5.

Plurality Naming

One of the big complaints in the first version of the Entity Framework was how naming conventions were applied to EDM objects such as entities and navigation properties when using the model wizards.

The first version of the Entity Framework gave the Entity Name and the Entity Set Name the same name. There was no attempt to singularize or pluralize names when generating a model from a database.

The problem is that this caused some confusion when referencing the database table or EntityType in code. For example, if your database has a table called Employees, then you will also get an EntityType called Employees as well. This causes confusion about whether you are referencing the table or the EntityType, such as in the code fragment below.

```
Customers customer = new Customers();
```

Luckily, this issue has been addressed. The model wizards, both the Entity Data Model and Update Model Wizards, now provide the option of using singular or plural forms of names for entities, entity sets, and navigation properties.

The goal of this change was to make the application code much easier to read and avoid a lot of the confusion between object names.

More on the EDM is discussed in Chapter 2.

Complex Types

A big addition to this version of the Entity Framework is the support for complex types. Complex types are like entities in that they consist of a scalar property or one or more complex type properties. Thus, complex types are non-scalar properties of entity types that enable scalar properties to be organized within entities.

Complex types are discussed in detail in Chapter 3.

Customized Object-Layer Code Generation

Object-layer code is generated, by default, by the EDM using the Entity Model Code Generator tool. This version of the Entity Framework allows developers to add text templates to a project that replaces the default tool to generate the object-layer code.

By using custom text templates, the EDM will generate the object context and entity classes. The Entity Framework makes it very easy to add custom templates via the EDM.

Complex Types are discussed in detail in Chapter 3.

Model Browser Improvements

Several improvements have been made to the model browser that make working with the EDM much more pleasant. Improvements include the following:

- Updating the model when changes are made to the underlying database.

- Deleting objects from the model.

- Searching for a specified string in the storage and conceptual models.

- Locating entity types on the design surface.

This list is by no means complete, as many more improvements have been made to the model browser.

The model browser enhancements will be discussed in detail in Chapter 2.

Back-End Support

The great thing about the Entity Framework is that in essence it does not really care about the data store from which the data is being queried. It doesn't need to. Neither the type of database nor the schema itself is completely unknown to the Entity Framework, and they will have no impact on your model.

Out of the box, the Entity Framework ships with two providers:

- *EntityClient Provider for the Entity Framework*: Used by Entity Framework applications to access data described in the EDM. This provider uses the .NET Framework Data Provider for SQL Server (SqlClient) to access a SQL Server database.

- NET Framework Data Provider for SQL Server (SqlClient) for the Entity Framework: Supports the Entity Framework for use with a SQL Server database.

The great thing about the Entity Framework is that it is database-, or data source–, independent, in that you can create custom providers to access other databases. For example, through third party providers you can access the following:

- Oracle

- MySql

- PostgreSQL

- SQL Anywhere

- DB2

- Informix

- U2

- Ingres

- Progress

- Firebird

- Synergy

- Virtuoso

This is quite a list and it shows you that the Entity Framework is gaining in popularity. This list is by no means complete, as providers are continuously being created by third-party vendors. At the time of this writing, a complete list of providers and their vendors can be found here:

http://msdn.microsoft.com/en-us/data/dd363565.aspx

The great thing about this is that the provider does all of the work for you pertaining to query reshaping. You are responsible for providing the connection information to the specific data store, but the provider takes care of the rest when working with the Entity Framework. Why? Because of the need to learn databases or figure out the nuances of different data stores. Instead, you use the Entity Framework's query syntax such as LINQ to Entities or Entity SQL and forgo the headache of remembering the database differences.

This book will use Microsoft SQL Server 2008 as its database and will use the .NET Framework Data Provider for SQL Server (SqlClient) for the Entity Framework as the data provider. Through this provider you can use SQL Server as far back as version SQL Server 2000 up through SQL Server 2008. Microsoft even supports SQL Server Compact Edition.

CHAPTER 2

■■■

The Entity Data Model

Chapter 1 spent quite a bit of time discussing the need for, and introducing, the Entity Framework. As part of that discussion the chapter introduced the EDM (Entity Data Model) and its many benefits to you. As you have learned, the EDM is the bridge between your application and your data and is the component that allows you to work with your data conceptually rather than going directly against your database and trying to figure out the back-end schema.

This chapter is going to build on the first chapter and spend the entire time taking an in-depth look at an EDM and how it works. This chapter will walk you through creating an EDM, and then we will lift the lid, take a look underneath, and explore every nook and cranny of the EDM. This chapter will spend quite a bit of time looking at the EDM Designer and its related files. The first thing this chapter is going to walk you through is the creation of your first Entity Data Model. From there, we'll lift the lid and discuss everything there is about it.

Creating an EDM

In the previous version of the Entity Framework you could generate a model from an existing database, and you could also start with an empty model and create the conceptual model from scratch.

However, that is where the functionality ended for creating an EDM. If you created a model from scratch, you could not create the database from that model and in some cases you were required to work with the raw XML (more on that later in this chapter).

There have been significant changes to the Entity Framework and the EDM. With the EF 4.0, some significant improvements have been made. Along with creating an EDM from an existing database schema (called database-first), you can now also do the following:

- *Model-first*: Allows you to start with an empty model, define your model and then generate the database, mappings, and classes from the defined model.

- *Code-only*: Allows you to use the Entity Framework using Plain Old CLR Objects (POCO) entities and without an EDMX file.

The database-first approach has been available since the very beginning of the EF with the release of .NET 3.5 SP1. The model-first approach is new to Visual Studio 2010 and .NET 4.0 and allows you to create an EDM from scratch. The code-only approach lets developers view their code as their model.

The following three sections will discuss each of the approaches for creating an EDM. I'm going to let you know now that there are a lot of screen shots, and they are included for two reasons. The first is to help those who are not familiar with the EF to get up and going with ease. The second is to help those already familiar with the EF to know where the new changes and enhancements are. All the examples in this book will use the AdventureWorks database for SQL Server 2008. That database can be downloaded from the CodePlex web site, from the following URL:

```
http://msftdbprodsamples.codeplex.com/Release/ProjectReleases.aspx?ReleaseId=18407
```

So, let's begin.

Taking a Database-First Approach

Fire up Visual Studio 2010 and create a new Windows Forms Application project. Make sure on the New Project dialog that you have the .NET Framework 4.0 selected (it should select this by default, however). I called my project EFDemo but you can call your project whatever you want.

Once the project is created, open solution explorer and right-click on the project. Select Add ➤ New Item from the context menu. This will open the Add New Item dialog shown below in Figure 2-1.

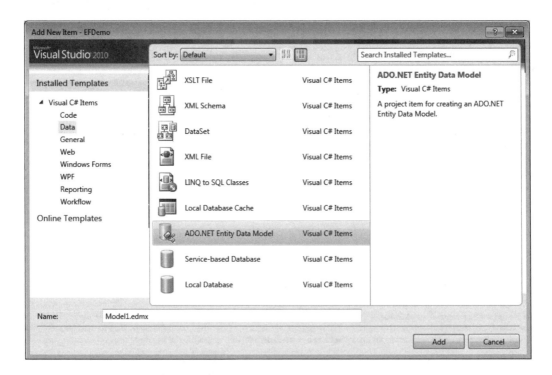

Figure 2-1. *The Add New Item dialog*

In the list of Installed Templates on the left side of the dialog, select the Data node. This will list all the Data object templates, among them the ADO.NET Entity Data Model template. Select the ADO.NET Entity Data Model template and click Add.

Selecting the ADO.NET Entity Data Model template will begin the Entity Data Model Wizard. The first step in the wizard lets you choose the type of model you want to use. In this step, you have the option of generating a model from a database or starting with an empty model.

This section deals with generating a model from an existing database schema; select that option as shown in Figure 2-2 and click Next.

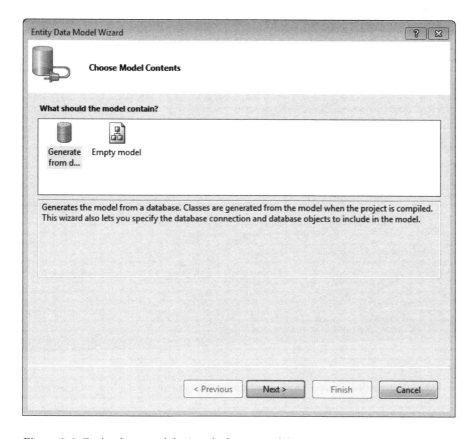

Figure 2-2. Entity data model wizard: choose model contents

The next page in the wizard lets you specify the data connection for your EDM. If you have previously created connections they will show up in the list. If you have a connection to the AdventureWorks database, select that connection. Figure 2-3 shows this step in the wizard prior to making any selections.

If you haven't created any connections you will need to create one, and this can be done by clicking the New Connection button. This button will open the Connection Properties dialog, shown in Figure 2-4.

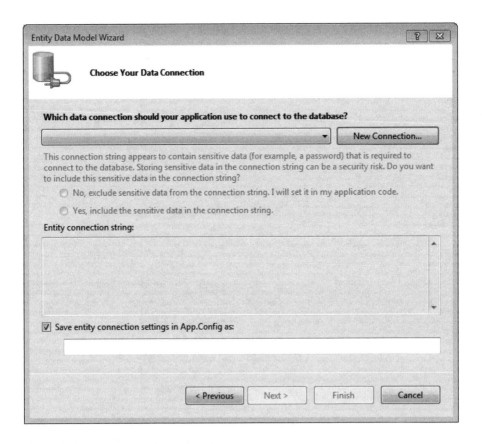

Figure 2-3. Choose your data connection

The Connection Properties dialog looks very similar to most other SQL Server connection dialogs in that you need to provide the server name, authentication method (Windows for SQL Server authentication), and the database name. Select the AdventureWorks2008 database and click the Test Connection button to make sure all the connection settings are correct. If everything checks out fine, click OK on the Connection Properties dialog. Figure 2-4 shows my Connection Properties dialog filled out.

Clicking OK on the Connection Properties dialog will take you back to the data connection page of the wizard with your new connection shown in the connection drop-down, shown in Figure 2-5.

The other options on that page of the wizard should now be enabled. These other options determine how the connection string in the EDM will be stored. The two options state that you will either include the username and password in the connection string or you will set the username and password in your code.

Figure 2-4. Database connection properties

As you toggle between the two connection string options on the Data Connection page of the wizard you will notice that the User ID and Password values in the Entity connection string section appear and disappear. For the purpose of this demo, select the option to include the sensitive data in the connection string. In a production environment you certainly would not want to select this option.

Lastly, you have the option to save the connection string in the application configuration file and provide a name of the section in which to save the information. If you do not select this option you will have to provide the entire connection string information through code. For the sake of this demo, accept the default, which is to save the settings in the application configuration file. Figure 2-5 shows a completed data connection page. Click Next once you have made all the necessary selections.

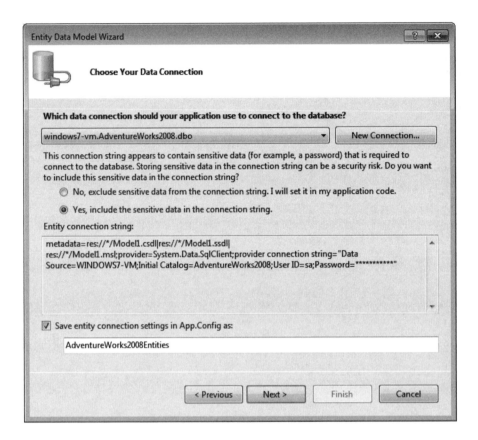

Figure 2-5. *Choose your data connection*

The next step of the wizard allows you to select the database objects to include in the EDM. On this page, shown in Figure 2-6, you can select tables, views, and stored procedures. Also included in the list of stored procedures are scalar-valued functions. Functions will be discussed in Chapter 5.

For this example, I have selected the following:

- *Tables*: Person.BusinessEntity, Person.Person, HumanResources.Employee

- *Views*: Sales.vPersonDemographic, person.vAdditionalContactInfo, HumanResources.vEmployee

- *Stored procedures*: uspGetManagerEmployees

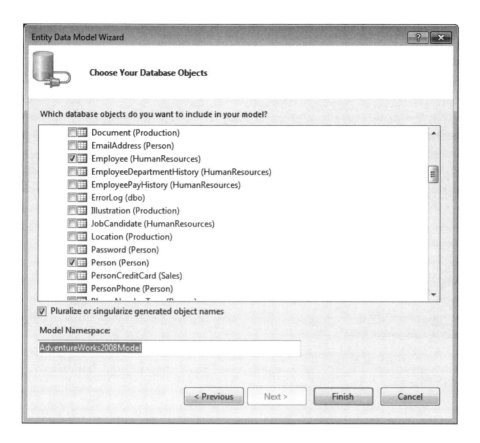

Figure 2-6. *Choosing the database objects*

At this point our model is ready to be built. But before you click the Finish button, there is a very important item that I need to discuss that has been added to this step in the wizard. If you take a good look at Figure 2-6 you will notice something that was not there before in the previous version, and that is the checkbox "Pluralize or singularize generated object names."

Making Generated Object Names Plural or Singular

If you have worked at all with the previous version of the Entity Framework (version 3.5) then the checkbox on in Figure 2-6 should make you stand up and shout for joy. The ability to pluralize or singularize object names is one of the biggest requested enhancements for 4.0.

In the previous version of EF, the Entity Set Name and the Entity Name properties were both the same. For example, if you mapped the Person table, the Entity Set Name and Entity Name properties were both named Person. This naming convention caused confusion because as you started coding against the model, the names of the objects did not quite make sense.

Naming is improved in Entity Framework 4.0. The checkbox on the Database Objects page of the model wizard shown in Figure 2-6 provides for the pluralization or singularization of Entity names. By default, this checkbox is checked, and if you leave it checked, the wizard will automatically pluralize or singularize Entity names. The wizard applies English-language rules for singulars and plurals by doing the following:

- Making all EntityType names singular

- Making all Entity Set names plural

For example, take a look at Figure 2-7. When we mapped the Person table a few moments ago, it pluralized the name Person to People. It left the Entity Name as Person but pluralized that name to People for the Entity Set Name property.

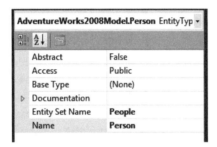

Figure 2-7. *Entity properties*

The same is true for the opposite scenario when the Entity Name is pluralized. For example, if the Entity Name property had a value of People, the EDM wizard would have set the Entity Set Name property to Person. Just think how much less confusing naming will be. Now when you code against the model, the names of objects will be logical.

Plural and Singular Navigation Properties

The checkbox at the bottom of Figure 2-6 also applies to navigation properties. Leaving the checkbox checked will set the following for navigation properties:

- Make the navigation property name singular for each navigation property that returns at most one entity

- Make the navigation property name plural for each navigation property that returns more than one entity

You'll read about navigation properties a little later in Chapter 3. As a quick introduction, navigation properties are shortcut properties used to identify entity relationships.

Go ahead and click the Finish button on Database Object page of the wizard. At this point the new EDM model will be generated and displayed in the Designer window, shown in Figure 2-8.

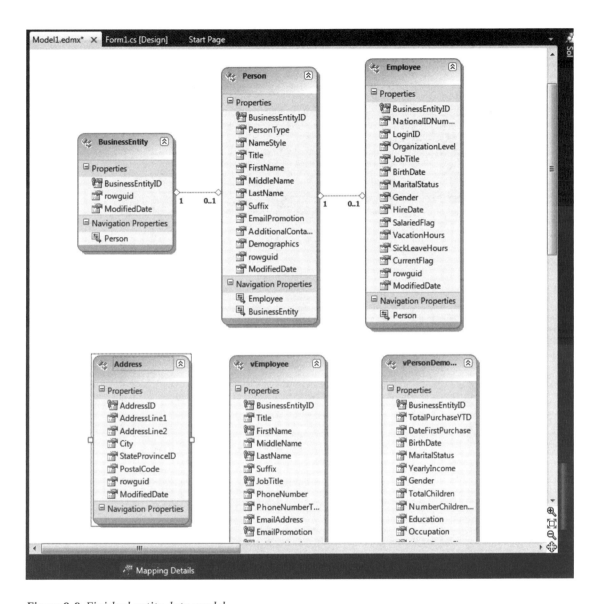

Figure 2-8. Finished entity data model

What you are looking at in Figure 2-8 is the Designer window of the entity data model. The file on which the figure is based is named Model1.edmx, and the contents of that file will be displayed in the Solution Explorer. The Designer windows will be discussed in greater detail in Chapter 3, in the section "The Designer Window and the EDM."

You have just created your first Entity Data Model generated from an existing database. We will be discussing the EDM further later in the book. For now, let's look at the model-first and code-only approaches to generating an EDM.

Taking a Model-First Approach

A new and welcomed feature to the EF 4.0 is the ability to create a conceptual model first and then derive the storage model, database, and mappings from that. This section will walk you through each step of generating a conceptual model, and will explain all the different properties and components involved in the model-first approach.

As you did in the first exercise, open the solution explorer and right-click on the project. Select Add ➤ New Item from the context menu and select the ADO.NET Entity Data Model template and click Add. This will start the Entity Data Model Wizard again.

This time select the Empty model template and click Finish (it's the only button option). A new and empty model will be displayed in the Designer window, such as the one shown in Figure 2-10.

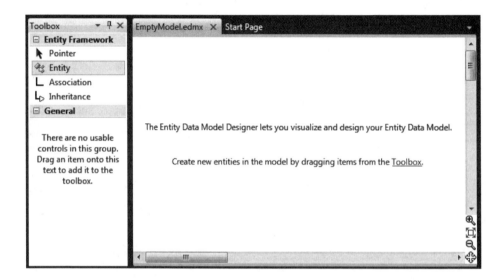

Figure 2-9. *The EDM designer*

Also shown in Figure 2-9 is the Toolbox. Inside the toolbox are the objects you can drag into your model in the Designer. There are three:

- *Entity*: Allows you to design and create an Entity.

- *Association*: Lets you create an association (or relationship) between two entities.

- *Inheritance*: Lets you create an Inheritance relationship between two entities.

■ **Note** Entities, Associations, and Inheritance are discussed in Chapter 7.

As the hint in the designer suggests, you can create entities by dragging the Entity object from the toolbox into the Designer. Another option is to right-click in the Designer itself and select Add ➤ Entity from the context menu.

Drag an Entity into the designer. This will create a new Entity called Entity1, with a single property called ID, as shown in Figure 2-10.

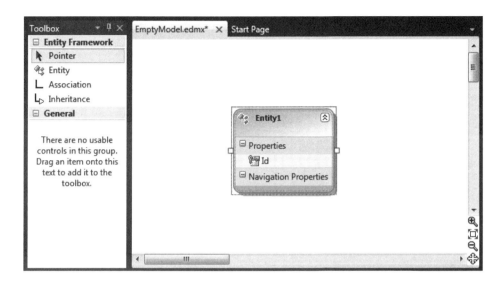

Figure 2-10. *EDM designer - entity*

The default ID property is created as a "Primary Key" for the Entity. You can change the name of the Entity property by opening the Properties page of the Entity property and changing it there, as shown in Figure 2-11. I am creating a Customer table so I called my property Customer ID.

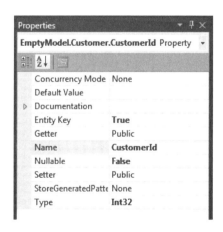

Figure 2-11. *Entity properties*

Notice also the other properties of the Entity Property. The Entity Key property is set to True, indicating that this column is used as the Entity "Primary Key." You can also set a default value, specify whether it can be nullified, and change its data type.

Additional properties can be added by right-clicking on the Entity itself and selecting Add ➤ Scalar Property or Complex Property, as shown in Figure 2-12.

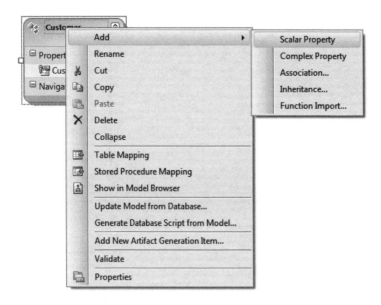

Figure 2-12. Adding a scalar property

You should also notice in Figure 2-12 a new Add menu option, called Complex Property. A complex property (or type) is a non-scalar property of entity types that facilitates the organization of scalar properties within entities. If that explanation didn't make sense, don't worry about it now because complex properties will be explained in Chapter 3.

We are going to add a few more properties to this Entity and add two more Entities and their properties as well to finish off this example; but first, let's add a new property to the Customer Entity called CustomerFirstName. From the Add menu, select Scalar Property and type in CustomerFirstName. Figure 2-13 shows the properties of this scalar property. Here you can set properties such as *Fixed Length, Max Length, Nullable,* and *Type.*

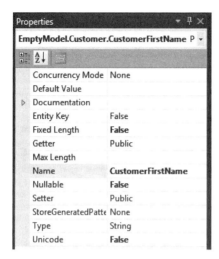

Figure 2-13. *Entity Scalar Properties*

Let's finish this example by adding the rest of the Customer properties, and two more Entities and their properties. For the Customer Entity, add the following properties and their types:

- CustomerLastName (String)
- CustomerAddress (String)
- CustomerCity (String)
- CustomerState (String)
- CustomerZipCode (String)
- CustomerPhone (String)
- ModifyDateTime (DateTime)

We need to add two more Entities: Item and Order. Add a new Entity to the Designer and change its name to Item. Change the ID property to ItemID. Add the following scalar properties:

- ItemName (String)
- ItemDescription (String)
- ModifyDateTime (DateTime)

Add one more entity to the Designer and name it Order. Change its ID property to OrderID. Add the following scalar properties and their types:

- OrderID (int32)
- CustomerID (int32)
- ItemID (int32)
- ModifyDateTime (DateTime)

We're almost done. The next thing we need to do is add relationships, or associations. From the toolbox select Association and create an association between the Customer and Order by selecting the CustomerID property in the Customer entity and, while holding the left mouse button down, drag over to the CustomerID property in the Order entity. Create a second association between Item and Order using the ItemID property in each entity.

When you are all done, your model should look like Figure 2-14.

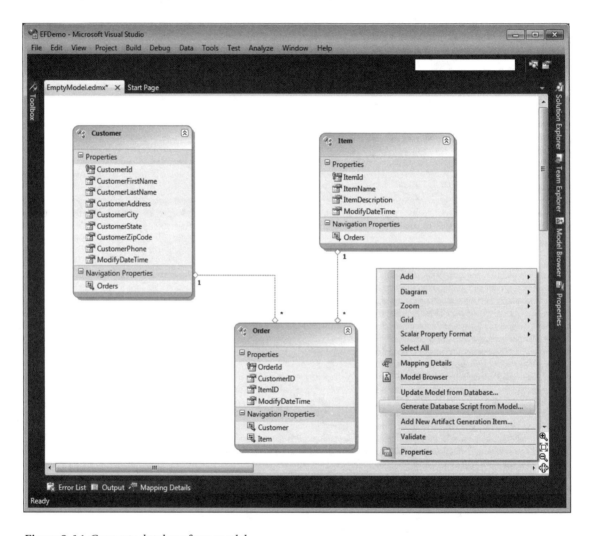

Figure 2-14. Generate database from model

Now comes the really cool part. In the previous version of the EF, this basically is as far as you could go. But not with 4.0! You asked for the ability to generate the schema model and database from the conceptual model and you got it!

Generating a Schema and Database

Figure 2-15 shows how you can continue on and generate a schema and database after creating a new model. Notice that there is a new menu item on the context menu when you right-click on the Designer (it is highlighted in the previous figure), called *Generate Database Script from Model*.

Since you are starting with an empty model you will need to specify the target database. As soon as you select the *Generate Database Script from Model* you will get the Data Connection screen, shown in Figure 2-15, which is identical to the one shown in Figure 2-5. The idea is that you need an available server and database that the system will use to determine what type of DDL to generate.

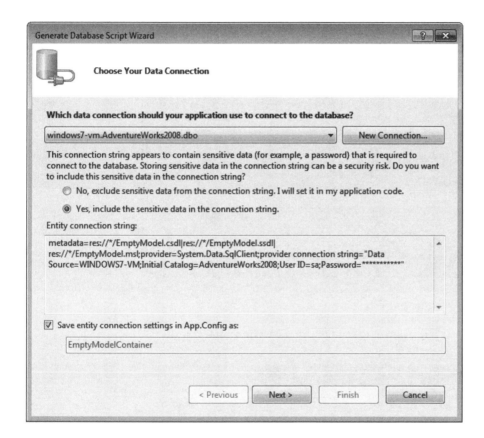

Figure 2-15. *Selecting the data connection*

Clicking the Next button on this step of the wizard will take you to the next step, which presents you with a preview of the DDL that will be generated, such as the one in Figure 2-16, which is the DDL generated for the model created previously.

The DDL in Figure 2-16 is generated by a template and is read-only. If you want to edit the format of the DDL you need to modify the template. The resulting DDL, such as that shown in the figure, should be placed in a separate DDL file that will not be regenerated.

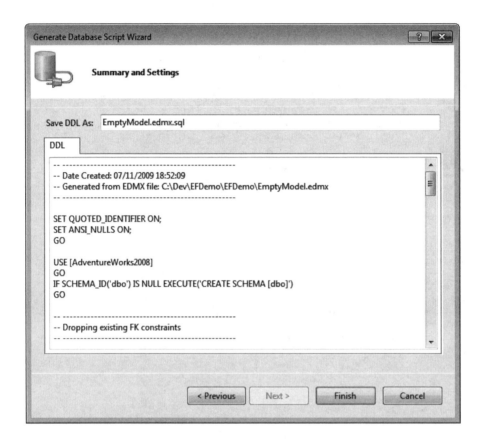

Figure 2-16. Database script summary

When you click Finish, you will be presented with the warning in Figure 2-17.

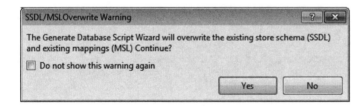

Figure 2-17. Schema overwrite warning

This warning in Figure 2-17 is simply to let you know that you are about to regenerate all existing Storage Schema (SSDL) and Mapping (MSL) from scratch. This means that if you modify your conceptual model and run the *Generate Database Script from Model* again, you will lose any customizations or modifications that you have made since the first time around.

Your resulting DDL will then be displayed in the Visual Studio IDE with a file name of *ModelName*.edmx.sql. For example, the model for this example was EmptyModel, and therefore the saved DDL file was named EmptyModel.edmx.sql. You can see this in Figures 2-18 and 2-19.

One of the things you will notice in Figure 2-19 is the toolbar used to Deploy the DDL with the appropriate database already selected.

Figure 2-18. *Generated DDL script*

Figure 2-19 also shows the DDL file added to your project. One thing to keep in mind about the generated DDL is that it will not migrate data or schema. Your database will be recreated from scratch when the DDL script is run. No existing data will be saved. If you have data that you wish to save, you must save and restore it yourself.

Figure 2-19. New model in solution explorer

Running the script will create the database objects. When the script has finished running, you will get a message stating that the script has run successfully, as shown in Figure 2-20.

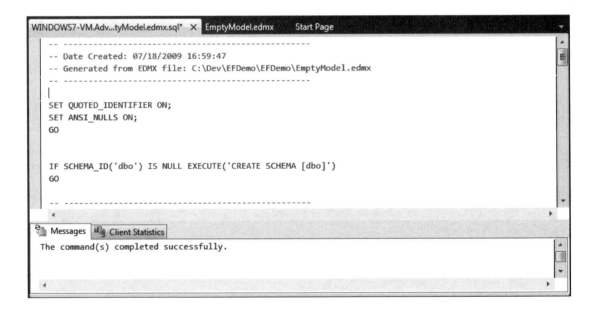

Figure 2-20. Running the SQL DDL script

The DDL script that you've just seen run in Figure 2-20 will generate the schema shown in Figure 2-21. That schema will correspond to the model shown earlier in Figure 2-14. Notice that all the primary key and foreign key constraints have been created between the tables. The engine will also create the appropriate clustered keys on primary keys, and indexes on foreign keys.

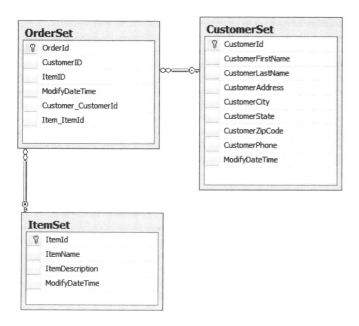

Figure 2-21. *Generated database schema*

One of the reasons the model-first approach of creating the EDM is so welcome is simply due to its extensibility. You can take control of the entire process of only sections or parts of it. An example of this extensibility would be modifying the DDL generation process so that you can customize the DDL to add support for your specific database or environment. We'll cover this type of customization later in Chapter 9.

Managing Table Inheritance

Table inheritance is a concept that will come in handy while developing with the Entity Framework. You have two options for how table inheritance is implemented within your model. They are

- *Table-per-type*: Uses a separate table in storage to maintain data for each type in the inheritance hierarchy.

- *Table-per-hierarchy*: Uses one table in storage to maintain data for all the types in an inheritance hierarchy.

Since the EF engine uses a table-per-type mapping strategy, that is, each entity is mapped to a single database table, certain rules are used to generate the database schema. These rules are outlined in Table 2-1, which contains information on how tables are created based on entity types.

Table 2-1. *Entity Types and Tables*

	Table Name	Created Columns	Primary Key	Foreign Keys
Non-derived type	Derived from the EntitySet property.	A column for each scalar property.	Column(s) that correspond to the entity key property or properties.	See Foreign Key section below.
Derived type	A combination of the base type's EntitySet element name and type name.	A column for each non-inherited scalar property and a column for each inherited key property.	Column or columns that correspond to inherited entity key property or properties.	The primary key of the child table is also a foreign key that references the primary key of its parent table.

Even though the engine creates a table column for each property, you can still create additional columns for navigation properties. We'll cover more of table mappings in the next chapter.

The last topic to cover is code-only EDM creation.

Taking a Code-Only Approach

So far we talked about two different ways to create your Entity Data Model: database-first and model-first. There is a third method, as was mentioned earlier, which allows developers to create their model using POCO (Plain Old CLR Objects) classes. This method is called code-only because the model that is created is done only through code. The code-only approach allows developers to write domain classes without ever looking at or touching a designer or dealing with XML.

The code-only approach simply requires that you create POCO classes that contain the same structure as the database schema you want to map to, such as the following Contact and Employee classes, which you will be creating later in Chapter 10.

```
public class Contact
{
    public Contact() { }
    public int ContactID { get; set; }
    public bool NameStyle { get; set; }
    public string Title { get; set; }
    public string FirstName { get; set; }
    public string MiddleName { get; set; }
    public string LastName { get; set; }
    public string Suffix { get; set; }
    public string EmailAddress { get; set; }
    public int EmailPromotion { get; set; }
    public string Phone { get; set; }
    public string PasswordHash { get; set; }
    public string PasswordSalt { get; set; }
    public Guid rowguid { get; set; }
    public DateTime ModifiedDate { get; set; }
    public ICollection<Employee> Employees { get; set; }
}
```

```
public class Employee
{
    public Employee() { }
    public int EmployeeID { get; set; }
    public string NationalIDNumber { get; set; }
    public string LoginID { get; set; }
    public int ManagerID { get; set; }
    public string Title { get; set; }
    public DateTime BirthDate { get; set; }
    public string MaritalStatus { get; set; }
    public string Gender { get; set; }
    public DateTime HireDate { get; set; }
    public bool SalariedFlag { get; set; }
    public int VacationHours { get; set; }
    public int SickLeaveHours { get; set; }
    public bool CurrentFlag { get; set; }
    public Guid rowguid { get; set; }
    public DateTime ModifiedDate { get; set; }
    public Contact Contact { get; set; }
}
```

Once you have your POCO classes created, the next step is to define a class that derives from the ObjectContext class. This newly created class is used to describe the shape of the model you are creating, along with the mechanism for accessing your POCO classes, such as the following code:

```
public class AWModel : ObjectContext
{
    public AWModel(EntityConnection connection)
        : base(connection)
    {
        DefaultContainerName = "AWModel";
    }

    public IObjectSet<Contact> Contact
    {
        get { return base.CreateObjectSet<Contact>(); }
    }

    public IObjectSet<Employee> Employee
    {
        get { return base.CreateObjectSet<Employee>(); }
    }
}
```

One of the great things about the code-only approach is the flexibility to define your model, such that you can easily put your Entity Framework-aware classes in one assembly while your POCO classes are located in a second assembly, much like you would do in a non-POCO project.

■ **Note** Code-only development is covered in Chapter 10.

■ ■ ■

CHAPTER 3

The Entity Data Model
Inside and Out

Chapter 2 introduced you to the different ways an EDM (Entity Data Model) can be created. Regardless of the method that was used to create the model (generate from a database, start with an empty designer or through POCO), you should have begun to see the purpose of the EDM, such as how it lets developers work on a data model conceptually instead of directly. We talked a lot in the first chapter about how the EDM "bridges the gap" between the application and the data, and by this point you should begin to see how the EDM does that.

If you still aren't making the connection, then this chapter should do that for you. While we have talked at length about what the Entity Framework is and what it does, we have yet to spend any time discussing the "how." This chapter discusses the "how" by taking a look at the Entity Data Model itself and the components of the EDM. This chapter will take a look "under the hood" so-to-speak, looking at the pieces that actually make up the EDM and the Designer (the composition) and see how it is all structured. Later on in the book we will discuss more advanced topics regarding the EDM, such as model customizations.

We'll first take a look at the visual aspect of the EDM by exploring all of the components of the Designer, followed by an internal look at the EDM by digging into the code and components that make up the EDM.

The Designer Window and the EDM

In Chapter 2 we created several models, illustrating how to create an EDM. This chapter will use the first example, which created an EDM from an existing database. When the EDM model wizard is all finished, you should be staring at the EDM Designer window.

The Designer Window

Figure 3-1 shows the EDM that you generated from the AdventureWorks database. In this conceptual view you see three tables (BusinessEntity, Person, and Employee), three views (Employee, AdditionalContactInfo, and PersonDemographics). There is also one stored procedure, but that does not show up in the Designer—instead it is listed in the Model Browser, which will be discussed shortly.

You should notice something a bit different in Figure 3-1 from the similar image in Chapter 2 (Figure 2-8). The entities in the image show extra information, specifically the property data type. By default, the EDM does not display the property type information, but that can easily be displayed by right-clicking on the EDM background and selecting Scalar Property Format ➤ Display Name and Type from the context menu. Notice that not only do the scalar property types display for the tables, but for the views as well, which is very nice. The result is a quick view so that you don't need to view the

Properties page to look at the data type. What the EDM does not show is the length. For example, for String scalar properties, it simply shows "String" but does not show the length. You will still need to look at the Properties page to view the string length information as well as other information pertaining to the selected scalar property.

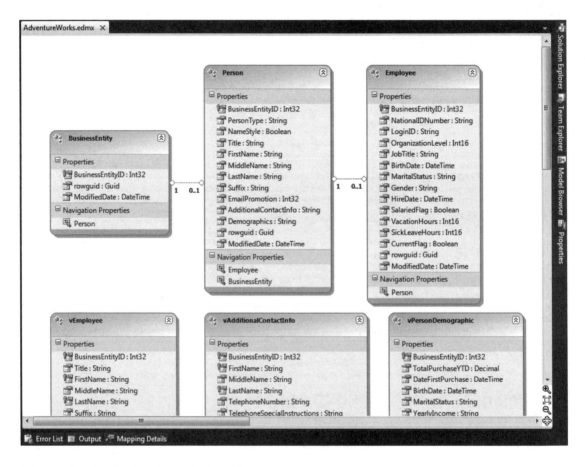

Figure 3-1. *AdventureWorks Entity Data Model*

The Designer window provides a graphical view of your Entity Data Model and the members that you included in your model. It is through the EDM that you can do tasks such as the following:

- Create and modify entities
- Create and modify associations between entities
- View and edit mappings
- Modify inheritance relationships

The Designer is the tool that allows you to work with the EDM and provides the functionality developers need to create, modify, and update the EDM. The Designer consists of several components to assist you in designing and editing your conceptual model. Figure 3-2 shows the different components, including the following:

- *Designer surface*: A visual surface for creating and modifying the conceptual model.

- *Mapping Details window*: The location where mappings are created or modified. The window is discussed later in the chapter.

- *Toolbox*: Contains controls that can be used to create entities, associations, and inheritance relationships.

- *Model Browser window*: Provides a view of the conceptual model and the associated storage model.

Model Browser Window

The Model Browser window provides a tree view of the conceptual and storage models that are defined in the EDM (specifically, the .edmx). The information in this window is organized by the type of information contained within the window, as shown in Figure 3-2. The first node displays the information found in the conceptual model, such as entities and associations. The second node displays the storage model components, i.e., those components of the database that have been imported into the model, such as tables, views, and stored procedures. Within the Model Browser window you can

- Locate an entity on the Designer surface by right-clicking the entity and selecting Show in Designer from the context menu

- Delete objects from the storage model, including stored procedures, tables, and views

- Create function imports from stored procedures by right-clicking on a stored procedure and selecting Add Function Import from the context menu

- Update the model from the database

As you select items in the Model Browser window, these items become the active object in the Properties and Mapping windows, making it easy to modify and work with EDM objects.

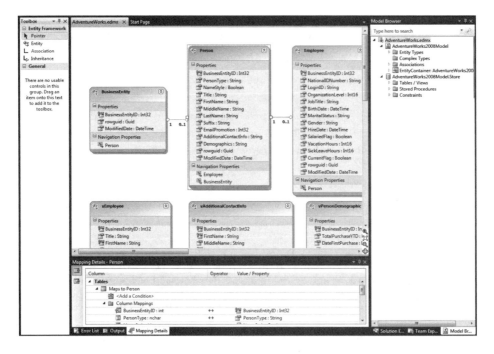

Figure 3-2. Designer surface and windows

Mapping Details Window

The Mapping Details window provides an interface enabling you to view and edit the physical mappings between the storage and conceptual models. Through this window you can view and modify the mappings for the tables and views as well as map entities to functions (stored procedures).

When an entity is selected in the Designer, the Mapping Details window shows the mapping between the entity properties and the table column in the storage model. For example, in Figure 3-2 you can see the Person entity is selected in the Designer as well as the Mapping Details window showing the mapping between the table columns and the properties of the Person entity. Within this window you can change the individual property mappings or assign imported stored procedures as functions to perform Insert, Update, and Delete operations.

With an understanding of the different windows in the Designer, let's move on and discuss the different components in the EDM Designer itself.

Entities

To understand the Entity Framework and how entities work, there are a few concepts that you should know:

- *Entity type*: This represents a particular type of data, such as Employee, Order, or Product. Entity types are highly structured records with a key.

- *Entity set*: This is a logical container for entities of a single type.

Entities, therefore, are instances of entity types, and entities can be grouped into entity sets. The model in Figure 3-3 illustrates this concept, which includes three entity types (*SalesPerson*, *SalesOrderHeader*, and *SalesOrderDetail*), two entity sets (*SalesPerson* and *SalesOrder*), and relationships between the three entity types.

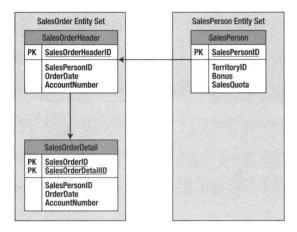

Figure 3-3. *Entity and EntitySets*

With the explicit concept of entities and relationships, developers can now describe schemas more precisely by using entities to provide the formal design for the details of a data structure. In other words, the formal design should specify how an application will encapsulate the different types and kinds of data in a logical structure. The EDM model we created earlier came from the AdventureWorks database, which contains Employees, Products, Sales, and more. Each of these represents a data structure and entities are the formal specifications of the details of those structures.

An Order type, for example, contains details such as salesperson, order date, and quantity. A SalesPerson type could contain name, address, and other pertinent information. The EDM represents a logical connection between the SalesPerson and the Order as a relationship, or association.

You'll also notice that the entity set is defined in the properties of the entity itself. For example, Figure 3-4 shows the Employee entity selected with the Properties page opened showing the properties for that entity. One of the properties of the entity is the *Entity Set Name*. In this example the property takes on the plural version of the entity name, in this case, Employees. This property is editable, and as such allows you to change the entity set name and add multiple entities to the same entity set.

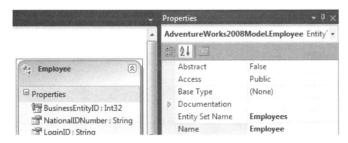

Figure 3-4. *Entity properties*

Scalar Properties

Entities are made up of properties. Scalar properties are properties whose values are physically and literally contained within the entity itself. As you saw earlier, you can modify the display of the entity to also show the scalar property data type, also shown in Figure 3-5. Also shown in the figure are the properties of a selected scalar property, including properties such as whether the property can be null or if the property is an entity key. String scalar properties include additional properties that define string length.

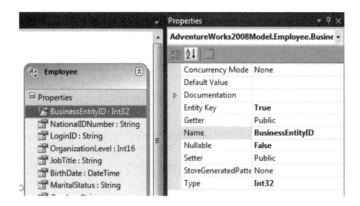

Figure 3-5. *Scalar properties*

You should also notice a property called *StoreGeneratedPattern*. This property is used to determine if the corresponding column in the database will be auto-generated during insert and update operations. This property is applied to all scalar properties.

Additional properties can be added to entities by right-clicking on the entity and selecting *Add ➤ Scalar Property* from the context menu, shown in Figure 3-6.

Figure 3-6. *Adding a scalar property*

You can then define the data type and other properties of the new scalar property.

Complex Types

Complex types are not new to the Entity Framework 4.0. They existed in 3.5, but you could not create them via the Designer—you had to create them manually. Creating them manually meant that you had to go into the CSDL (Conceptual Schema) and add the necessary XML to create the complex type. The problem with this is that once you created your complex type, you could not open the EDM Designer anymore because the Designer didn't support complex types.

With the Entity Framework 4.0, the process of manually creating the complex type is gone. With EF 4.0 you now have the ability to add complex types via the Designer. Before we walk through how to create them, let's first back the bus up and discuss what they are.

Complex Types Defined

Complex types provide a handy mechanism for storing and encapsulating properties related to one or more entities. For example, you may have more than one entity that needs to store phone and email information. Complex types can also be used to add additional structure to your entities. Regardless of how you use them, they are very useful. As you will see shortly, complex types are made up of scalar properties as well as additional complex types.

Complex types in EF 4.0 are anything but complex in the sense of what it takes to create one. Complex types are types, meaning that you can instantiate them outside of the parent entity. Yet as such they still provide the ability to navigate to them through the related entity or entities. Let's take a look at how to create them and how they work.

Creating a Complex Type

Creating a complex type is quite easy. Open the Model Browser window and expand the top node (the conceptual model node). Within that node is a complex types node, shown in Figure 3-7. The complex types node will contain all the complex types for your model. Complex types can be added, deleted, and modified directly through the Model Browser. As you will see shortly, creating and defining complex types are quite easy to do.

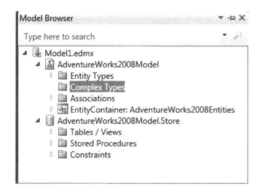

Figure 3-7. Model Browser

To add a new complex type, right-click on the complex type node and select Create Complex Type from the context menu, as shown in Figure 3-8. This will create a complex type with a default name of ComplexType1. You can rename the complex type by right-clicking the complex type and selecting Rename from the context menu. I renamed my complex type to AddntlContactInfo.

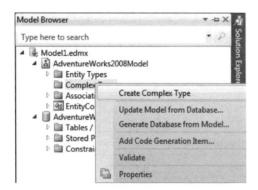

Figure 3-8. *Create complex type*

At this point the complex type is useless because we have not defined any properties. To add properties to the complex type, right-click in the complex type and select Add ➤ Scalar Property, then select the data type of the scalar property you want to create. You can see this in Figure 3-9. As you can see, you have the same data types for complex type scalar properties as you do with regular entity scalar properties. And this should be no surprise because a complex type is simply an extension of your entity or entities.

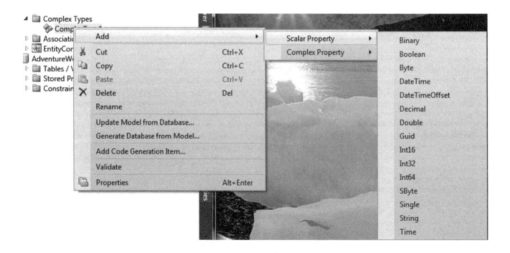

Figure 3-9. *Adding scalar properties to the complex type*

For this example, I added three scalar properties called Active, CellPhone, and EmailAddress, which you can see in Figure 3-10. CellPhone and EmailAddress are type String while Active is type Byte. If you have followed along, congratulations—you have created your first complex type.

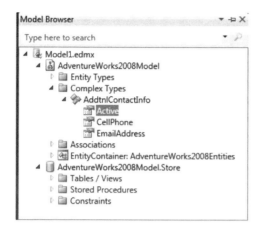

Figure 3-10. Finished complex type

The next step is to add it to our desired entity. Going back to the EDM, let's add it to the Contact entity. Adding a complex type is just like adding a scalar property to an entity. Right-click on the entity you want to add the complex type to and select Add ➤ Complex Property from the context menu, as shown in Figure 3-11.

Figure 3-11. Adding the complex type to the entity

You should now have a complex property added to the entity with a default name of ComplexProperty, shown in Figure 3-12. It would be wise to rename this new complex property something more meaningful.

Figure 3-12. Entity with complex type property

Even though you have added a complex property to the entity, you haven't told it which complex type you want this property based on. This is very easy to do. With the new complex property highlighted, you can either right-click the complex property and select Properties from the context menu, or you can simply open the Properties window. In either case, you will be presented with the properties for the complex property, shown in Figure 3-13. The complex property has a type property, which lists all the complex types defined. Simply expand the drop-down and select the complex type (in this case there is only one) that you want your new complex property based on.

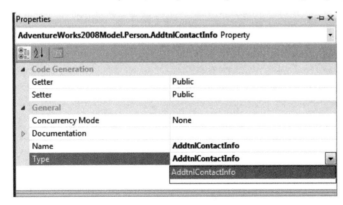

Figure 3-13. Setting the type property

Voila, you're done! You have successfully created and implemented a complex type. Querying this new complex property is as simple as navigating to it from the Contact entity, as follows:

```
Contact.AddntlContactInfo.EmailAddress
```

Throughout this exercise we used the terms complex type and complex property. These terms are not interchangeable. As we have discussed, complex types are made up of scalar properties and other complex types. A complex property is what is added to an entity and based on the complex type.

Foreign Keys and Relationships (Associations)

As you become familiar with the Entity Framework and the EDM, you'll find a definite appreciation for how the EF creates associations. Creating the associations is not trivial, and the engine follows specific DDL rules to generate each association.

In an EDM, relationships look much like logical relationships at the database schema level and therefore are logical connections between entities. Each entity that participates in an association is called an *end*. Each end has a *role* attribute that names and describes each end of the association logically (or in other words, specifies the entities related by the association). Associations have what is called a *multiplicity* attribute, which specifies the number of instances that each end can take part in the association.

For example, Figure 3-14 shows properties of the association (relationship) between the *Employee* and *Person* entities. These properties define the association, which include all of the aspects discussed previously. In this example, the roles are the *Employee* and *Person* entities, and it is a one-to-many relationship. Although denoted by "0..1" (which means "zero or one") this can be misinterpreted. This simply means that one Person might have multiple Employee roles, but only one employee can be related to a single Person.

A better explanation might be taken from Figure 3-3, a few pages earlier. A salesperson can have multiple sales (in the SalesOrderHeader table), but only one sale can be related to a single salesperson.

The OnDelete properties specify an action to be taken when an entity on the corresponding end is deleted. In database terms, this is called "cascading deletes" and provides a way to delete a child record when the parent record is deleted, preventing what are called "orphaned" child records.

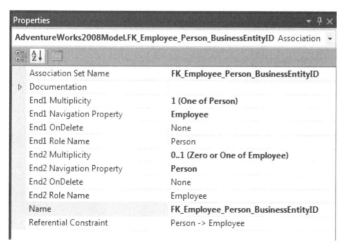

Figure 3-14. Association properties

In this example, every Employee must be related to a corresponding Person. Person and Employee are logically related but they exist as independent entities. As such, it is possible to have a Person without an associated Employee, but not possible to have an Employee without an associated Person. This is the "zero or one" part. Table 3-1 describes those association generation rules.

Table 3-1. Rules for Generating Associations

Relationship (Association) Type	Generation Rule
One-to-many (1:*)	Columns are added to the table that corresponds to the entity type on the 0..1 or * end of the association. The added columns have foreign key constraints that reference the primary key or the table that corresponds to the entity type on the other end of the association.
One-to-one (1:1)	Columns are added to one of the tables that corresponds to entity types on the ends of the association. The table to which the columns are added is chosen at random. The added columns have foreign key constraints that reference the primary key of the table that corresponds to the entity type on the other end of the association.
Many-to-many (*:*)	A join table is created, and for each key property in each entity type, a column is added to the table. The columns have foreign key constraints that reference the primary keys in the tables created based on the entity types on the ends of the association. The primary key of the created table will be a compound primary key that consists of all the columns in the table.

The goal of the EDM in regards to relationships is to provide flexible modeling capabilities, allowing explicit reference and navigation based on a pure peer-to-peer relationship model.

Navigation Properties

We talked about properties a bit ago when we discussed scalar properties. Entities also have navigation properties. Navigation properties are simply pointers to related entities, shortcut properties used to locate the entities at the ends of an association. Navigation properties help describe navigable paths between associations.

Figure 3-15 shows the EDM created earlier, highlighting the entities contained in the EDM. In the figure, the Employee navigation property in the Person entity is highlighted. The properties of that navigation property are shown on the right in the Properties pane. In this figure you can see that the navigation properties of each entity inherit the name of their related entity.

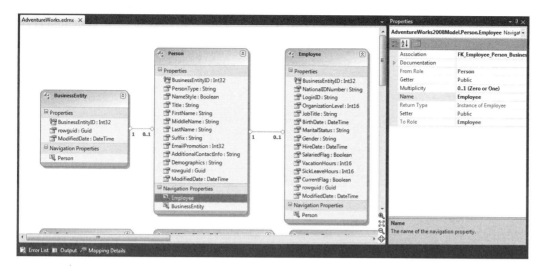

Figure 3-15. *Navigation properties*

From the figure you can see that there is indeed a foreign key defined between the Person and Employee entities on the BusinessEntityID property. You can also see much of the same type of information that you see when looking at the association information in Figure 3-14, such as multiplicity for the corresponding end of the association as well as the role the navigation property belongs to.

Due to the way associations and navigation properties are handled, navigation between entities is very easy. For example, Figure 3-15 shows the *Person* and *Employee* entities each with an associated navigation property to the corresponding related entity, providing a path that allows navigation between the two entities. As such, it is now possible to easily locate an instance of the *Person* entity from the *Employee* entity, or vice-versa.

Navigation properties also provide collection functionality. Let's use the case of the *SalesPerson* and *SalesOrderHeader* for this example. In my EDM, the object model will contain an Add method on the *SalesOrderHeader* property, which allows new *SalesOrderHeader* instances to be created and added.

Mapping Details

The Mapping Details window the lets you view and edit mappings between the conceptual model and the storage model within the EDM. Changes made here are applied immediately to the .edmx file. Through this window you can map entity types or associations.

Figure 3-16 shows table column mapping. There are three columns: the *Column* column lists the table column name and data type, the *Operator* column provides the mapping type, and the *Value/Property* column is the entity column that the table column is directly mapped to.

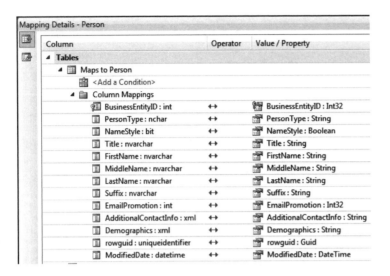

Figure 3-16. Mapping details

Lifting the EDM Hood

Now that we know how the visual part of the EDM works, the next step is to look at the makeup of the EDM. Visually, only a small part of the model is viewable via the Designer, but most of the work is done under the hood and it will really help you to know what goes on underneath there.

Double-clicking on the .edmx files always opens up the EDM in the Designer, so to look under the hood you'll need to implement a "right-click" approach. So, right-click on the .edmx file and select Open With... from the context menu. This will open the Open With dialog box, shown in Figure 3-17.

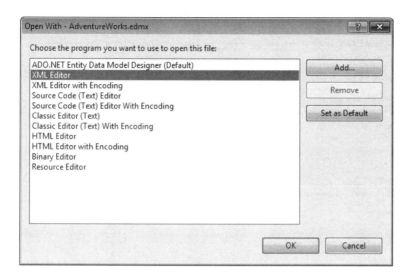

Figure 3-17. Opening the EDM in XML

We want to look at the EDM in its raw form, so select XML Editor (as shown in Figure 3-17) and click OK. If you have the EDM Designer open it will ask you to close it before continuing. Click Yes.

What you are now looking at are 547 lines of raw XML. If you added more or fewer tables, views, or stored procedures your XML might be more or fewer rows, but in my example, there are 547 lines. However, the line count is not important—what is important is the content of the XML. It might look intimidating, but it really is not. The .edmx file is really a combination of three EDM metadata files: the conceptual schema definition language (CSDL), store schema definition language (SSDL), and mapping specification language (MSL) files. The best way to view these is to collapse the individual sections, as shown in Figure 3-18. This will break it down into about 14 lines.

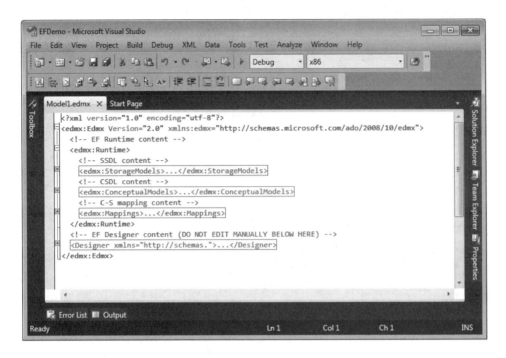

Figure 3-18. EDM in raw XML

From here, we'll look at the individual sections.

The EDM Model Parts

As stated earlier, the EDM is really comprised of several different pieces within two different sections. In Figure 3-18 you can see the two different sections, the Runtime and the Designer sections.

The Runtime section is made up of three additional sections, which were mentioned briefly earlier:

- *SSDL*: Storage Schema Definition Language, also known as the conceptual model

- *CSDL*: Conceptual Schema Definition Language, also known as the storage model

- *CS (MSL)*: Mapping information

Each of these sections is discussed in the following pages.

The SSDL Section

As the name suggests, the SSDL (StorageModel) section is an XML schematic representation of the mapped data store. In this case, it is the tables selected from the AdventureWorks2008 database. Figure 3-19 shows the top of this section expanded. This section itself is about 240 lines long for the objects selected from the database in our example.

```
1    <?xml version="1.0" encoding="utf-8"?>
2    <edmx:Edmx Version="2.0" xmlns:edmx="http://schemas.microsoft.com/ado/2008/10/edmx">
3      <!-- EF Runtime content -->
4      <edmx:Runtime>
5        <!-- SSDL content -->
6        <edmx:StorageModels>
7          <Schema Namespace="AdventureWorks2008Model.Store" Alias="Self" Provider="System.Data.SqlClient" ProviderManifestToken="2008" xmlns:store="http://schema
8            <EntityContainer Name="AdventureWorks2008ModelStoreContainer">
9              <EntitySet Name="Employee" EntityType="AdventureWorks2008Model.Store.Employee" store:Type="Tables" Schema="HumanResources" />
10             <EntitySet Name="BusinessEntity" EntityType="AdventureWorks2008Model.Store.BusinessEntity" store:Type="Tables" Schema="Person" />
11             <EntitySet Name="Person" EntityType="AdventureWorks2008Model.Store.Person" store:Type="Tables" Schema="Person" />
12             <EntitySet Name="vEmployee" EntityType="AdventureWorks2008Model.Store.vEmployee" store:Type="Views" store:Schema="HumanResources" store:Name="vEmplo
13               <DefiningQuery>SELECT
14      [vEmployee].[BusinessEntityID] AS [BusinessEntityID],
15      [vEmployee].[Title] AS [Title],
16      [vEmployee].[FirstName] AS [FirstName],
17      [vEmployee].[MiddleName] AS [MiddleName],
18      [vEmployee].[LastName] AS [LastName],
19      [vEmployee].[Suffix] AS [Suffix],
20      [vEmployee].[JobTitle] AS [JobTitle],
21      [vEmployee].[PhoneNumber] AS [PhoneNumber],
22      [vEmployee].[PhoneNumberType] AS [PhoneNumberType],
23      [vEmployee].[EmailAddress] AS [EmailAddress],
24      [vEmployee].[EmailPromotion] AS [EmailPromotion],
25      [vEmployee].[AddressLine1] AS [AddressLine1],
26      [vEmployee].[AddressLine2] AS [AddressLine2],
27      [vEmployee].[City] AS [City],
28      [vEmployee].[StateProvinceName] AS [StateProvinceName],
29      [vEmployee].[PostalCode] AS [PostalCode],
30      [vEmployee].[CountryRegionName] AS [CountryRegionName],
31      [vEmployee].[AdditionalContactInfo] AS [AdditionalContactInfo]
32      FROM [HumanResources].[vEmployee] AS [vEmployee]</DefiningQuery>
33             </EntitySet>
34             <EntitySet Name="vAdditionalContactInfo" EntityType="AdventureWorks2008Model.Store.vAdditionalContactInfo" store:Type="Views" store:Schema="Person"
35               <DefiningQuery>SELECT
36      [vAdditionalContactInfo].[BusinessEntityID] AS [BusinessEntityID],
37      [vAdditionalContactInfo].[FirstName] AS [FirstName],
38      [vAdditionalContactInfo].[MiddleName] AS [MiddleName],
39      [vAdditionalContactInfo].[LastName] AS [LastName],
40      [vAdditionalContactInfo].[TelephoneNumber] AS [TelephoneNumber],
41      [vAdditionalContactInfo].[TelephoneSpecialInstructions] AS [TelephoneSpecialInstructions],
42      [vAdditionalContactInfo].[Street] AS [Street],
```

Figure 3-19. SSDL

Obviously it wouldn't be prudent to paste the entire XML section in here, but I have tried to include enough to give you an idea of what this section is all about. I'll also include some code snippets as well to illustrate how the SSDL is implemented.

First, there are a few things that need to be highlighted that will help distinguish this section from others. Take a look at the *Schema* element. The *Namespace* includes ".Store"—an apparent indication that this mapped to the data store and not to the conceptual model or anything else. There are other name/value pairs that provide visual clues as to the source of the storage. You'll notice a Provider attribute and a ProviderManifestToken attribute. These two attributes show what provider was used to connect to the data store and the version of the data store. In this case, the System.Data.SqlClient provider was used to access a SQL Server version 2008 database.

There is also an EntityContainer element, which in the SSDL describes the persisted data store. This is usually a database such as SQL Server. The name for this element is typically the name of the database with the words "StoreContainer" appended to the end.

You'll also notice in Figure 3-19 a <DefiningQuery> element. This element defines a query that maps to data-store views through client-side projection inside the EDM. These mappings are read-only. Client-side projection is useful in that users would need to map all store-view columns manually.

OK, with that let's take a look at some of the content further on in the SSDL section.

EntityType Element

As you scroll down in the XML you'll see one or more `<EntityType>` elements. There will be one for each table included in the EDM. The entity type names are the actual names of the tables in the database.

The `<EntityType>` element is used in the SSDL to define metadata about entities in the storage model that is used by the EDM. For example, the following was taken from the SSDL from our example:

```
<EntityType Name="Person">
  <Key>
    <PropertyRef Name="BusinessEntityID" />
  </Key>
  <Property Name="BusinessEntityID" Type="int" Nullable="false" />
  <Property Name="PersonType" Type="nchar" Nullable="false" MaxLength="2" />
  <Property Name="NameStyle" Type="bit" Nullable="false" />
  <Property Name="Title" Type="nvarchar" MaxLength="8" />
  <Property Name="FirstName" Type="nvarchar" Nullable="false" MaxLength="50" />
  <Property Name="MiddleName" Type="nvarchar" MaxLength="50" />
  <Property Name="LastName" Type="nvarchar" Nullable="false" MaxLength="50" />
  <Property Name="Suffix" Type="nvarchar" MaxLength="10" />
  <Property Name="EmailPromotion" Type="int" Nullable="false" />
  <Property Name="AdditionalContactInfo" Type="xml" />
  <Property Name="Demographics" Type="xml" />
  <Property Name="rowguid" Type="uniqueidentifier" Nullable="false" />
  <Property Name="ModifiedDate" Type="datetime" Nullable="false" />
</EntityType>
```

One thing to keep in mind is that the Type attribute of the Property element is the provider data types, meaning the SQL Server data types. The `<Key>` element specifies which properties make up the identity key of the table.

Association Element

The Association element defines how the database defines the relationships between the given tables. In the following code sample taken from the SSDL, the Association element defines the primary key and foreign key relationships between the *Employee* table and the *Person* table.

```
<Association Name="FK_Employee_Person_BusinessEntityID">
  <End Role="Person" Type="AdventureWorks2008Model.Store.Person" Multiplicity="1" />
  <End Role="Employee" Type="AdventureWorks2008Model.Store.Employee"↩
Multiplicity="0..1" />
    <ReferentialConstraint>
      <Principal Role="Person">
        <PropertyRef Name="BusinessEntityID" />
      </Principal>
      <Dependent Role="Employee">
        <PropertyRef Name="BusinessEntityID" />
      </Dependent>
    </ReferentialConstraint>
  </Association>
```

Much of the information is pulled directly from the database. For example, the Name attribute is the name of the foreign key found in the database.

One of the most important elements in the association is the *ReferentialConstraint* element. This element serves two main purposes:

- *Relationship direction*: Using the Principle and Dependent elements, this specifies the direction in a relationship. In the previous code, Employee is dependent on Person.

- *Ensures data integrity*: Specifies data integrity between entities. For example, a row in the Employee table cannot exist in the Person table. This rule exists in the database via the foreign key, but this is also enforced in the Entity Framework because of the ReferentialConstraint element.

As data is sent to the database, the Entity Framework APIs will use the ReferentialConstraint element to check any and all data against this rule before it is sent to the database. Anything that does not pass the ReferentialConstraint rule will result in the data not even being sent to the database.

Related to the <Association> element is the <AssociationSet> element. Directly below the <DefiningQuery> element you will find one or more <AssociationSet> elements. This element specifies the associations in the SSDL metadata. For example, the following XML defines the association shown previously.

```
        <AssociationSet Name="FK_Employee_Person_BusinessEntityID"↩
Association="AdventureWorks2008Model.Store.FK_Employee_Person_BusinessEntityID">
            <End Role="Person" EntitySet="Person" />
            <End Role="Employee" EntitySet="Employee" />
        </AssociationSet>
```

An AssociationSet is simply a container for an association. This might be confusing because you also have an EntityContainer for entities, which is ideal because it is very possible and expected to have many Employee entities, for example. But does that mean you can have a collection of associations? The answer is that associations between entities are also objects, and therefore you can have multiple association objects. An example of this would be where you have a single SalesPerson with multiple orders (SalesOrderHeader), and as such you would have an association (FK object) for each relationship.

OK, now on to the CSDL.

The CSDL Section

The CSDL (Conceptual Schema Definition Language), as the name suggests, is simply a conceptual schema. In other words, it is a conceptual design template for the object model that applications will use to build their applications against. Figure 3-13 shows the top of this section expanded. This section itself is about 170 lines long.

If you think that this looks similar to the SSDL, you are correct. However, there are some differences in the elements and differences in the purposes of the elements. This section also has a Schema element as well as EntityType elements and Association elements.

The CSDL also has an EntityContainer element, but for the CSDL this element controls the scope of entity and associations in the defined object model. As you can see in the next figure, the EntityType and AssociationSet definitions are all contained within the EntityContainer. The EntityContainer exposes the EntitySets, making it the entry point for executing queries against the model. When you write queries, you write them against the EntitySet, and it is the responsibility of the EntitySet to pass permission on to the entity itself.

For the CSDL, the name of this element is typically the name of the database with the word "Entities" appended to the end. You can see this in Figure 3-20.

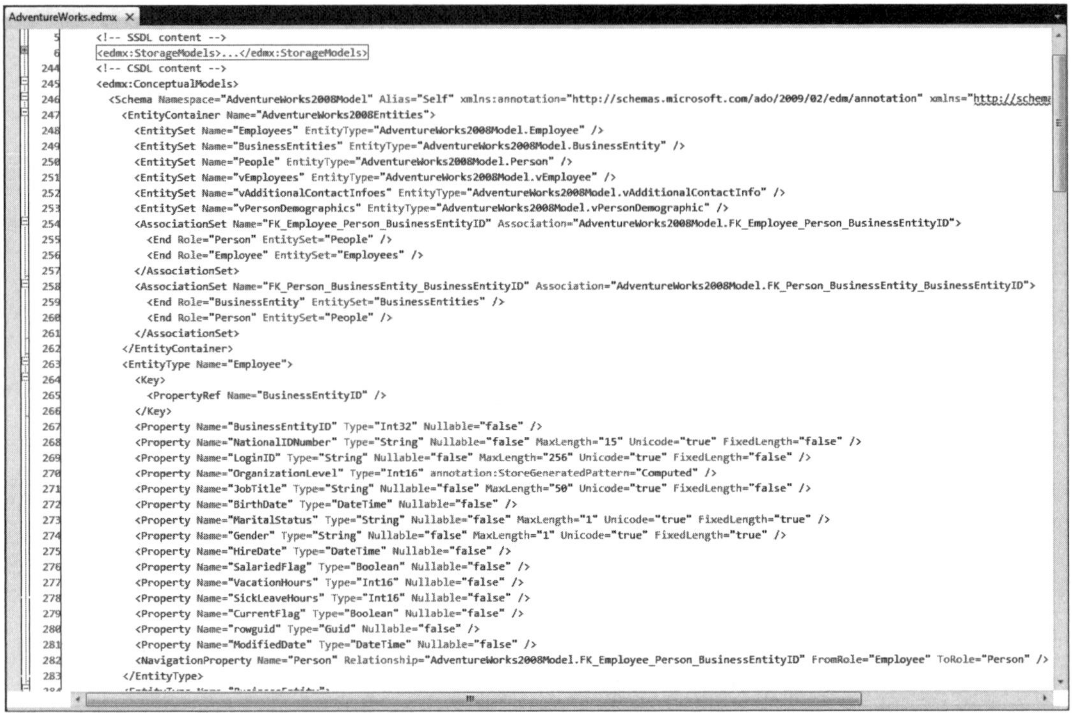

Figure 3-20. CSDL

Let's take a look at a few things we also looked at in the SSDL section, starting with the *Schema* element. The *Namespace* is missing the ".Store" appendage. The name/value pairs found in the SSDL that were used to map and connect to a data store and specify data store version are also gone. This makes sense because we are dealing conceptually and not with physical storage.

OK, with that let's take a look at some of the content further on in the CSDL section.

EntityType Element

In the CSDL, the EntityType element is used to specify an object in the domain of the designed application. Another way to say that is an EntityType is a data type in the conceptual model. The following code shows the EntityType for the Employee entity taken from our example.

```
<EntityType Name="Employee">
  <Key>
    <PropertyRef Name="BusinessEntityID" />
  </Key>
  <Property Name="BusinessEntityID" Type="Int32" Nullable="false" />
  <Property Name="NationalIDNumber" Type="String" Nullable="false" MaxLength="15"↩
Unicode="true" FixedLength="false" />
  <Property Name="LoginID" Type="String" Nullable="false" MaxLength="256"↩
Unicode="true" FixedLength="false" />
```

```
        <Property Name="OrganizationLevel" Type="Int16"↵
annotation:StoreGeneratedPattern="Computed" />
        <Property Name="JobTitle" Type="String" Nullable="false" MaxLength="50"↵
Unicode="true" FixedLength="false" />
        <Property Name="BirthDate" Type="DateTime" Nullable="false" />
        <Property Name="MaritalStatus" Type="String" Nullable="false" MaxLength="1"↵
Unicode="true" FixedLength="true" />
        <Property Name="Gender" Type="String" Nullable="false" MaxLength="1"↵
Unicode="true" FixedLength="true" />
        <Property Name="HireDate" Type="DateTime" Nullable="false" />
        <Property Name="SalariedFlag" Type="Boolean" Nullable="false" />
        <Property Name="VacationHours" Type="Int16" Nullable="false" />
        <Property Name="SickLeaveHours" Type="Int16" Nullable="false" />
        <Property Name="CurrentFlag" Type="Boolean" Nullable="false" />
        <Property Name="rowguid" Type="Guid" Nullable="false" />
        <Property Name="ModifiedDate" Type="DateTime" Nullable="false" />
        <NavigationProperty Name="Person" Relationship="AdventureWorks2008Model↵
.FK_Employee_Person_BusinessEntityID" FromRole="Employee" ToRole="Person" />
      </EntityType>
```

This code looks much like the EntityType of the SSDL, but you'll notice some additional information:

- *Types*: Unlike the SSDL, the data types that define these properties are primitive types, or simple types, of the Entity Framework object model that align with the .NET Framework data types.

- *String data types*: String data types have additional attributes such as Unicode and FixedLength.

Also, you'll notice the addition of a NavigationProperty element. This element defines a shortcut that is used to navigate between entities that are related using the Association type.

The Key element is used differently in the CSDL than in the SSDL. The Key element defines which property or properties make up the identity key for the entity. It also provides tracking at the entity level, meaning that you can track changes to the entity and track updates and entity refreshes.

Associations

Lastly, let's look at the association for the CSDL. It looks nearly identical to an association defined in the SSDL, but the one difference in this example is that where the Type attribute included ".Store" while the Type attributes for the CSDL do not.

```
    <Association Name="FK_Employee_Person_BusinessEntityID">
      <End Role="Person" Type="AdventureWorks2008Model.Person" Multiplicity="1" />
      <End Role="Employee" Type="AdventureWorks2008Model.Employee"↵
Multiplicity="0..1" />
        <ReferentialConstraint>
          <Principal Role="Person">
            <PropertyRef Name="BusinessEntityID" />
          </Principal>
          <Dependent Role="Employee">
            <PropertyRef Name="BusinessEntityID" />
          </Dependent>
        </ReferentialConstraint>
```

```
</Association>
```

You should be able to look at these associations and see that they include all of the same information that you see in Figure 3-7. Two ends are defined, one with a role of *Person* and one with a role of *Employee*. The association *Name* comes from the predefined relationship established in the database. The multiplicity is also defined, and you can see that for every *Person* there will be at least one *Employee*, but only a single *Employee* can be associated to a single *Person*.

OK, now on to the CSDL.

The CS (MSL) Section

The mapping section is a specification that is used to connect the CSDL types to the database metadata defined in the SSDL. Figure 3-21 shows the mapping from our example.

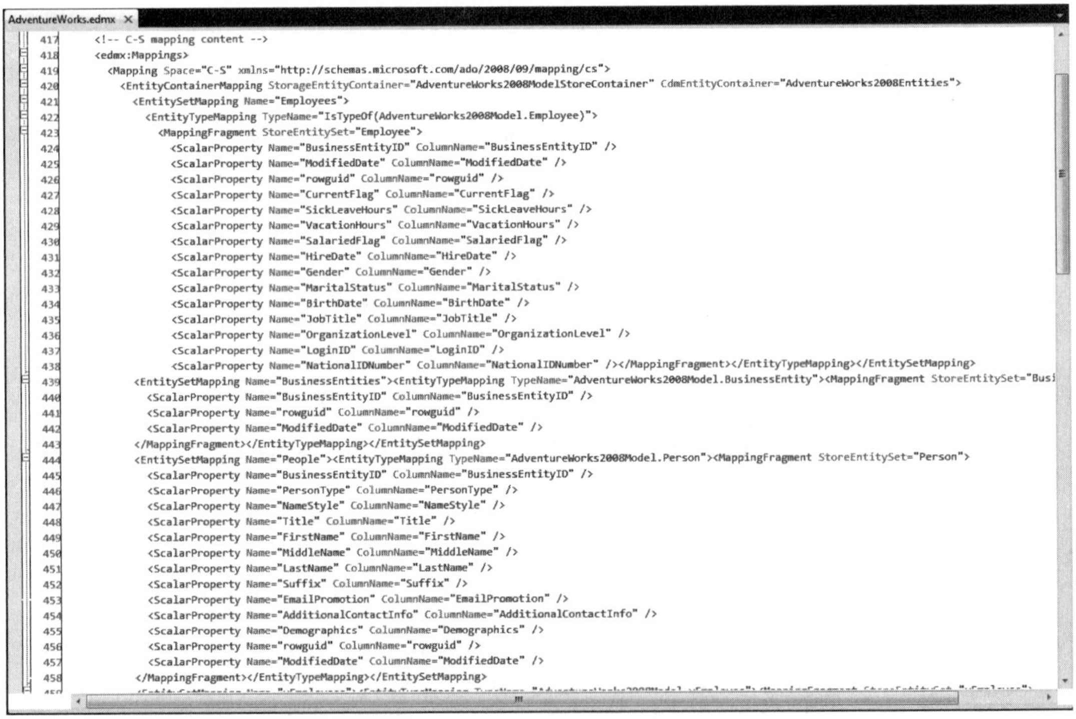

Figure 3-21. MSL

The mapping is a layer that resides between the conceptual and store layers. Its entire purpose is to provide the mapping between entities (entity properties) to the tables and columns in the data store. Notice in the previous figure that the section is actually called C-S Mapping, referring to conceptual storage mapping.

Can these mappings be modified? Absolutely. The mapping layer provides model customization if you like to work with XML. However, there is a better way to work with the mapping and that is discussed in a few pages. What we want to take a look at here are the elements contained in the mapping layer, as they are different from the CSDL and SSDL sections. The elements are defined as follows:

- *Mapping*: This is the root element. You'll notice that the element contains MSL (Mapping Specification Language) Space = "C-S" abbreviation. This simply signifies that the mapping is between the Conceptual and Storage schemas.

- *EntityContainerMapping*: This maps the entity container defined in the conceptual schema to the entity container in the storage schema. This element contains the name of the two entity containers and uses those to identify the same container names provided in the CSDL and SSDL.

- *EntitySetMapping*: This connects an EntitySet defined in the CSDL to an EntitySet in the SSDL.

- *EntityTypeMapping*: This connects an entity type and each of its properties in the CSDL to a table and column defined in the SSDL.

- *Mapping Fragment*: This is used for entity splitting. It does not apply in the current example and will be discussed in detail later in the book.

- *AssociationSetMapping*: This identifies columns in the tables that directly correspond to *EndProperty* elements of related entities. Entities can only be related when a foreign key column in the data table contains a property of another table (usually a key property of another entity).

- *ScalarProperty*: This maps the property name of the entity type property in the CSDL to the column name of the mapped table.

Let me say a few words about association mapping. Figure 3-22 shows how association properties work using foreign keys. This example uses the SalesPerson and SalesOrderHeader table. Think of this like mapping entities using the EntitySetMapping, except here the AssociationSetMapping is being used to map associations.

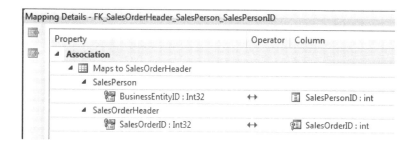

Figure 3-22. Association mapping details

The key in this example is the foreign key, FK_*SalesOrderHeader_SalesPerson_SalesPersonID*. The AssociationSetMapping maps this foreign key association in the CSDL to the SalesOrderHeader table in the SSDL.

EDM-Generated Classes

When your EDM is created, a file is also added to the project that is auto-generated by a tool called the EntityModelCodeGenerator, which is used by the ADO.NET Entity Data Model Designer. This tool is called by the Entity Data Model Wizard when you generate your EDM. The file that is created has a file name patterned after the name of your model with the extension of designer.cs. Thus, if you name your model EFDemo, this file will be called EFDemo.Designer.cs.

Figure 3-23 shows the high levels of this class. By expanding the different regions in this file you will notice that this file is made up of partial classes that define the contexts and entities used by the EDM. In the Contexts region you will find a partial class that inherits from the ObjectContext class, used to provide facilities for querying and working with entity data as objects. Within this region are also the different constructors used to initialize AdventureWorks2008Entities objects.

```
 1  //--------------------------------------------------------------------------
 2  // <auto-generated>
 3  //     This code was generated from a template.
 4  //
 5  //     Manual changes to this file may cause unexpected behavior in your application.
 6  //     Manual changes to this file will be overwritten if the code is regenerated.
 7  // </auto-generated>
 8  //--------------------------------------------------------------------------
 9
10  using System;
11  using System.Data.Objects;
12  using System.Data.Objects.DataClasses;
13  using System.Data.EntityClient;
14  using System.ComponentModel;
15  using System.Xml.Serialization;
16  using System.Runtime.Serialization;
17
18  [assembly: EdmSchemaAttribute()]
19  EDM Relationship Metadata
25
26  namespace EFDemo
27  {
28      Contexts
226
227      Entities
2618     ComplexTypes
2631
2632  }
2633
```

Figure 3-23. Code generation

The following code shows the constructors within the Contexts region. As you can see in the code, the top constructor utilizes the app.config file to retrieve the connection string.

```
#region Constructors

/// <summary>
```

```
/// Initializes a new AdventureWorks2008Entities object using the connection string found↩
 in the 'AdventureWorks2008Entities' section of the application configuration file.
/// </summary>
public AdventureWorks2008Entities() : base("name=AdventureWorks2008Entities",↩
 "AdventureWorks2008Entities")
{
    this.ContextOptions.LazyLoadingEnabled = true;
    OnContextCreated();
}

/// <summary>
/// Initialize a new AdventureWorks2008Entities object.
/// </summary>
public AdventureWorks2008Entities(string connectionString) : base(connectionString,↩
 "AdventureWorks2008Entities")
{
    this.ContextOptions.LazyLoadingEnabled = true;
    OnContextCreated();
}

/// <summary>
/// Initialize a new AdventureWorks2008Entities object.
/// </summary>
public AdventureWorks2008Entities(EntityConnection connection) : base(connection,↩
 "AdventureWorks2008Entities")
{
    this.ContextOptions.LazyLoadingEnabled = true;
    OnContextCreated();
}

#endregion
```

Expanding the Entities region, you will find multiple partial classes, one for each object defined in the EDM, such as tables and views. These partial classes define the methods, properties, and navigation methods of each entity. Looking at the Person partial class you will also see the complex type you defined earlier.

```
/// <summary>
/// No Metadata Documentation available.
/// </summary>
[EdmEntityTypeAttribute(NamespaceName="AdventureWorks2008Model", Name="Person")]
[Serializable()]
[DataContractAttribute(IsReference=true)]
public partial class Person : EntityObject
{
#region Factory Method

/// <summary>
/// Create a new Person object.
/// </summary>
/// <param name="businessEntityID">Initial value of the BusinessEntityID property.</param>
/// <param name="personType">Initial value of the PersonType property.</param>
/// <param name="nameStyle">Initial value of the NameStyle property.</param>
```

```
/// <param name="firstName">Initial value of the FirstName property.</param>
/// <param name="lastName">Initial value of the LastName property.</param>
/// <param name="emailPromotion">Initial value of the EmailPromotion property.</param>
/// <param name="rowguid">Initial value of the rowguid property.</param>
/// <param name="modifiedDate">Initial value of the ModifiedDate property.</param>
public static Person CreatePerson(global::System.Int32 businessEntityID,↵
 global::System.String personType, global::System.Boolean nameStyle,↵
 global::System.String firstName, global::System.String lastName,↵
 global::System.Int32 emailPromotion, global::System.Guid rowguid,↵
 global::System.DateTime modifiedDate)
{
    Person person = new Person();
    person.BusinessEntityID = businessEntityID;
    person.PersonType = personType;
    person.NameStyle = nameStyle;
    person.FirstName = firstName;
    person.LastName = lastName;
    person.EmailPromotion = emailPromotion;
    person.rowguid = rowguid;
    person.ModifiedDate = modifiedDate;
    return person;
}

#endregion
#region Primitive Properties

/// <summary>
/// No Metadata Documentation available.
/// </summary>
[EdmScalarPropertyAttribute(EntityKeyProperty=true, IsNullable=false)]
[DataMemberAttribute()]
public global::System.Int32 BusinessEntityID
{
    get
    {
        return _BusinessEntityID;
    }
    set
    {
        if (_BusinessEntityID != value)
        {
            OnBusinessEntityIDChanging(value);
            ReportPropertyChanging("BusinessEntityID");
            _BusinessEntityID = StructuralObject.SetValidValue(value);
            ReportPropertyChanged("BusinessEntityID");
            OnBusinessEntityIDChanged();
        }
    }
}
private global::System.Int32 _BusinessEntityID;
partial void OnBusinessEntityIDChanging(global::System.Int32 value);
partial void OnBusinessEntityIDChanged();
```

The Entity Framework allows you to extend these classes to add your own logic and protect the custom code you write. When not using partial classes, you run the risk of losing the changes you make to auto-generated code when you regenerate the EDM. Instead of making changes directly to the auto-generated classes, you can put your custom code in a separate file that won't be overwritten whenever you regenerate or update the EDM. The goal is to declare your class as partial. In Chapter 10 we'll see how to create all of these classes by hand using POCO (Plain Old CLR Objects) without the need of the Designer.

CHAPTER 4

■■■

Querying the EDM

You have spent the previous two chapters creating and exploring an Entity Data Model. Chapter 2 discussed the different ways an EDM can be created, and Chapter 3 explored the many facets of the EDM both internally and externally. It is now finally time to write some code.

This chapter will discuss how to write queries against the EDM by using the LINQ-to-Entities syntax and the Entity SQL syntax, both provided by the Entity Framework. This chapter will also discuss the difference between query syntax and method syntax and when you might use one over the other. We'll also spend a few pages discussing how queries are executed so that you can write effective queries for optimal performance.

We won't go too deep in this chapter, since we'll save the more advanced topics for later. The important thing this chapter will do will be to build a foundation you can use for writing and optimizing queries.

Querying with the Entity Framework

The key to remember when working and querying with the Entity Framework is that you are querying a data model, not directly against a database. Over the last couple of chapters you have created several EDMs, and in this chapter you are going to query against the EDM. This is much different than querying directly against a database, for several reasons. First, the syntax is different. Instead of writing T-SQL queries, you will use LINQ to Entities or Entity SQL to construct and execute queries. Second, when you query the EDM you are letting the Entity Framework do a lot of the work for you, such as processing your queries and handling results.

The Entity Framework employs the ADO.NET providers to handle query operations. Specifically, the System.Data.SqlClient is utilized to turn your query into something the SQL Server database engine will understand. On the return side, this same provider will do the work of translating the results into objects that your application can work with.

I know by now you are itching to starting querying, so let's get to that.

Syntax Options

When writing queries to query your EDM, there are several syntax options available to you. Before you begin writing queries it will be helpful to know the differences between the two syntaxes and why you would use one or the other. Thus, the following two sections will discuss the available syntaxes, query expression and method-based.

Query-Expression Syntax

The most common syntax used with writing LINQ queries (LINQ to Entities, LINQ to SQL, etc.) is the query-expression syntax. This is simply because it is easier to read and understand. With query-expression syntax, queries are written using operators and functions. This section will spend a page or two showing some examples of query expression, and most if not all of the examples throughout this book will use this syntax.

For your first example, open Form1.cs in design mode and place a button and list box on the form. In the Click event of the button, place the following code:

```
using (var context = new AdventureWorks2008Entities())
{
    var people = context.People;
    foreach (var person in people)
    {
        listBox1.Items.Add(string.Format("{0} {1}", person.FirstName, person.LastName));
    }
}
```

Run the code by pressing F5. When the form appears, click the button. After several seconds, the list will populate, as shown in Figure 4-1.

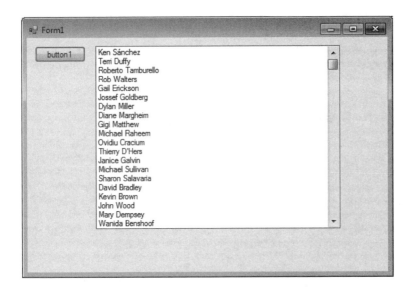

Figure 4-1. First query

If this is your very first LINQ-to-Entities query, congratulations. Let's spend a few minutes looking at the syntax. The very first line we are interested in is the following:

```
var context = new AdventureWorks2008Entities()
```

In Chapter 3 you learned all about the context and how the context is used in the Entity Framework. The context is discussed again shortly.

The next line we want to look at is this one:

```
var people = context.People
```

This line is the query itself. This is the simplest form of a query. The last line executes the query and then iterates through the results.

```
foreach (var person in people)
```

Before we move on, I need to point out a change between .NET 3.5 Entity Framework and .NET 4.0 Entity Framework. Put a breakpoint on the closing brace (}) of the foreach block. Run the app again and click the button. When the execution hits the breakpoint, hold your mouse pointer over the word people in the foreach line. You'll notice that the type is a System.Data.Objects.ObjectSet.

```
foreach (var person in people)
{
    ⊞ ● people │ {System.Data.Objects.ObjectSet<EFDemo.Person>} ⊟
    listBox1.Items.Add(string.Format("{0} {1}", person.FirstName, person.LastName));
}
```

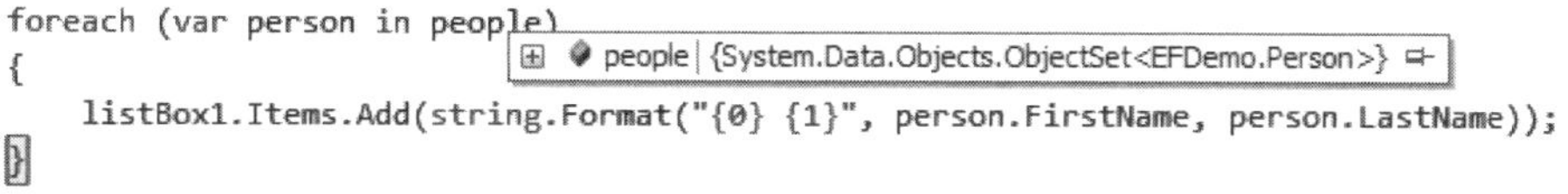

Figure 4-2. ObjectSet

The ObjectSet class lets you work with typed entity sets without the need to specify the entity set name as an argument to each method call. The Object set class also provides object context functionality by expanding the ObjectQuery(T) functionality that allows you to execute actions directly against objects such as deleting and adding objects. The System.Data.Objects namespace contains a number of classes that provides query functionality that the Entity Framework utilizes. These classes enable you to query data by working with strongly typed CLR object instances of entity types. These classes also provide insert, update, and delete capabilities as well.

The previous example is the simplest form of a query expression. Let's get a bit more complicated than that because the previous query just said "give me every record from the People entity." This is not very good because there are 19,972 records in that table. Let's modify that query as follows:

```
using (var context = new AdventureWorks2008Entities())
{
    var people = from p in context.People
                 where p.LastName == "King"
                 select p;
    foreach (var person in people)
    {
        listBox1.Items.Add(string.Format("{0} {1}", person.FirstName, person.LastName));
    }
}
```

Press F5 to run the query and click the button when the form loads. This time the list box will populate with all people with a last name of "King," as shown in Figure 4-3.

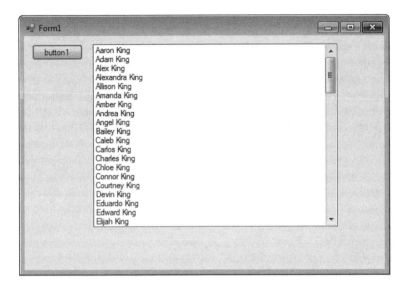

Figure 4-3. *Specific results*

The query you wrote in the previous example is a LINQ-to-Entities query. LINQ queries begin with the FROM clause and end with the SELECT clause. This is much like how the SQL Server Query Engine processes a query. If you were to take the previous LINQ query and write it in T-SQL format it would look something like this:

```
SELECT * FROM Person.Person WHERE LastName = 'King'
```

This is the type of syntax all T-SQL developers are familiar with. When a T-SQL query is written, at the very minimum the query includes, and begins with, a SELECT clause, which specifies the columns you want to be returned by the query, followed by a FROM clause, which lists the tables and/or views containing columns identified in the SELECT clause.

Depending on the T-SQL query, it could include one or more joins, such as INNER JOIN or OUTER JOIN, followed by some filtering using the WHERE clause. It could also contain a HAVING clause, and quite possibly some ordering using the ORDER BY clause.

How many of you stopped to think how SQL Server processes the queries such as the previous one? Does SQL Server execute the query from top to bottom starting with the SELECT clause and work its way down? Initially one might think that, but that is not how a query is processed in SQL Server at all. SQL Server logically processes a query in the following order (by number):

```
(8) SELECT (9) TOP
(1) FROM
(3) JOIN
(2) ON
(4) WHERE
(5) GROUP BY
(6) WITH
(7) HAVING
(1) ORDER BY
```

Notice that the FROM clause is processed first, while the SELECT clause is processed almost last. Any clause that is not specified in the query is simply skipped by the query processing engine. So, why is this important?

While this discussion won't go into the intricacies of the SQL Server query processing, it was discussed to point out the similarities between a LINQ query syntax and how SQL Server processes a query.

Thus, we can take the previous example and write it as follows, keeping in mind how similar it looks to the recent order:

```
from p in context.People
where p.LastName == "King"
orderby p.FirstName
select p;
```

The previous code selected all the columns from the People entity, so let's modify that a bit to only select the first name and last name, as shown in the following code:

```
from p in context.People
where p.LastName == "King"
orderby p.FirstName
select new { p.FirstName, p.LastName };
```

As you typed these queries you should have immediately noticed the presence of IntelliSense. This is also an indication that you are dealing with a LINQ-to-Entities query. As you typed the "p." you were presented with a list of available properties from which to select to include in your query. This is simply because you identified the People EntitySet in the outset of your code, and LINQ to Entities immediately was able to determine the items in the collection that you will need in your query, specifically items from the People EntitySet.

Context

Before we move on to method-based syntax, let's revisit the topic of context again just so we can fully understand what it is and what it does. At the end of Chapter 3 we spent a few pages looking at the code behind the EDM, which contained a number of properties and partial classes.

It is through these properties and partial classes that AdventureWorks2008Entities() class is found. This class represents the EntityContainer, which you saw in the EDM XML that you saw earlier in Chapter 3. The EntityContainer inherits from an EntityFramework class called the ObjectContext. This ObjectContext class is the primary class that has the responsibility of managing data as objects of defined EDM entity types.

It is through the ObjectContext that connections to the actual data store are made and through which object state and identity management for entity type instances are maintained.

Thus, the very first line in our code examples has been the following:

```
using (var context = new AdventureWorks2008Entities())
```

This line establishes and manages our database connection and provides of the functionality of working with entity data as objects as well as managing object state.

OK, enough about query expression syntax. Let's move on to method-based syntax.

Method-Based Syntax

Method-based syntax, while not as elegant and easily readable as query-expression syntax, is no less functional or effective than query-expression syntax. As I stated earlier, most of the examples will be given in query-expression syntax, but this section will describe the method-based syntax so that you have a second option when writing LINQ-to-Entities queries.

Method-based syntax at first might seem a bit daunting and confusing, but the key to understanding method-based syntax is to understand Lambda expressions. Lambda expressions, first introduced in .NET Framework 3.0, are anonymous functions that can contain expressions and statements. Lambda expressions use the operator =>, which is read as "goes to," meaning that the left side of the operator specifies any input parameters while the right side of the operator holds the expression or statement block. For example, the following is a simple example of a lambda expression:

```
y =>y + y
```

The previous expression is read as "y goes to y plus y." In a lambda expression the => operator has the same precedence as the = assignment. So, how does this apply to LINQ queries? Lambdas are used in method-based LINQ queries as arguments to query operator methods. For example, the following code sample shows lambda expressions used as arguments to the Where and OrderBy standard query operator methods.

```
var people = context.People.Where(c => c.LastName == "King").OrderBy(d => d.FirstName);

foreach (var person in people)
{
    listBox1.Items.Add(string.Format("{0} {1}", person.FirstName, person.LastName));
}
```

In the previous code, a simple lambda expression is used to create a LINQ-to-Entities query similar to the query used earlier. While they are syntactically different, the results are the same. This query returns people who have a last name of "King" and orders the results by first name. This query, however, such as the query-expression query used earlier in the chapter, returns all the rows and then pulls out the first name and last name properties to populate the list box.

To fix this, we can add another lambda expression to return only the first name and last name properties from the entity, as shown here.

```
var people = context.People.Where(c => c.LastName == "King").OrderBy(d =>
d.FirstName).Select(r => new { r.FirstName, r.LastName });
```

So, other than syntax, what is the difference between a method-based query and a query-expression query? The answer to this lies in the way the CLR processes these two types of queries. Visual Basic and C# understand LINQ syntax, but the CLR does not understand it. When a LINQ query expression is sent for execution, it is first translated to a set of method calls that the CLR can understand. Since method-based syntax is already in "method" form, there is no need for the translation.

As an exercise, run the previous method-based query in your code. However, before you run the code, open SQL Server Profiler and create a trace against the AdventureWorks2008 database. Run the code that contains the previous query, and when the code is finished executing, open the SQL Profiler trace and look for the query that was executed.

You'll notice that the query that was actually executed looks much different than the LINQ query. Here is the SQL that the SQL Profiler showed that was executed.

```
SELECT
[Project1].[C1] AS [C1],
[Project1].[FirstName] AS [FirstName],
```

```
[Project1].[LastName] AS [LastName]
FROM ( SELECT
        [Extent1].[FirstName] AS [FirstName],
        [Extent1].[LastName] AS [LastName],
        1 AS [C1]
        FROM [Person].[Person] AS [Extent1]
        WHERE N'King' = [Extent1].[LastName]
)  AS [Project1]
ORDER BY [Project1].[FirstName] ASC
```

The idea here is that while LINQ evaluates the query one method at a time, the query is not processed one method at a time. LINQ to Entities evaluates each method one at a time, and when it is done evaluating it will create a store command based on all the evaluated methods. Again, even though the methods are evaluated individually, they are not executed individually (or separately).

Also notice that each lambda expression in the recent method-based query uses different variable names. This is not necessary, as I could have used the same variable in each expression, as shown here.

```
var people = context.People.Where(c => c.LastName == "King").OrderBy(c =>
c.FirstName).Select(c => new { c.FirstName, c.LastName });
```

I use different variables just for clarity and so that I can easily see how the query is evaluated in the compiler.

So, why use one syntax over the other? Developer preference. Develop in the syntax or style you prefer. It's a personal choice.

With an understanding of the two query syntaxes, let's move on to the available query options.

Querying Options

When the Entity Framework was first being developed, the Entity SQL language was actually being developed as the query language to use to query the EDM. However, the EF team caught wind of a "LINQ" language and quickly realized that the LINQ language would be a great benefit to the EF product. Thus occurred the birth of LINQ to Entities. However, that does not mean that Entity SQL has gone away. That option still exists and is certainly a viable option for querying your EDM.

This section, then, will discuss these two options.

LINQ to Entities

LINQ to Entities is typically the query syntax of choice simply because it is easier to learn as well as familiar to those who already know the LINQ syntax. The LINQ syntax has been in existence since Visual Studio 2008 and is gaining popularity fast. LINQ (Language INtegrated Query) was first created to query in-memory CLR objects but quickly expanded to include querying capabilities for XML, databases, DataSets, and EF Entities.

In this chapter you have a seen a few LINQ-to-Entities queries, but this section is going to drill a little deeper. As you have already learned, LINQ to Entities is one of the LINQ implementations and provides the ability to query EF Entities. Since LINQ is integrated into the Visual Studio IDE you get the benefits of IntelliSense and working in an object-oriented environment.

As a quick refresher, a LINQ query begins with the FROM clause and ends with the SELECT clause. Why does a LINQ query begin with the FROM clause? Identifying the type right out of the gate enables the IntelliSense to provide correct and consequential suggestions when constructing the rest of the query.

You saw the following LINQ-to-Entities query earlier:

```
from p in context.People
where p.LastName == "King"
orderby p.FirstName
select new { p.FirstName, p.LastName };
```

In this query, p is simply a query variable name that will be used in the rest of the query to reference the entity object you are working with. Also in the query are four LINQ standard query operators: from, where, orderby, and select.

There are 53 standard query operators that provide sorting, filtering, grouping, join, and other functionality that can be included in a LINQ query. While a discussion of all of the standard query operators is outside the scope of this book, a few of them will be discussed in this chapter as well as later in the book in a discussion of advanced query topics.

For the most part, except for the from being the first clause and the select being the last clause, the order of any other operator does not matter. For example, the preceding query can also have the orderby and where reversed:

```
from p in context.People
orderby p.FirstName
where p.LastName == "King"
select new { p.FirstName, p.LastName };
```

Yet when this query is executed and viewed via SQL Profiler you'll notice that the query executed at the database is exactly as before:

```
SELECT
[Project1].[C1] AS [C1],
[Project1].[FirstName] AS [FirstName],
[Project1].[LastName] AS [LastName]
FROM ( SELECT
        [Extent1].[FirstName] AS [FirstName],
        [Extent1].[LastName] AS [LastName],
        1 AS [C1]
        FROM [Person].[Person] AS [Extent1]
        WHERE N'King' = [Extent1].[LastName]
)  AS [Project1]
ORDER BY [Project1].[FirstName] ASC
```

OK, a quick comment before we get to a few LINQ-to-Entities examples. We need to discuss the IQueryable interface. The IQueryable interface is a LINQ query type, providing the ability to evaluate queries against specific typed data sources (in other words, where the type is known).

Figure 4-4 shows you what the compiler thinks the type is when you hover your mouse over people in the foreach statement.

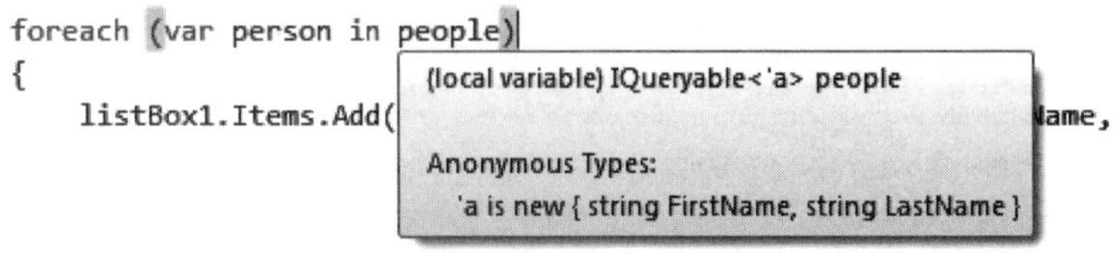

Figure 4-4. IQueryable

In this example, the compiler recognizes that this is a LINQ query, but it doesn't know that it is a LINQ-to-Entities query and therefore really can't tell you the return type because we used an anonymous type to declare people. Although the query will be processed by the Entity Framework, it will result in an ObjectQuery, which implements IQueryable.

OK, let's do a few LINQ-to-Entities query examples. These queries will build on our earlier examples. This first example selects everyone with a first name of King or a first name of Jones, orders them by first name, and then selects only the FirstName and LastName properties to be returned in the results.

```
var people = from p in context.People
             where p.LastName == "King"
                || p.LastName == "Jones"
             orderby p.FirstName
             select new { p.FirstName, p.LastName };
```

This query is similar to the following T-SQL query:

```
SELECT p.FirstName, p.LastName
FROM Person.Person AS p
WHERE p.LastName = 'King'
OR p.LastName = 'Jones'
ORDER BY p.FirstName
```

Modify the LINQ query behind button1 to look like the previous LINQ-to-Entities query. Press F5 to run the project, and when the form appears, click button 1. Figure 4-5 shows the results of the query.

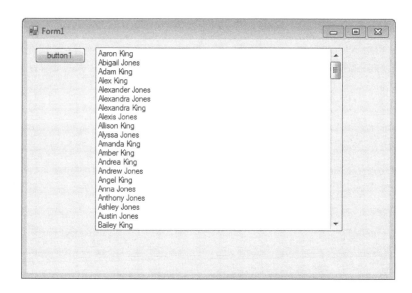

Figure 4-5. Order by first name

Since we ordered by first name, the Kings and Joneses are intermixed. What if we didn't want them intermixed (grouping by last name)? We can accomplish this two ways.

Modify the LINQ-to-Entities query as shown here. We change the Order By to order first by LastName, then by FirstName.

```
var people = from p in context.People
             where p.LastName == "King"
             || p.LastName == "Jones"
             orderby p.LastName, p.FirstName
             select new { p.FirstName, p.LastName };
```

Now when we run the application and click the button, we see that the Joneses are listed first (ordered by first name), then the Kings are listed second (ordered by first name), as you can see in Figure 4-6.

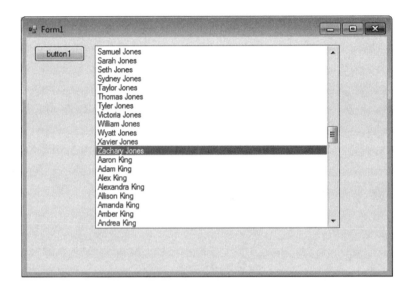

Figure 4-6. *Order by last name and first name*

However, there is another way to not intermix the names, and that is by using the group operator. Modify the query and foreach as you see it here.

```
var people = from p in context.People
             orderby p.FirstName
             where p.LastName == "King"
             || p.LastName == "Jones"
             group p by p.LastName;

foreach (var person in people)
{
    foreach (var per in person)
    {
        listBox1.Items.Add(string.Format("{0} {1}", per.FirstName, per.LastName));
    }
}
```

```
}
```

Running this query will return the same results as the previous query (shown in Figure 4-6). In this example we use the group operator to group the last names, still ordering by first name. This way, all last names are grouped together.

You're probably asking yourself, "Why doesn't this query end in a SELECT?" Well, I sort of fibbed earlier. A LINQ query can end in either a SELECT or GROUP. I wanted to make understanding LINQ queries easy and didn't want to over-complicate things. Now that you have a pretty good grasp of LINQ queries, I feel it is time to throw this at you, but I promise I'll try not to fib any more.

This next query is similar to the original query, but it orders the first name in descending order.

```
var people = from p in context.People
             where p.LastName == "King"
             || p.LastName == "Jones"
             orderby p.LastName, p.FirstName descending
             select new { p.FirstName, p.LastName };

foreach (var person in people)
{
    listBox1.Items.Add(string.Format("{0} {1}", person.FirstName, person.LastName));
}
```

Running this query will result in the names being ordered by LastName, then FirstName in descending order, as shown in Figure 4-7.

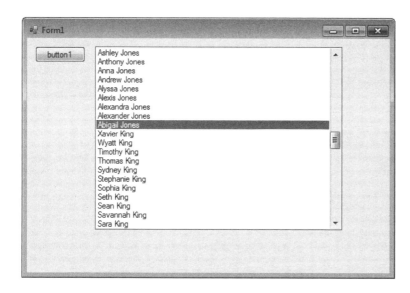

Figure 4-7. Order FirstName descending

OK, one last example. This query uses the join operator to pull in a third piece of data, the hire date. For this query, I removed the where operator filter, but joined on the Employees entity to get the hire date of the person.

```
var people = from p in context.People
             join emp in context.Employees on p.BusinessEntityID equals emp.BusinessEntityID
             orderby p.LastName, p.FirstName descending
             select new { p.FirstName, p.LastName, emp.HireDate };

foreach (var person in people)
{
    listBox1.Items.Add(string.Format("{0} {1} {2}", person.FirstName, person.LastName,↵
 person.HireDate ));
}
```

Notice that the join syntax looks very similar to that of T-SQL. Running this query produces the following results:

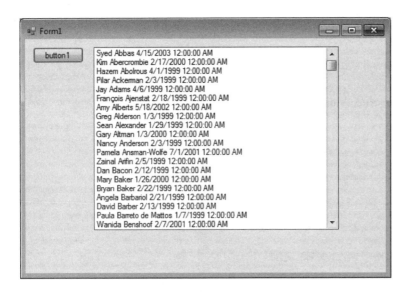

Figure 4-8. *Join results*

In this section we have looked at some pretty basic LINQ-to-Entities queries, but it should give you a foundation on which to start writing and authoring queries. Later on in the book we'll explore more detailed and advanced queries.

Entity SQL

The ADO.NET-provided Entity SQL language is a storage-independent syntax and language that looks very similar to T-SQL. It was the original language designed to work with the Entity Framework to query EDM objects, and as such it supports EDM constructs, letting users query data represented by an EDM.

As much as it looks like T-SQL, there are some differences between the two languages. For example, Entity SQL does not support the * syntax (for example SELECT *, or COUNT(*)). Another example is that T-SQL allows for ORDER BY clauses to be specified only at the topmost SELECT statement, whereas in

Entity SQL you can use a nested ORDER BY expression and be placed anywhere in the query. There are many differences and a complete list can be found here:

```
http://msdn.microsoft.com/en-us/library/bb738573(VS.100).aspx
```

Let's get to the first example. Open Form1 in design and add another button to it. In the Click event of the new button, add the following code:

```
using (var context = new AdventureWorks2008Entities())
{
    var str = "SELECT VALUE p FROM AdventureWorks2008Entities.People AS p WHERE p.LastName↵
 = 'King' Order by p.FirstName";

    var people = context.CreateQuery<Person>(str);

    foreach (var person in people)
    {
        listBox1.Items.Add(string.Format("{0} {1}", person.FirstName, person.LastName));
    }
}
```

Press F5 to run the application and when the form appears click the new button. The list box will populate with the same data as did our very first LINQ-to-Entities example from this chapter. Functionally, the two queries are the same, but syntactically they are very much different.

To understand how an Entity SQL query works, let's take a look at the query itself and its different components. Here is the query itself:

```
SELECT VALUE p FROM AdventureWorks2008Entities.People AS p
```

Now let's spend a few minutes and look at the individual components that make up this query:

- *VALUE*: Used to return an object, not a row. If returning a single item then this is not used.

- *p*: A variable reference.

- *AdventureWorks2008Entities.People*: The collection (EntityContainer.EntitySet) to be evaluated.

- *p*: A defining variable.

The VALUE clause is required only when you want to return a single item such as an entity, property, or collection. However, as stated previously, the VALUE clause cannot be used when selecting multiple items.

Immediately you should see a problem with the Entity SQL approach. While the previous code works and we get the desired results back, the query is a string value and you won't know it works until you run the program. But with LINQ to Entities and IntelliSense, you'll know immediately prior to running the application.

```
var str = "SELECT p.FirstName, p.LastName FROM AdventureWorks2008Entities.People AS p WHERE
p.LastName = 'King' Order by p.FirstName";
```

This last example will utilize the same query but pass a parameter to it.

```
var str = "SELECT p.FirstName, p.LastName FROM AdventureWorks2008Entities.People↵
```

```
 AS p WHERE p.LastName = @LastName Order by p.FirstName";

var people = new System.Data.Objects.ObjectQuery<Person>(str, context);
people.Parameters.Add(new System.Data.Objects.ObjectParameter("LastName", "King"));
```

We haven't spent as much time on Entity SQL simply because it is string-based and is not as elegant as LINQ to Entities. However, that does not mean that the Entity SQL language is not a viable option. It most certainly is. Entity SQL uses a return type of ObjectQuery, in the case of the previous example and ObjectQuery<Person>, not an IQueryable as we discussed earlier. As an ObjectQuery it has all the methods and properties that are not available to IQueryable (however, keep in mind that IQueryable inherits from ObjectQuery).

The EntityClient

Besides using LINQ to Entities and Entity SQL, there is one more way you can query the EDM, and that is through the EntityClient. The EntityClient provider can be used by the Entity Framework to access data described in an EDM. This provider uses supplementary .NET Framework data providers to access data sources, such as SQL Server. For example, the SqlClient provider for SQL Server is used by the EntityClient provider to access the SQL Server database.

The key to using this provider is found in the System.Data.EntityClient namespace. Through this provider operations that are performed on conceptual entities are translated into operations performed on physical sources, and returned results are translated from physical data sources into conceptual entities.

The EntityClient, unlike LINQ to Entities or Entity SQL, does not have its own language, but rather uses the Entity SQL language to execute commands against an entity model. As such, the Entity Framework facilitates the communication and translation of Entity SQL into storage specific queries. Since the Entity SQL language is not tied to any particular database, Entity SQL works great for the EntityClient provider.

Using the EntityClient is extremely similar to using other .NET data access technologies such as the SqlClient. If you are familiar with the SqlClient (and subsequent SqlDataReader) then you won't have a problem with the EntityClient at all.

Let's walk though a quick example to illustrate how the EntityClient works. Open Form1 in design again and add a third button to the form. In the code behind the form, add the following to the declaration section:

```
using System.Data.EntityClient
```

Next, behind the code for the new button, add the following:

```
var firstname = "";
var lastname = "";

using (EntityConnection conn = new EntityConnection("name = AdventureWorks2008Entities"))
{
    conn.Open();
    var query = "SELECT p.FirstName, p.LastName FROM AdventureWorks2008Entities.People↩
 AS p WHERE p.LastName = 'King' Order by p.FirstName";

    EntityCommand cmd = conn.CreateCommand();
    cmd.CommandText = query;

    using (EntityDataReader rdr↩
```

```
    = cmd.ExecuteReader(System.Data.CommandBehavior.SequentialAccess))
    {
        while (rdr.Read())
        {
            firstname = rdr.GetString(0);
            lastname = rdr.GetString(1);
            listBox1.Items.Add(string.Format("{0} {1}", firstname, lastname));
        }
    }
    conn.Close();
}
```

Run the project by pressing F5 again. When Form1 displays, click the new button. The list box will populate with data we have seen in previous examples, such as that in Figure 4-3.

In this example, you'll notice that it executes an Entity SQL query that you have seen a few times in previous sections. But what needs to be highlighted are several new classes, the EntityConnection class and the EntityCommand class.

EntityConnection

Unlike other connection classes, the EntityConnection class is what provides a connection to an EDM, not directly to a data store. The EntityConnection class has several constructors, one of which accepts a string such as the one we used in the recent example, which is the name of the compiled EDM.

```
using (EntityConnection conn = new EntityConnection("name = AdventureWorks2008Entities"))
```

The connection information is tied to the EDM schema with pointers to the connection overloads. Notice in the following code the connection information for the EntityConnection.

```
#region Constructors

/// <summary>
/// Initializes a new AdventureWorks2008Entities object using the connection string↵
  found in the
///     'AdventureWorks2008Entities' section of the application configuration file.
/// </summary>
public AdventureWorks2008Entities() : base("name=AdventureWorks2008Entities",↵
  "AdventureWorks2008Entities")
{
    OnContextCreated();
}

/// <summary>
/// Initialize a new AdventureWorks2008Entities object.
/// </summary>
public AdventureWorks2008Entities(string connectionString) : base(connectionString,↵
  "AdventureWorks2008Entities")
{
    OnContextCreated();
}

/// <summary>
/// Initialize a new AdventureWorks2008Entities object.
```

```
///  </summary>
public AdventureWorks2008Entities(EntityConnection connection) : base(connection,↵
  "AdventureWorks2008Entities")
{
    OnContextCreated();
}
```

```
#endregion
```

You can also see how all of this information is mapped together by exploring the app.config file in the Solution Explorer. In the app.config file is a <ConnectionString> section with the same name found in the previous code as well as what we specified in our EntityClient example.

EntityCommand

The EntityCommand is really no different than other provider commands you have used. It essentially represents a command that will be executed against an EDM. Like other command providers, the EntityCommand has similar properties and events such as the CommandText property and ExecuteReader method. The CommandText property points to the Entity SQL statement that is to be executed. The ExecuteReader method executes the command and returns a data reader.

Immediate vs. Deferred Query Execution

This chapter has focused specifically on queries and query execution. But there is a bit more that needs to be discussed regarding when and how queries are executed. The point at which query expressions are executed varies. The query is not executed when the query is created, and in fact if you step through the code and try to look at the results of a query prior to iteration it will tell you that the results will automatically be enumerated if you try to look at the results. You can see this in Figure 4-9.

The key is to know when queries will be executed and what triggers queries execution, along with what you can do to tell a query to have it execute it immediately. By default, all LINQ queries are executed when the query variable is iterated over. The query is not executed when it is built, which means the following code does not execute a query:

```
var query = from p in context.people
                  select new { p.LastName, p.FirstName, p.MiddleName }
```

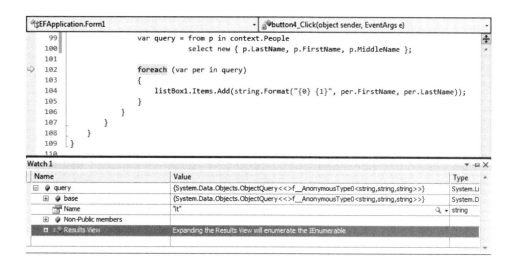

Figure 4-9. Query execution timing

Deferred Execution

The select statement in the previous code does not execute the query. The query is executed when the query variable (in this case, the variable query) is iterated over in the foreach statement. This form of query execution is called *deferred* execution. With deferred query execution, the query variable does not hold the query results—it only stores the query command. The query is actually executed at some point after the construction of the query. Deferred query execution has the benefit of being able to execute the query more than once, or as frequently as needed.

Deferred query execution also has the added benefit of being able to extend the query. For example, in the following code the initial query is created, then a second query extends (modifies) the first query to include an additional filter. Both queries are then executed during iteration, but the second iteration returns only a single row.

```
var query = from p in context.People
            select new { p.LastName, p.FirstName, p.MiddleName, p.BusinessEntityID };

var secondquery = query.Where(p => p.BusinessEntityID == 8);

foreach (var per in query)
{
    listBox1.Items.Add(string.Format("{0} {1}", per.FirstName, per.LastName));
}

foreach (var per in secondquery)
{
    textBox1.Text = per.FirstName + " " + per.LastName;
}
```

When queries return a sequence of values, then deferred query execution is the norm. However, what happens when you need the results immediately or if the query returns a singleton value? This is where immediate query execution comes into play.

Immediate Execution

Any query that returns a singleton value is executed immediately. You can also force a query to be executed immediately. Both of these scenarios are accomplished by using one of the LINQ query operators that provide this functionality. LINQ provides several operators that force the query to be executed immediately and also return a singleton value. These operators include the following:

- *ToList*: Create a List(T) from an IEnumerable(T).

- *ToDictionary*: Creates a Dictionary from an IEnumerable(T).

- *ToLookup*: Creates a generic Lookup from an IEnumerable(T).

- *ToArray*: Creates an array from an IEnumerable(T).

- *Average*: Computes the average of a sequence of numeric values.

- *First*: Selects first value in a sequence of values.

- *Count*: Counts number of values in a sequence of values.

- *Max*: Returns the maximum value in a sequence of values.

Let's take a look at how to force an immediate query execution first. The following code causes the query to be executed immediately by using the ToList operator, which returns the query results in a List object.

```
var query = (from p in context.People
            select new { p.LastName, p.FirstName, p.MiddleName, p.BusinessEntityID
}).ToList();
```

Again, if we step through the code and look at the query variable we can see that the query was executed even before the query was iterated over. We can see this in Figure 4-10.

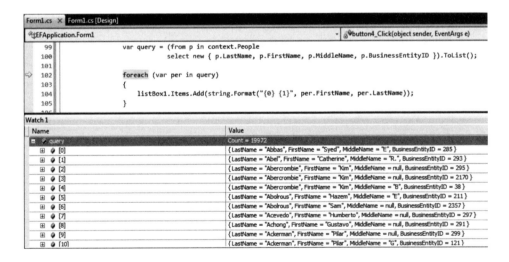

Figure 4-10. Immediate query execution

The following is an example of using the Count operator to execute the query immediately to return a count of all people in the Person table whose last name begins with the letter "K."

```
var query = (from p in context.People
             where p.LastName.StartsWith("K")
          select new { p.LastName, p.FirstName, p.MiddleName, p.BusinessEntityID
}).Count();
```

When we run the code and look at the query variable we can see that it returned 482 rows and that there is no need to do any iteration. Queries that return a singleton value do so because the query must produce the results to calculate the singleton value.

CHAPTER 5

■■■

Working with Entities

By now, you should have a good understanding of how the Entity Data Model (EDM) is organized and how to query it. I've focused a bit on entities and will examine them in more detail later in the book when I look at advanced topics, but I've barely scratched the surface. You can do much more with entities when dealing with data, and that is what this chapter discusses.

The last chapter focused on querying the EDM; but what do you do after you receive the data? In real-world scenarios, you typically add, modify, and even delete data. All these things are possible in the Entity Framework (EF). You can add a new entity or edit or delete existing entities. You'll also look at how changes are tracked via the EF and how changes are ushered back and forth between the EDM and the database.

The ObjectContext

The end of Chapter 3 discussed the ObjectContext and the important role it plays in the EDM, and Chapter 4 referenced it again as it talked about how the ObjectContext is necessary when you're querying the EDM. Every query you wrote in the last chapter used the ObjectContext via the AdventureWorks2008Entities class (which inherits from the ObjectContext). You use this context to execute queries and work with resulting objects returned by those queries.

Let's examine the last sentence in the previous paragraph. The EF deals with objects. Queries are executed against a data source, and the query results data records are never returned; the results are materialized into common language runtime (CLR) types and then returned to the client. This process is called *object materialization* and is performed by the EF. You learned in Chapter 3 that this functionality is provided by the Object Services implemented in the System.Data.Objects and System.Data.Objects.DataClasses namespaces.

The ObjectContext resides through these namespaces. This class encapsulates an ObjectStateManager object that tracks objects during CUD (Create, Update, Delete) operations. There is only one ObjectStateManager for each object context. The ObjectContext also maintains an ObjectStateEntry for each and every entity stored in the ObjectContext cache. This class is the focus of the next section.

ObjectStateEntry

The ObjectStateEntry class is responsible for maintaining state and key information for entities. An instance of the class is created for each entity type in the cache, and it has the sole responsibility of tracking and maintaining the original values of the object, its relationships, and any properties that have been modified on the entity. The ObjectStateEntry class also tracks EntityState (such as whether the entity has been detached, deleted, modified, and so on) and EntityKey values.

One ObjectStateEntry can't have the same key as another ObjectStateEntry within the same ObjectStateManager.

When an entity is first created (enters the ObjectContext cache), the ObjectStateEntity takes a snapshot of it. This snapshot contains the original values of the entity, and as the entity is modified the current values are also stored. At the point of entity modification, the EntityState property is set to one of the following values:

- *Detached:* The object exists, but it isn't being tracked by the Object Services.

- *Unchanged:* The object hasn't been modified since it was loaded into the context or since the SaveChanges method was last called.

- *Added:* The object is newly added to the context, and the SaveChanges method hasn't been called.

- *Deleted:* The object has been deleted from the context.

- *Modified:* The object has changed, but the SaveChanges method hasn't been called.

The great thing about working with entities is that the EF and the ObjectContext do all the change tracking for you. As changes are made to the entity, the ObjectContext tracks these changes and automatically sets the EntityState property. Before you work on some examples, the next section examines change tracking and how changes are saved.

Tracking and Saving Changes

I briefly discussed how changes are tracked using the EntityState, but let's dig a bit deeper to understand how change tracking works. When a new object is added to the ObjectQuery (returned by the query), it's added to the object cache. This cache is maintained by the ObjectStateManager. There is one ObjectStateManager for each object context, and within that object context you can add, modify, and delete objects.

Only a single instance of an object, by entity key, is kept in the cache and managed by Object Services. As such, and by default, queries only return objects that aren't already in the cache. This provides the added functionality of not overwriting the data (objects) in the cache. This functionality is provided by the MergeOption enumeration (which is specified for queries and load options), consisting of the following enumeration members:

- *Append Only:* The default behavior. Existing objects in the object context aren't loaded from the data source.

- OverwriteChanges: Objects are always loaded from the data source. Property changes made to objects in the object context are overwritten by data-source values.

- PreserveChanges: Objects are always loaded from the data source. Property changes made to objects are preserved in the object context.

- NoTracking: Objects aren't tracked in the ObjectStateManager and are maintained in a detached state.

After all changes to the entities have been made, the changes need to be ushered back to the data source. This is done by a single method of the ObjectContext called SaveChanges. This method is responsible for persisting all entity changes to the data store and resetting the change tracking on the object context.

For the ADO.NET 4.0 Entity Framework, a couple of changes have been made to the SaveChanges method. In the ADO.NET 3.5 Entity Framework, the SaveChanges method had two constructors. The first constructor, SaveChanges(), saved all updates to the data store and reset all change tracking. The second constructor, SaveChanges(Boolean), saved all updates to the data store and optionally reset all change tracking.

For the ADO.NET 4.0 Entity Framework, SaveChanges(Boolean) has been deprecated and replaced with a new SaveChanges(SaveOptions) constructor. Thus, the SaveChanges method has the following two constructors:

- SaveChanges():Saves all updates to the data store and resets all change tracking.

- SaveChanges(SaveOptions): Saves all updates to the data store with the associated SaveOptions.

The second constructor allows you to specify an Enum (enumeration) that dictates the behavior of the object context when the SaveOptions method is called. The enumeration members are as follows:

- AcceptAllChangesAfterSave: After all the changes are saved, the AcceptAllChangesAfterSave() method is called, resetting change tracking.

- DetectChangesBeforeSave: Before changes are saved, the DetectChanges() method is called to synchronize the property values of objects. These objects are those that are associated to the object context with data in the ObjectStateManager.

- None: Changes are saved without the DetectChanges() method or the AcceptAllChangesAfterSave() method being called.

An example of this enumeration in use is shown here:

```
context.SaveChanges(SaveOptions.AcceptAllChangesAfterSave);
```

The SaveOptions overload should be used to make sure either that DetectChanges is called before you save changes to the data store or that the AcceptAllChanges method is called after you save the changes to the data store. Why would you one over the other? The DetectChanges method ensures that all ObjectStateEntry changes are identified and synchronized in all objects managed and tracked by the ObjectStateManager. The AcceptAllChanges method allows all the changes on all related entries in ObjectStateManager so that the resulting state is either unchanged or detached. Really, you don't need to use one or the other, because the enumeration has a FlagsAttribute attribute that allows a bitwise combination of the values.

Let's get to some examples. The following sections discuss updating, adding, and deleting entities.

Updating Entities

Updating an entity is simple, as the following examples illustrate. Open your Visual Studio project, and, on the form you worked with earlier, place a new button and a label. This example updates a record in the Person table.

Prior to adding the code, let's look at the data in SQL Server. Open SQL Server Management Studio, open a new query window, and select the AdventureWorks2008 database. In the query window, execute the following query:

```
select * from Person.Person where LastName = 'Kleinerman'
```

You should get two records for Kleinerman, one with a Title value and one without. Let's update the Title value on the record that doesn't have a title. BusinessEntityID 1243 contains a Title value, but id 228 doesn't. This example updates row id 228 to include a Title value.

In the code behind the new button, add the following code (including the commented-out line):

```
try
{
    using (var context = new AdventureWorks2008Entities())
```

```
        {
            var per = context.People.First(p => p.BusinessEntityID == 228);
            // var per = context.People.Where(p => p.BusinessEntityID == 228).First();
            per.Title = "Mr.";
            per.ModifiedDate = DateTime.Now;
            context.SaveChanges();
            label1.Text = "Save Successful";
        }
    }
}
catch (Exception ex)
{
    MessageBox.Show(ex.Message);
}
```

Run the project by pressing F5. When the form displays, click the new button you added. The label on the form displays "Save Successful" when it has executed successfully. Go back to SQL Server Management Studio (SSMS), and rerun the previous query. You see that row id 228 now includes a Title value.

In the code, you create a new AdventureWorks2008Entities object (as you have in previous examples). You then create an object query that returns the record you're looking for. You set (update) the title, update the ModifiedDate, and finally call SaveChanges on the context to persist the changes back to the data store.

Let's look what happens behind the scene. Open SQL Server Profiler, and run the code again. When the code has finished executing, examine the output in SQL Server Profiler. Figure 5-1 highlights one of the lines you're interested in.

SQL:BatchStarting	SELECT TOP (1) [Extent1].[BusinessEntityID] AS [Bu...	.Net SqlClie...
SQL:BatchCompleted	SELECT TOP (1) [Extent1].[BusinessEntityID] AS [Bu...	.Net SqlClie...
Audit Logout		.Net SqlClie...
RPC:Completed	exec sp_reset_connection	.Net SqlClie...
Audit Login	-- network protocol: LPC set quoted_identifier on ...	.Net SqlClie...
RPC:Completed	exec sp_executesql N'update [Person].[Person] set [...	.Net SqlClie...
Trace Pause		

```
SELECT TOP (1)
[Extent1].[BusinessEntityID] AS [BusinessEntityID],
[Extent1].[PersonType] AS [PersonType],
[Extent1].[NameStyle] AS [NameStyle],
[Extent1].[Title] AS [Title],
[Extent1].[FirstName] AS [FirstName],
[Extent1].[MiddleName] AS [MiddleName],
[Extent1].[LastName] AS [LastName],
[Extent1].[Suffix] AS [Suffix],
[Extent1].[EmailPromotion] AS [EmailPromotion],
[Extent1].[AdditionalContactInfo] AS [AdditionalContactInfo],
[Extent1].[Demographics] AS [Demographics],
[Extent1].[rowguid] AS [rowguid],
[Extent1].[ModifiedDate] AS [ModifiedDate]
FROM [Person].[Person] AS [Extent1]
WHERE 228 = [Extent1].[BusinessEntityID]
```

Figure 5-1. Query execution in SQL Server Profiler

A SELECT was issued against the data store to return the data for the specific row you're looking for. This SELECT is in the form of standard T-SQL. Here you can see that the EF, and more specifically the

ObjectContext, translated the LINQ query into a T-SQL statement that the database engine can understand.

Go back into SQL Server Profiler, and click the row that has the update statement in it (the far-left column says "RPD:Completed," as shown in Figure 5-1). The statement was executed to update the data store by calling the SaveChanges method.

What is important here is that only the Title and ModifiedDate columns were updated because those were the only values you changed. Again, as you've learned, the EF sends values to the data store only for those entity properties that have changed. The following code is proof of that:

```
exec sp_executesql N'update [Person].[Person]
set [Title] = @0, [ModifiedDate] = @1
where ([BusinessEntityID] = @2)
',N'@0 nvarchar(8),@1 datetime2(7),@2 int',@0=N'Mr.',@1='2009-09-07 11:41:25.1656711',@2=228
```

One last item before you move to adding entities. Go back to the code behind the button, comment out the first line, and un–comment out the following line. Before you run the code, ask yourself whether the statement sent to SQL and executed will be any different than the previous code.

Next, place a breakpoint on the line you just uncommented, and make sure SQL Server Profile is still running. Now, rerun the code, keeping an eye on Profiler. When the execution stops at the breakpoint, press F10. Notice that the SELECT statement is immediately executed. I discuss this in a second.

Press F5 to finish running the code. Go back to SQL Server Profiler, and look at the update statement. Is it any different? No, it isn't. Why not? Because both statements are essentially the same. The First operator allows you to specify a condition for which to test each element. It then returns the first element of a sequence that satisfies the supplied condition. In essence, it's a filer.

Go back to the SELECT statement. Why was it sent immediately to the data store when you ran the code highlighted by the breakpoint? Standard query operators differ in the timing of their execution. If a query returns a singleton value executes immediately. If they return a sequence of values defer their execution and return an enumerable object. The First operator returns a singleton value and thus executes immediately.

Adding Entities

Let's move on to adding entities. For this example, you use a different set of tables. For the sake of simplicity, create a new EDM, pointing to the AdventureWorks2008 database, and include the following tables:

- Production.ProductModel
- Production.Product

The EDM wizard takes care of all the naming, so you should be ready to move forward with this example.

Back in SSMS, run the following query:

```
SELECT * FROM Production.ProductModel ORDER BY ProductModelID
```

Scroll down in the Results window, and you see that there are 128 rows in the ProductModel table. This example adds a new row to that table.

Add a new button to the form in Visual Studio. Behind that button, add the following code (if you didn't change the context name, it should be called AdventureWorks2008Entities1):

```
try
{
```

```
        using (var context = new AdventureWorks2008Entities1())
        {
            ProductModel prodModel = new ProductModel();
            prodModel.Name = "Front Forks";
            prodModel.rowguid = Guid.NewGuid();
            prodModel.ModifiedDate = DateTime.Now;
            context.ProductModels.AddObject(prodModel);
            context.SaveChanges();
            label1.Text = "Save Successful";
        }
    }
    catch (Exception ex)
    {
        MessageBox.Show(ex.Message);
    }
```

Run the project, and click the new button when the form displays. When the code finishes executing, the label again displays "Save Successful." Go back to SSMS, and rerun the query. Scroll to the bottom of the Results window, and you should see a new row added with an id of 129, as shown in Figure 5-2.

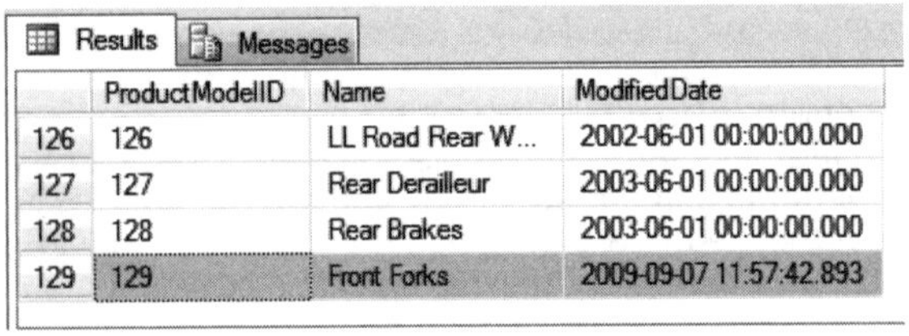

Results | Messages

	ProductModelID	Name	ModifiedDate
126	126	LL Road Rear W...	2002-06-01 00:00:00.000
127	127	Rear Derailleur	2003-06-01 00:00:00.000
128	128	Rear Brakes	2003-06-01 00:00:00.000
129	129	Front Forks	2009-09-07 11:57:42.893

Figure 5-2. *New product model*

In the code, you first create a new instance of the ProductModel class object and then set the Name, rowguid, and ModifiedDate properties. You add the object to the context by calling the AddObject method, and you call the SaveChanges method on the context. Calling the AddObject method adds the object to the ObjectStateManager in the Added state.

There is another way to add an entity, as shown in the following code:

```
try
{
    using (var context = new AdventureWorks2008Entities())
    {
        var prodModel = ProductModel.CreateProductModel(0, "Rear Shock", Guid.NewGuid(),↵
 DateTime.Now);
        context.AddToProductModels(prodModel);
        context.SaveChanges();
        label1.Text = "Save Successful";
    }
}
catch (Exception ex)
{
    MessageBox.Show(ex.Message);
}
```

In this example, you use the CreateProductModel method to create a new ProductModel object. This method lets you specify the property values in the method overload. Then, as in the previous example, you add that object to the ProductModel using the AddToProductModel method.

Relational Inserts

So far in this chapter, you've worked with single entities without dealing with any of their associations or relationships. In the previous examples, you've updated or inserted into tables that act in a parent role, such as ProductModel and Person. But in reality, developers work with relational data, and that means working with child entities. Product suppliers may add product models on occasion, but they add related products much more often. The EF needs to be able to insert related child data easily. Fortunately, it does this quite well. Let's illustrate this functionality with an example.

For this example, add another button to your form, and add the following code to the button's Click event:

```
try
{
    using (var context = new AdventureWorks2008Entities())
    {
        var prodMod = context.ProductModels.Where(pm => pm.ProductModelID == 129).First();
        var prod = new Product();
        prod.Name = "Inverted Kayaba";
        prod.ProductNumber = "IKAYA-R209";
        prod.MakeFlag = true;
        prod.FinishedGoodsFlag = true;
        prod.Color = "Red";
        prod.SafetyStockLevel = 250;
        prod.ReorderPoint = 250;
        prod.StandardCost = 2500;
        prod.ListPrice = 3900;
        prod.Size = "40M";
        prod.SizeUnitMeasureCode = "CM";
        prod.WeightUnitMeasureCode = "LB";
        prod.Weight = (decimal)45.2;
        prod.DaysToManufacture = 5;
        prod.ProductLine = "S";
        prod.Class = "M";
        prod.Style = "M";
        prod.ProductSubcategoryID = 1;
        prod.SellStartDate = DateTime.Now;
        prod.ModifiedDate = DateTime.Now;
        prod.rowguid = Guid.NewGuid();
        prod.ProductModel = prodMod;
        context.SaveChanges();
        label1.Text = "Save Successful";
    }
}
catch (Exception ex)
{
    MessageBox.Show(ex.InnerException.Message);
}
```

In this example, a new Product is created in memory and then attached to the related ProductModel that was queried and returned from the data store. After it's attached, the SaveChanges method is called.

Prior to running the example, open SQL Server Profiler again so you can evaluate the query that is executed. Run the project, and click the new button when the form displays. As in the previous examples, the label displays the success message after the code executes successfully.

In SSMS, execute the following query:

```
SELECT * FROM Production.Product ORDER BY ProductModelID
```

Scroll down to the bottom of the Results window, and you see the newly added row, shown in Figure 5-3.

	ProductID	Name	ProductNumber	MakeFlag	FinishedGoodsFlag	Color	SafetyStockLevel	ReorderPoint	StandardCost	ListPrice	Size	SizeUnitMe
496	842	Touring-Panniers, L...	PA-T100	0	1	Grey	4	3	51.5625	125.00	NULL	NULL
497	878	Fender Set - Mountain	FE-6654	0	1	NULL	4	3	8.2205	21.98	NULL	NULL
498	879	All-Purpose Bike Sta...	ST-1401	0	1	NULL	4	3	59.466	159.00	NULL	NULL
499	823	LL Mountain Rear ...	RW-M423	1	1	Black	500	375	38.9588	87.745	NULL	NULL
500	824	ML Mountain Rear ...	RW-M762	1	1	Black	500	375	104.7951	236.025	NULL	NULL
501	825	HL Mountain Rear ...	RW-M928	1	1	Black	500	375	145.2835	327.215	NULL	NULL
502	826	LL Road Rear Wheel	RW-R623	1	1	Black	500	375	49.9789	112.565	NULL	NULL
503	894	Rear Derailleur	RD-2308	1	1	Silver	500	375	53.9282	121.46	NULL	NULL
504	907	Rear Brakes	RB-9231	0	1	Silver	500	375	47.286	106.50	NULL	NULL
505	1005	Inverted Kayaba	IKAYA-R209	1	1	Red	250	250	2500.00	3900.00	40M	CM

***Figure 5-3.** Relational insert*

In this example, you first query for the ProductModel you want to attach the Product to. You then create a new instance of the Product class and fill in its properties. You attach the new Product to the ProductModel.

However, look at the code that creates the new Product. After the new product is created in memory, it's attached to the ProductModel, but where is the relation? If you look at the table in SSMS, you see a foreign key column called ProductModelID; but it isn't set in the previous code. If you query the Product table for the record that was just inserted, it does have the correct ProductModelID value.

Go back to SQL Server Profiler, and find the INSERT statement. I've included it here as well. Notice that the ProductModelID column is included in this T-SQL statement with the correct value:

```
exec sp_executesql N'insert [Production].[Product]([Name], [ProductNumber], [MakeFlag],
  [FinishedGoodsFlag], [Color], [SafetyStockLevel], [ReorderPoint], [StandardCost],
  [ListPrice], [Size], [SizeUnitMeasureCode], [WeightUnitMeasureCode], [Weight],
  [DaysToManufacture], [ProductLine], [Class], [Style], [ProductSubcategoryID],
  [ProductModelID], [SellStartDate], [SellEndDate], [DiscontinuedDate], [rowguid],
  [ModifiedDate])
values (@0, @1, @2, @3, @4, @5, @6, @7, @8, @9, @10, @11, @12, @13, @14, @15, @16, @17,
  @18, @19, null, null, @20, @21)
select [ProductID]
from [Production].[Product]
where @@ROWCOUNT > 0 and [ProductID] = scope_identity()',N'@0 nvarchar(50),@1
  nvarchar(25),@2 bit,@3 bit,@4 nvarchar(15),@5 smallint,@6 smallint,@7 decimal(19,4),@8
  decimal(19,4),@9 nvarchar(5),@10 nchar(3),@11 nchar(3),@12 decimal(8,2),@13 int,@14
  nchar(2),@15 nchar(2),@16 nchar(2),@17 int,@18 int,@19 datetime2(7),@20
```

```
uniqueidentifier,@21 datetime2(7)',@0=N'Inverted Kayaba',@1=N'IKAYA-R209',↵
@2=1,@3=1,@4=N'Red',@5=250,@6=250,@7=2500.0000,@8=3900.0000,@9=N'40M',@10=N'CM ',@11=N'LB↵
',@12=45.20,@13=5,@14=N'S ',@15=N'M ',@16=N'M ',@17=1,@18=129,@19='2009-09-07↵
12:07:26.0439482',@20='00000000-0000-0000-0000-000000000000',@21='2009-09-07↵
12:07:26.0439482'
```

The relationship defined in the EDM between ProductModel and Product is accomplished via the new foreign key support in EF 4.0 and the associated mappings that interact with the ProductModelID foreign key value.

You should be starting to understand the inner workings of the EF and what happens when the SaveChanges method is called. Long before the query is translated to the data store native command, the ObjectContext identifies the appropriate relationships and uses the defined EDM model mappings to determine the foreign key field's needs. In this case, the ProductModelID in the related ProductModel is needed for the ProductModelID in the new Product.

Deleting Entities

You can delete an entity several different ways, depending on what your code is currently doing. This section explores the options.

Add another button to the form, and add the following code to the button's Click event:

```
try
{
    using (var context = new AdventureWorks2008Entities())
    {
        var prod = context.Products.Where(p => p.ProductID == 1005).First();
        context.DeleteObject(prod);
        context.SaveChanges();
    }
}
catch (Exception ex)
{
    MessageBox.Show(ex.InnerException.Message);
}
```

In this example, you create an object query that returns the record you're looking for—in this case, the new product you just added. You then call the DeleteObject method on the context, pass it the object you returned in the query, and call the context SaveChanges method. The DeleteObject method marks an object for deletion from the ObjectStateManager. After SaveChanges is called, the object is deleted from the data store. If DeleteObject is called on a parent object, all child objects are also deleted.

Run the project, and click the new button. Again, after the success message is displayed in the label, query the product table; you see that the newly added product has been deleted.

The next example illustrates another way to delete entities. In this example, you get the object by entity key by creating an instance of the EntityKey class. By using the EntityKey class, you can specify the EntitySet name, the primary key column name, and the key value. You use the GetObjectByKey method to return the object of the specified key and then call the same DeleteObject method used in the previous example:

```
try
{
    using (var context = new AdventureWorks2008Entities())
    {
```

```
        var prodKey = new EntityKey("AdventureWorks2008Entities.Products",↵
    "ProductID", 1005);
        var prod = context.GetObjectByKey(prodKey);
        context.DeleteObject(prod);
        context.SaveChanges();
    }
}
catch (Exception ex)
{
    MessageBox.Show(ex.Message);
}
```

This chapter wraps up with one final example, illustrating another way to delete entities. You use the same technique of querying the data store immediately for the record to be deleted, and then you call the same DeleteObject method and SaveChanges method to delete the record. This approach isn't the best performing, because you query and return the record you want to delete. It isn't efficient, but it shows you several options:

```
try
{
    using (var context = new AdventureWorks2008Entities())
    {
        ProductModel prodMod = context.ProductModels.Where(pm => pm.ProductModelID↵
    == 129).First();
        context.DeleteObject(prodMod.Products.Where(p => p.ProductID == 1007));
        context.SaveChanges();
    }
}
catch (Exception ex)
{
    MessageBox.Show(ex. Message);
}
```

Now that you know how to work with entities and query them, the next chapter builds on that knowledge by showing you how to work with stored procedures. Several new features have been added to the ADO.NET 4.0 Entity Framework to help you use stored procedures more effectively.

■ ■ ■

CHAPTER 6

Stored Procedures and the EDM

The last couple of chapters, specifically Chapters 4 and 5, focused on querying the Entity Data Model (EDM) and using entities to add, update, and delete data. Chapter 4 provided a good background on the different methods and technologies used to query the EDM using LINQ to Entities and Entity SQL. Chapter 5 provided the foundation for understanding how to work with entities: using entities to update objects, add new objects, and delete existing objects. This information provides the foundation for this chapter.

Given the strengths of LINQ to Entities and Entity SQL, many developers still prefer to use stored procedures when executing database logic, such as CRUD (Create, Read, Update, and Delete) operations. Dynamic commands are proving to be just as efficient as their stored procedure counterparts—but I am of the firm opinion that if the world was coming to an end amid earthquakes and tornados and hurricanes, there would be two developers ignoring the devastation because they were still debating dynamic SQL versus stored procedures.

This chapter doesn't debate which approach is better. There are cases where both are warranted. You may have current stored procedures that you want to take advantage of, or you may want the control over what is executed and how it's executed that stored procedures can give.

This chapter shows you how the Entity Framework (EF) utilizes stored procedures and how this approach differs from using the SaveChanges method you learned about in the last chapter.

Stored Procedures in the EDM

The first EDM you built back in Chapter 2 included a few tables and views from the AdventureWorks database, but it included only a single stored procedure that returned employees for a given manager. For this chapter, you need a few more stored procedures that insert into, update, and delete from a table; but the AdventureWorks database doesn't include any stored procedures for the tables you're using, so let's create some.

The following code creates three stored procedures on the Person table: one to insert a new person, one to update an existing person, and one to delete an existing person. This code is also available from this book's catalog page on www.apress.com:

```
USE [AdventureWorks2008]
GO

IF  EXISTS (SELECT * FROM sys.objects WHERE object_id = OBJECT_ID(N'[dbo]↩
.[UpdatePerson]') AND type in (N'P', N'PC'))
DROP PROCEDURE [dbo].[UpdatePerson]
GO

SET ANSI_NULLS ON
GO
```

```
SET QUOTED_IDENTIFIER ON
GO

CREATE PROCEDURE [dbo].[UpdatePerson]
(
        @BusinessEntityID int,
        @PersonType nchar(2),
        @NameStyle NameStyle,
        @Title nvarchar(8),
        @FirstName Name,
        @MiddleName Name,
        @LastName Name,
        @Suffix nvarchar(10),
        @EmailPromotion int,
        @rowguid uniqueidentifier,
        @ModifiedDate datetime
)
AS
BEGIN
        UPDATE [AdventureWorks2008].[Person].[Person]
        SET
                [PersonType] = @PersonType,
                [NameStyle] = @NameStyle,
                [Title] = @Title,
                [FirstName] = @FirstName,
                [MiddleName] = @MiddleName,
                [LastName] = @LastName,
                [Suffix] = @Suffix,
                [EmailPromotion] = @EmailPromotion,
                [rowguid] = @rowguid,
                [ModifiedDate] = @ModifiedDate
            WHERE [BusinessEntityID] = @BusinessEntityID
END;


USE [AdventureWorks2008]
GO

IF  EXISTS (SELECT * FROM sys.objects WHERE object_id = OBJECT_ID(N'[dbo]↵
.[InsertPerson]') AND type in (N'P', N'PC'))
DROP PROCEDURE [dbo].[InsertPerson]
GO

SET ANSI_NULLS ON
GO

SET QUOTED_IDENTIFIER ON
GO


CREATE PROCEDURE [dbo].[InsertPerson]
(
        @BusinessEntityID int,
        @PersonType nchar(2),
```

```
        @NameStyle NameStyle,
        @Title nvarchar(8),
        @FirstName Name,
        @MiddleName Name,
        @LastName Name,
        @Suffix nvarchar(10),
        @EmailPromotion int,
        @rowguid uniqueidentifier,
        @ModifiedDate datetime
)
AS
BEGIN

        INSERT INTO [AdventureWorks2008].[Person].[Person]
        (
                [BusinessEntityID],
                [PersonType],
                [NameStyle],
                [Title],
                [FirstName],
                [MiddleName],
                [LastName],
                [Suffix],
                [EmailPromotion],
                [rowguid],
                [ModifiedDate]
        )
        VALUES
        (
                @BusinessEntityID,
                @PersonType,
                @NameStyle,
                @Title,
                @FirstName,
                @MiddleName,
                @LastName,
                @Suffix,
                @EmailPromotion,
                @rowguid,
                @ModifiedDate
        )
END;

USE [AdventureWorks2008]
GO

IF  EXISTS (SELECT * FROM sys.objects WHERE object_id = OBJECT_ID(N'[dbo]↩
.[DeletePerson]') AND type in (N'P', N'PC'))
DROP PROCEDURE [dbo].[DeletePerson]
GO

SET ANSI_NULLS ON
GO
```

```
SET QUOTED_IDENTIFIER ON
GO


CREATE PROCEDURE [dbo].[DeletePerson]
(
        @BusinessEntityID int
)
AS
BEGIN

        DELETE FROM Person.Person WHERE Person.Person.BusinessEntityID = @BusinessEntityID

END;

GO
```

After you've created the stored procedures, it's time to add them to the model. Fortunately, the EF makes adding an object to an existing model easy. With the Designer open, right-click anywhere in the designer window and select Update Model from Database from the context menu, as shown in Figure 6-1.

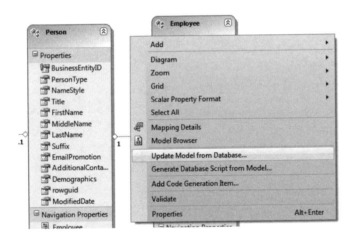

Figure 6-1. Choose Update Model from Database.

Choosing Update Model from Database opens the Update Wizard shown in Figure 6-2.

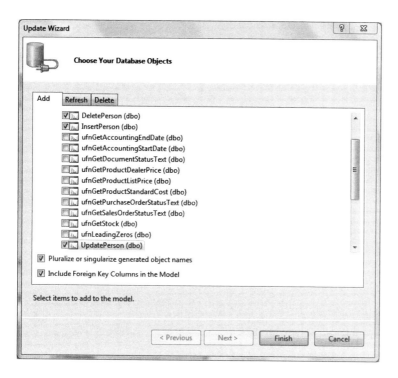

Figure 6-2. Adding new stored procedures

You use this wizard to update your model (the .edmx file). The Update Wizard has three tabs: Add, Refresh, and Delete. The Delete tab displays a list of database objects that will be deleted from the storage model. The Refresh tab displays a list of database objects whose definitions will be refreshed in the storage model. The Add tab lets you choose which objects you want to add to your model that you have not previously added.

On the Add tab, expand the Stored Procedures node, and select the three stored procedures you created earlier: DeletePerson, SelectPerson, and UpdatePerson. Then, click the Finish button. You use these stored procedures momentarily; first, I you need to discuss the Model Browser window.

The Model Browser

Whenever you have an EDM open and are viewing the Designer, a new windows appears to the right in the Visual Studio IDE: the Model Browser. This window is integrated into the EDM Designer to provide a view into the conceptual and storage models defined into the .edmx file.

The Model Browser window has two main nodes. The first (or top) node lists the entity types, complex types, and associations in the conceptual model. The second node lists all the objects you've imported into your EDM from the target database. Figure 6-3 shows the Model Browser from this chapter's example; I've expanded the first and second nodes and then expanded the Stored Procedures node under the data store node. The figure shows the stored procedures that I've imported into my EDM.

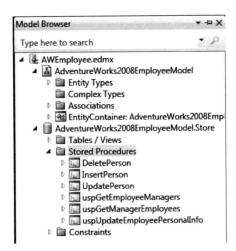

Figure 6-3. *The Model Browser*

You use the Model Browser later in the chapter; it's an important part of the EDM. In the Model Browser window, you can modify properties and mappings, locate an entity type on the design surface, and search the tree view of the conceptual and storage models.

What Is an EF Function?

You'll find out very quickly that the EDM doesn't incorporate the concept of a stored procedure. The EDM deals with functions, and in the model a function can represent either a stored procedure or a user-defined function (UDF). When you added stored procedures to the EDM, the SOAP Service Description Language (SSDL) represents the stored procedures as functions. For example, the following XML was taken from the SSDL from this chapter's example for the InsertPerson stored procedure:

```
<Function Name="InsertPerson" Aggregate="false" BuiltIn="false" NiladicFunction="false"
        IsComposable="false" ParameterTypeSemantics="AllowImplicitConversion" Schema="dbo">
  <Parameter Name="BusinessEntityID" Type="int" Mode="In" />
  <Parameter Name="PersonType" Type="nchar" Mode="In" />
  <Parameter Name="NameStyle" Type="bit" Mode="In" />
  <Parameter Name="Title" Type="nvarchar" Mode="In" />
  <Parameter Name="FirstName" Type="nvarchar" Mode="In" />
  <Parameter Name="MiddleName" Type="nvarchar" Mode="In" />
  <Parameter Name="LastName" Type="nvarchar" Mode="In" />
  <Parameter Name="Suffix" Type="nvarchar" Mode="In" />
  <Parameter Name="EmailPromotion" Type="int" Mode="In" />
  <Parameter Name="rowguid" Type="uniqueidentifier" Mode="In" />
  <Parameter Name="ModifiedDate" Type="datetime" Mode="In" />
</Function>
```

As you can see, the stored procedure is represented via a <Function>. This element contains several attributes that define the characteristics and behavior of the stored procedure, such as schema, which defines the database schema the object belongs to, and IsComposable, which indicates that the results returned by the procedure can't be used in the FROM clause of other SQL Statements (the value of this attribute must be `false`).

The `<Parameter>` element lists and describes any and all parameters, whether input or output. In this case, they're all input parameters.

From here, it's time to map the stored procedures (functions) to the appropriate entity.

Mapping Functions

Mapping a function is straightforward. By default, the EF constructs its own insert, update, and delete commands and sends them to the data store to be executed. You saw some of that in the previous chapter. This default behavior can be overwritten by mapping functions to a specific entity. After the mapping is done and your code calls SaveChanges(), the stored procedure is called instead of the native commands.

This section shows you how to map functions to entities, which is quite simple. With the EDM Designer open, click the entity to which you want to map the stored procedures. For this example, map the stored procedures to the Person entity. When you've selected the Person entity, open the Mapping Details window at the bottom of the Visual Studio IDE.

In this window, you see two icons at left. The top icon lets you map the selected entity to a table or view. You want the option shown in Figure 6-4, which lets you map entities to functions.

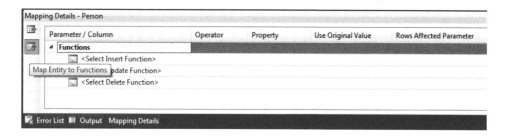

Figure 6-4. The Mapping Details window

Let's map the insert function first. In the Mapping Details window, click <Select Insert Function>. When you do, you're presented with a drop-down list of the available functions. Select the InsertPerson function. Your Mapping Details window now looks like Figure 6-5.

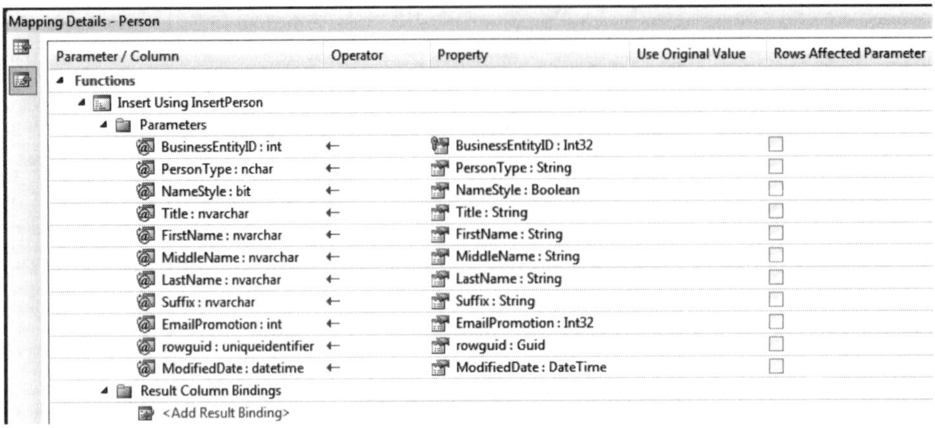

Figure 6-5. *Mapping the insert function*

Figure 6-5 shows the results of mapping a function to an entity. The Parameter/Column column lists all the columns or parameters (in this case, parameters) in the function. The Operator column shows the mapping or condition operator. In this example, it's showing what parameters are being mapped to what columns in the table (or entity). The Property column displays the entity property to which the parameter or column is being mapped.

Next, map the update function by selecting the UpdatePerson stored procedure from the drop-down list. Figure 6-6 shows the results of that mapping.

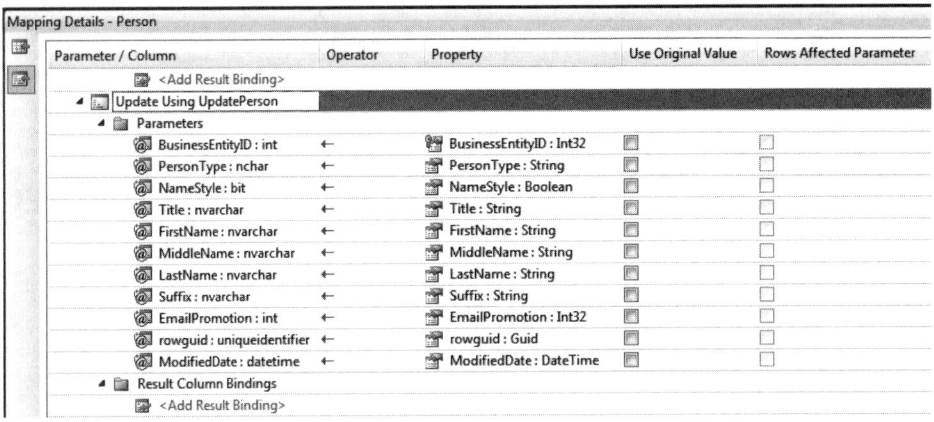

Figure 6-6. *Mapping the update function*

Last, map the delete function by selecting the DeletePerson stored procedure from the drop-down list. Figure 6-7 shows the results of that mapping.

Figure 6-7. *Mapping the delete function*

With the mappings complete, let's look at what happened under the covers. This information can be found in the mapping information (mapping specification language [MSL]) of the .edmx file. The following code shows what was added to the MSL. Here you see that a second EntityTypeMapping element has been added, mapping the functions to the Person entity:

```
<EntitySetMapping Name="People">
    <EntityTypeMapping TypeName="AdventureWorks2008Model.Person">
        <MappingFragment StoreEntitySet="Person">
            <ScalarProperty Name="BusinessEntityID" ColumnName="BusinessEntityID" />
            <ScalarProperty Name="PersonType" ColumnName="PersonType" />
            <ScalarProperty Name="NameStyle" ColumnName="NameStyle" />
            <ScalarProperty Name="Title" ColumnName="Title" />
            <ScalarProperty Name="FirstName" ColumnName="FirstName" />
            <ScalarProperty Name="MiddleName" ColumnName="MiddleName" />
            <ScalarProperty Name="LastName" ColumnName="LastName" />
            <ScalarProperty Name="Suffix" ColumnName="Suffix" />
            <ScalarProperty Name="EmailPromotion" ColumnName="EmailPromotion" />
            <ScalarProperty Name="AdditionalContactInfo" ColumnName↵
="AdditionalContactInfo" />
            <ScalarProperty Name="Demographics" ColumnName="Demographics" />
            <ScalarProperty Name="rowguid" ColumnName="rowguid" />
            <ScalarProperty Name="ModifiedDate" ColumnName="ModifiedDate" />
        </MappingFragment>
    </EntityTypeMapping>
    <EntityTypeMapping TypeName="AdventureWorks2008Model.Person">
        <ModificationFunctionMapping>
            <InsertFunction FunctionName="AdventureWorks2008Model.Store.InsertPerson">
                <ScalarProperty Name="ModifiedDate" ParameterName="ModifiedDate" />
                <ScalarProperty Name="rowguid" ParameterName="rowguid" />
                <ScalarProperty Name="EmailPromotion" ParameterName="EmailPromotion" />
                <ScalarProperty Name="Suffix" ParameterName="Suffix" />
                <ScalarProperty Name="LastName" ParameterName="LastName" />
                <ScalarProperty Name="MiddleName" ParameterName="MiddleName" />
                <ScalarProperty Name="FirstName" ParameterName="FirstName" />
                <ScalarProperty Name="Title" ParameterName="Title" />
                <ScalarProperty Name="NameStyle" ParameterName="NameStyle" />
                <ScalarProperty Name="PersonType" ParameterName="PersonType" />
                <ScalarProperty Name="BusinessEntityID" ParameterName="BusinessEntityID" />
            </InsertFunction>
```

```
        <UpdateFunction FunctionName="AdventureWorks2008Model.Store.UpdatePerson">
            <ScalarProperty Name="ModifiedDate" ParameterName="ModifiedDate"↵
Version="Current" />
            <ScalarProperty Name="rowguid" ParameterName="rowguid" Version="Current" />
            <ScalarProperty Name="EmailPromotion" ParameterName="EmailPromotion"↵
Version="Current" />
            <ScalarProperty Name="Suffix" ParameterName="Suffix" Version="Current" />
            <ScalarProperty Name="LastName" ParameterName="LastName"↵
Version="Current" />
            <ScalarProperty Name="MiddleName" ParameterName="MiddleName"↵
Version="Current" />
            <ScalarProperty Name="FirstName" ParameterName="FirstName"↵
Version="Current" />
            <ScalarProperty Name="Title" ParameterName="Title" Version="Current" />
            <ScalarProperty Name="NameStyle" ParameterName="NameStyle"↵
Version="Current" />
            <ScalarProperty Name="PersonType" ParameterName="PersonType"↵
Version="Current" />
            <ScalarProperty Name="BusinessEntityID" ParameterName="BusinessEntityID"↵
Version="Current" />
        </UpdateFunction>
        <DeleteFunction FunctionName="AdventureWorks2008Model.Store.DeletePerson">
            <ScalarProperty Name="BusinessEntityID" ParameterName="BusinessEntityID" />
        </DeleteFunction>
      </ModificationFunctionMapping>
    </EntityTypeMapping>
</EntitySetMapping>
```

As a child element of the `EntityTypeMapping` element, the `ModificationFunctionMapping` element specifies the functions (stored procedures) in the storage schema that handle change processing for an entity type. This element lists the insert, update, and delete function elements. The `Function` elements—that is, the `InsertFunction`, `UpdateFunction`, and `DeleteFunction` child elements—define the function to be called for the associated operation and the parameter bindings.

Functions (Stored Procedures) in Action

Now you put your new stored procedures and function mappings to the test. Open your form from the last example in design mode, and add four more buttons and another list box (if there is a list box already on the form, you can use it). Set the Text properties of the buttons to Insert, Update, Delete, and Select. You're going for functionality here, not pretty form design.

The next four sections test the functions you created.

Insert

Let's test the insert function first. In the code behind the Insert button, add the following code:

```
try
{
    using (var context = new AdventureWorks2008EmployeeEntities())
    {
        var busent = context.BusinessEntities.Where(p => p.BusinessEntityID == 292).First();
        var per = new Person();
```

```
        per.PersonType = "SC";
        per.NameStyle = true;
        per.Title = "Geek";
        per.FirstName = "Scott";
        per.MiddleName = "L";
        per.LastName = "Klein";
        per.Suffix = "Mr";
        per.EmailPromotion = 1;
        per.rowguid = Guid.NewGuid();
        per.ModifiedDate = DateTime.Now;
        busent.Person = per;
        context.SaveChanges();
        MessageBox.Show("record inserted");
    }
}
catch (Exception ex)
{
    MessageBox.Show(ex.InnerException.Message);
}
```

This code should look extremely familiar, because it's much like the code you wrote in the last chapter. First the context is created. Then, you query for a specific BusinessEntity, because in this example you insert a related Person record for an existing BusinessEntity record that doesn't already exist in the Person table.

You then create a new Person object, populate its properties, and call SaveChanges(). However, before you run this example, open SQL Server Profiler and start a new trace. When the trace is running, switch to Visual Studio, and run the project. Click the Insert button; if you coded everything correctly, you get a message box stating that the insert was successful.

Go back to the SQL Server Profiler, and pause the trace. Scroll up or down in the trace until you see the statement showing the execution of the InsertPerson stored procedure (see Figure 6-8).

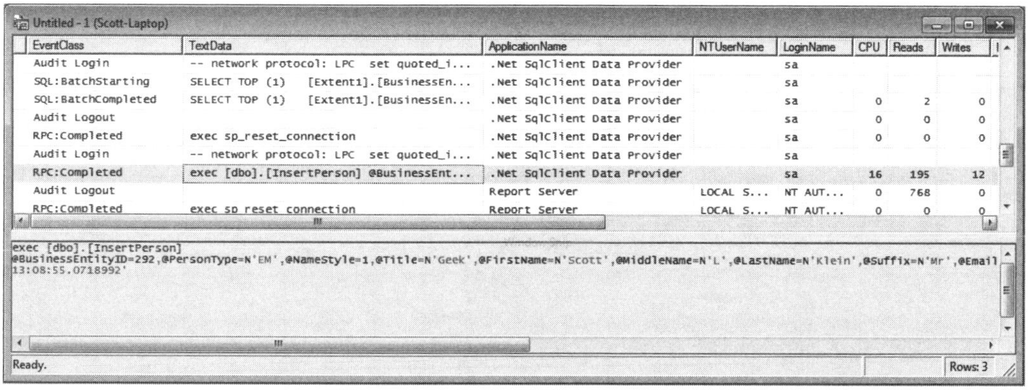

Figure 6-8. SQL Server Profiler insert

Instead of the native SQL commands being executed, the EF and the EDM utilized the stored procedure to do the insert, passing as parameters all the values you specified.

Now, a note: You may be asking, "What about stored procedures that return a new identity value?" These examples use the AdventureWorks2008 Person tables, and they use the same BusinessEntityID as the primary key in the tables. What you're wondering about, however, is doable, and I discuss it in another chapter.

Update

Let's move on to the update function. Behind the Update button, add the following code:

```
try
{
    using (var context = new AdventureWorks2008EmployeeEntities())
    {
        var per = context.People.Where(p => p.BusinessEntityID == 292).First();
        per.Title = "Head Geek";
        per.ModifiedDate = DateTime.Now;
        per.PersonType = "EM";
        context.SaveChanges();
        MessageBox.Show("record updated");
    }
}
catch (Exception ex)
{
    MessageBox.Show(ex.InnerException.Message);
}
```

This code is much like the first example, in that you're creating a new context instance; but this time you query the People entity for the record you just inserted, because you want to update that record. Start SQL Server Profiler again, and run the project. Click the Update button, and you should get a message stating that the update was successful. Switch over to SQL Server Profiler, and pause the trace so you can scroll up to find the update execution statement (see Figure 6-9).

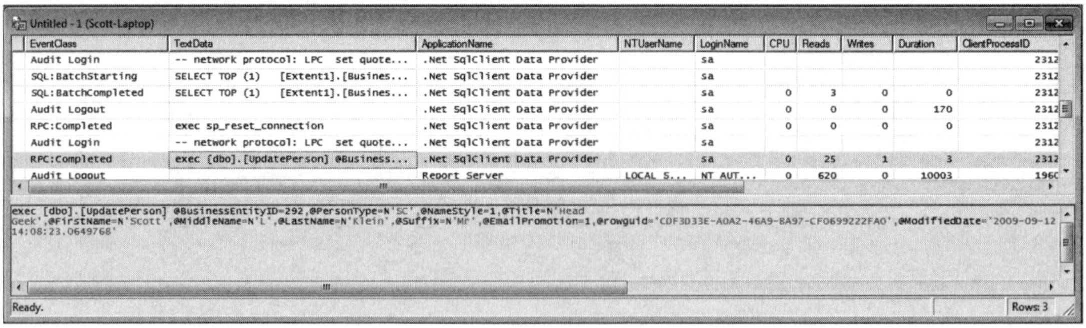

Figure 6-9. SQL Server Profiler update

Notice that even though you only updated the Title, PersonType, and ModifiedDate properties, the update statement included all the property values and sent them to the stored procedure. Why? Because the update stored procedure, based on the earlier mapping, expects 11 parameters, not just 3.

Delete

Finally, the delete function. Behind the Delete button, add the following code:

```
try
{
    using (var context = new AdventureWorks2008EmployeeEntities())
    {
        var per = context.People.Where(p => p.BusinessEntityID == 292).First();
        context.DeleteObject(per);
        context.SaveChanges();
        MessageBox.Show("record deleted");
    }
}
catch (Exception ex)
{
    MessageBox.Show(ex.Message);
}
```

Nothing too complicated here. You ask for the record you just inserted/updated, call the DeleteObject() method on the context (just as you did in the last chapter), and call the SaveChanges() method. Figure 6-10 shows the results of this code execution in SQL Server Profiler.

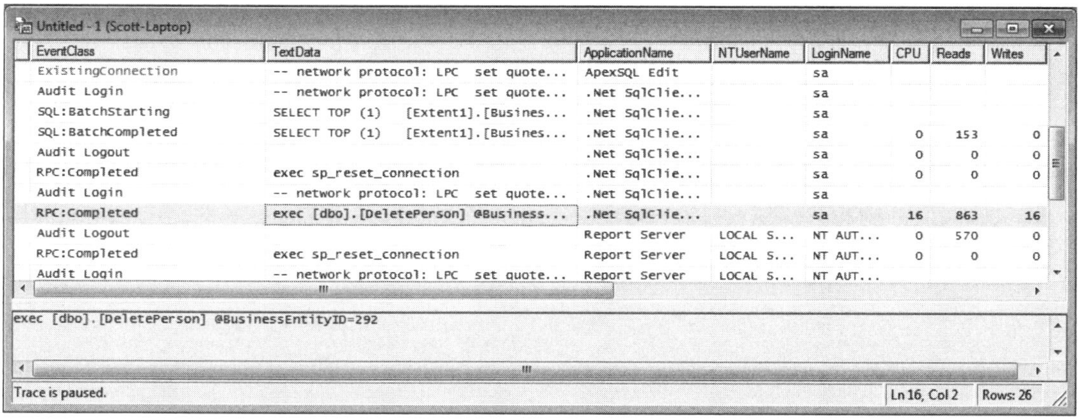

Figure 6-10. SQL Server Profiler delete

Now you've seen how easy it is to map stored procedures in the EF. Granted, these examples are simple, but the goal is to show you how function-mapping works. I'll get into more in-depth examples (such as using complex types) later in the book.

Select

But wait—you're not finished. What about stored procedures that return data? This is where the Model Browser comes in. Select stored procedures aren't mapped like their other CRUD brethren. You need to use the Model Browser for select procedures. First you need a select stored procedure, so let's create one. The following code creates a stored procedure that simply selects from the Person.Person table:

```
USE [AdventureWorks2008]
GO

IF  EXISTS (SELECT * FROM sys.objects WHERE object_id = OBJECT_ID(N'[dbo]↵
.[SelectPeople]') AND type in (N'P', N'PC'))
DROP PROCEDURE [dbo].[SelectPeople]
GO

SET ANSI_NULLS ON
GO

SET QUOTED_IDENTIFIER ON
GO


CREATE PROCEDURE [dbo].[SelectPeople]
AS
BEGIN

        SELECT
                [BusinessEntityID],
                [PersonType],
                [NameStyle],
                [Title],
                [FirstName],
                [MiddleName],
                [LastName],
                [Suffix],
                [EmailPromotion],
                [AdditionalContactInfo],
                [Demographics],
                [rowguid],
                [ModifiedDate]
        FROM
                [AdventureWorks2008].[Person].[Person]

END;

GO
```

You still need to add this stored procedure to the EDM, following the steps outlined earlier. The next section walks you through using your new stored procedure.

Using Functions in Queries

With the new stored procedure added, you need to go into the Model Browser so you can map it for reading. You do that by creating a Function Import mapping. In the Model Browser window, navigate to the stored procedures, and right-click the SelectPerson stored procedure. Doing so displays a context menu; select Add Function Import, as shown in Figure 6-11.

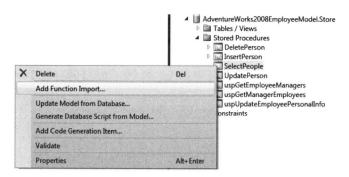

Figure 6-11. Add Function Import menu option

Note that the Add Function Import menu item is renamed for the ADO.NET 4.0 Entity Framework—it used to be Create Function Import. Selecting this option opens the Add Function Import dialog, shown in Figure 6-12.

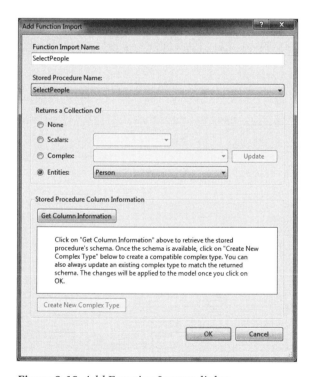

Figure 6-12. Add Function Import dialog

If you're familiar with this form in ADO.NET 3.5, you'll immediately notice that it looks much different. The top part of the dialog looks like the previous version except for the ability to return a collection of a complex type. The lower half of the dialog is completely new. This section allows you to create a new complex type to use in your stored procedure mapping. Again, I don't look at this here, but I'll return to it in a later chapter.

You want to select an Entity return type collection and then select the Person entity. Click OK.

Now you know why you added four buttons to the form. Add the following code behind the Select button:

```
using (var context = new AdventureWorks2008EmployeeEntities())
{
    var query = from p in context.SelectPeople()
                    where p.LastName.StartsWith("Kl")
                    select p;

    foreach (var per in query)
    {
        listbox1.Items.Add(string.Format("{0} {1}", per.FirstName, per.LastName);
    }
}
```

In SQL Server Profiler, run the project. Click the Select button, and a few names appear in the list box. Figure 6-13 shows the results of the stored procedure execution.

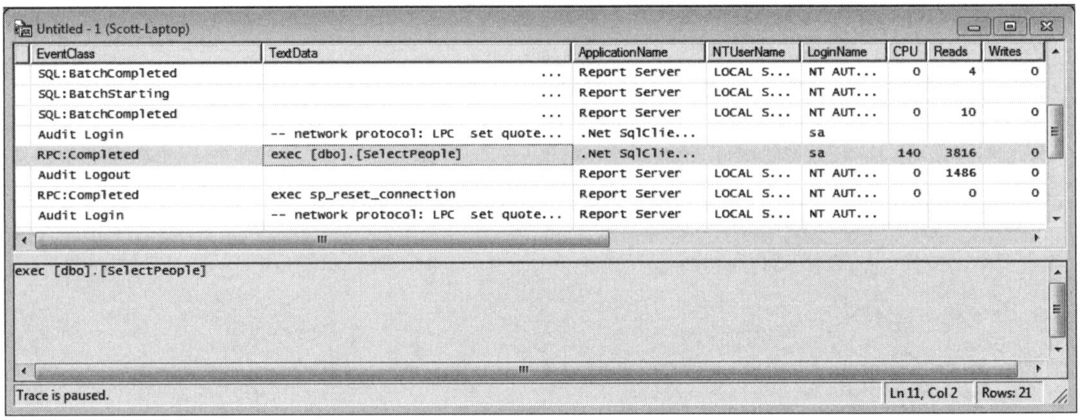

EventClass	TextData	ApplicationName	NTUserName	LoginName	CPU	Reads	Writes	
SQL:BatchCompleted	...	Report Server	LOCAL S...	NT AUT...	0	4	0	
SQL:BatchStarting	...	Report Server	LOCAL S...	NT AUT...				
SQL:BatchCompleted	...	Report Server	LOCAL S...	NT AUT...	0	10	0	
Audit Login	-- network protocol: LPC set quote...	.Net SqlClie...		sa				
RPC:Completed	exec [dbo].[SelectPeople]	.Net SqlClie...		sa	140	3816	0	
Audit Logout		Report Server	LOCAL S...	NT AUT...	0	1486	0	
RPC:Completed	exec sp_reset_connection	Report Server	LOCAL S...	NT AUT...	0	0	0	
Audit Login	-- network protocol: LPC set quote...	Report Server	LOCAL S...	NT AUT...				

```
exec [dbo].[SelectPeople]
```

Trace is paused.   Ln 11, Col 2   Rows: 21

Figure 6-13. SQL Server Profiler select

Again, this mapping is fairly straightforward. In Chapter 11, I discuss advanced queries as well as more complex stored procedures and function mappings.

■ ■ ■

CHAPTER 7

Relationships and Associations

Whether you're a seasoned EF veteran or this is your first foray into the Entity Framework, it should be obvious that when you're working with entities that are related to other entities, it's vital to remember that an Entity Data Model (EDM) isn't just made up of just entities but also includes relationships. Why is that? Because an EDM is based on an Entity Relationship Model (ERM), and these relationships are actual objects carrying the same importance and weight that an entity does.

The EF instantiates relationships as objects automatically as you work with the EDM, although you can still access the associations if you really need to. The great news is that as a developer, you don't need to work with them directly in most cases. Keep in mind that in scenarios where you need to map stored procedures to an entity, you must take into consideration any related entities (via association).

There is better news: Microsoft made some very significant improvements to how relationships and associations are handled in EF 4.0. This chapter focuses on those changes and discusses what that means to you as a developer. I spent a few pages in Chapter 3 discussing relationships within the EDM, and this chapter begins by revisiting that information and providing a brief overview of relationships and association types. I'll follow that up by taking a short look at how EF 3.5 dealt with relationships, because it's important for you to know what impact the new changes will have on your current EF projects. Most of the chapter focuses on the new EF 4.0 changes and their effect on the EDM.

Overview

One of the hardest concepts for developers to grasp, when dealing with the EF, is that of relationships and their use and application within the EDM. This confusion makes it difficult for developers to write efficient queries against the EDM. Let's begin this section by discussing the fundamentals of relationships and looking at a simple model example. This gives you a foundation on which to build your knowledge of how EF 3.5 and 4.0 handle relationships.

Relationships in General

Within the EDM designer, you see several representations of relationships between entities. These relationships, or *associations*, are displayed as lines between entities that are related one to another. At the end of each line is displayed the multiplicity between the entities—that is, how many items each end of line (entity) can and may have. The multiplicity is defined in one of the following three ways:

- *One:* Displayed as a numerical 1, this end of the relationship can have only one item—not less than one, and not more than one.

- *Many:* Displayed as the character *, this end of the relationship can and may have one or many (more than one) items.

- *Zero or One:* Displayed as the character string 0..1, this end of the relationship can have either zero items or one item, but no more than one item. Thus, 0..1 means Zero or One.

The One side of a relationship is typically a parent in a parent-child relationship. The Many side of a relationship is commonly a collection of children (or items) in a parent-child relationship. An example of a One-to-Many is customers and orders. One customer can have many orders. However, keep in mind that you can have a parent without a child, meaning you can have a customer who hasn't placed any orders.

Many relationships are the Zero or One-to-Many type. For example, a customer may have multiple phone numbers but may have only one of those numbers designated as a primary phone. When the customer record is first entered, perhaps several phone numbers are entered but none is designated as the primary phone. If a primary phone is later defined, then only one number can be defined as the primary number.

Relationships in EF 3.5

Let's jump into a brief EF 3.5 discussion and look at how the first version of the EF handled relationships. For this discussion, you use two tables from the AdventureWorks database: Person.Contact and HumanResources.Employee. Figure 7-1 shows the SQL Server Management Studio (SSMS) database diagram of these two tables and their relationships.

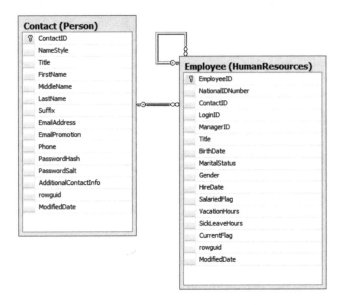

Figure 7-1. *A simple relationship*

This example ignores the self-referencing relationship on the HumanResources.Employee table and focuses strictly on the relationship between the two tables. You use Visual Studio 2008 SP1, in order to illustrate relationships defined in EF 3.5. In Visual Studio 2008, create a new project (either a Windows Forms or Class Library project). Add a new ADO.NET Entity Data Model item. When the Entity Data Model Wizard begins, create a connection to the AdventureWorks database, and click Next. In the Choose Your Database Objects step shown in Figure 7-2, select the two tables from Figure 7-1.

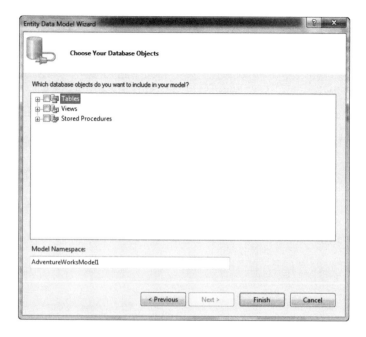

Figure 7-2. *Choose Your Database Objects*

Click Finish. You're then presented with your EDM with the two entities shown in Figure 7-3.

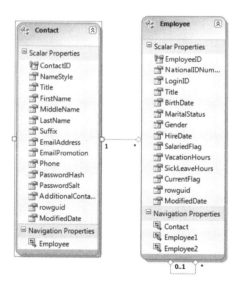

Figure 7-3. *Entities defined in EF 3.5*

You should immediately notice in Figure 7-3 that there are only 14 properties in the Employee table versus the 16 columns in the Employee table in Figure 7-1. What is missing? Foreign keys. ContactID and ManagerID are missing from the Employee entity. This is because foreign keys are typically mapped to a separate *association set* within the model.

You can also see that this example contains the three relationship types discussed earlier and is a perfect example of relationships and associations. In this example, a One-to-Many association exists between Contact and Employee, and there is also a Zero-or-One-to-Many on Employee.

You can see the association set in Figure 7-4, which shows the properties of the association defined between the two entities. The Association Set Name property, by default, holds the name of the association set that contains the association. You can view the association properties by right-clicking the association line between the two entities and selecting Properties from the context menu. This association was created when the EDM wizard read the AdventureWorks database and created the association based on the information it found in the database—namely, the information found in Figure 7-1.

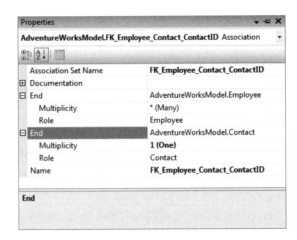

Figure 7-4. Association properties

Along with the association, a few other things are created in the model based on the relationship:

- *Navigation properties:* You can see the navigation properties in Figure 7-3, just below the scalar properties. Navigation properties aren't required, but they provide bidirectional navigation between entities via its association. The association tells the navigation which association in the model holds the information regarding how to navigate to the related entity.

- *Association sets*: These are containers for associations that have been instantiated at runtime. For example, for every Customer and related orders, you have that many instances of the association. If the ObjectContext contains five customers and their one or more related orders, you also have five instances of the association in the context.

- *AssociationSetMapping element:* This contains all the relationship information, identifying columns in data tables that correspond to related entities.

You look at the AssociationSetMapping element in a few pages when I discuss XML differences between EF 3.5 and 4.0.

In EF 3.5, associations were called *first class* associations. For 3.5, *first class* means that the EF treats associations at the same level as entities and other objects. You may have heard Microsoft say that associations aren't second-class citizens. This is certainly not the case—in fact, the opposite is true. Associations are first class because the EDM has a specific way to talk about and work with them.

EF 4.0 Relationships

Let's move on to EF 4.0 and look at the improvements Microsoft has made. To begin with, this section walks through the same example as for 3.5, but this time you use Visual Studio 2010.

Creating a WinForms Project

Fire up Visual Studio 2010, and create a new WinForms project (you're creating a WinForms project because you use the UI later). Add a new ADO.NET Entity Data Model item to the project, and follow the same steps as before (generate from a database, and create a connection to the AdventureWorks database).

On the Choose Your Database Objects step of the wizard, select the same two tables as in Figure 7-1: Person.Contact and HumanResources.Employee. Before you click Next, look at the dialog shown in Figure 7-5. This dialog is very similar to Figure 7-2. In EF 4.0, however, two new options are added:

- Pluralize or singularize generated object names

- Include foreign key columns in the model

As you learned in Chapter 2, the first option affects the naming of objects in your model (such as making all EntityType names singular and all EntitySet names plural). However, it's the second option you should focus your attention on. Checking the "Include foreign key columns in the model" option tells the model to use the new FK associations rather than the previous 3.5 type associations. Can you still use the EF 3.5 type associations? Absolutely, and I'll cover that shortly. For now, keep this option checked, and click Finish.

Figure 7-5. *Choose Your Database Objects 4.0*

When the model is built, notice that the entities in the model look extremely similar to those built in EF 3.5. Comparing figures 7-6 and 7-3, you should see that they're nearly identical. The only difference between the two figures is the addition of the two scalar properties ContactID and ManagerID in the HumanResources.Employee table, the foreign keys to Person.Contact table, and the HumanResources.Employee table itself. Visually, everything else in the EDM is the same, including the associations and the navigation properties.

But that isn't to say that things didn't change under the covers. Microsoft made some great improvements to be able to include foreign keys in conceptual and object models. I discuss this shortly.

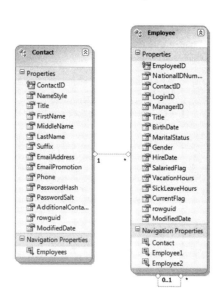

Figure 7-6. *Entities defined in EF 4.0*

Many of the changes that Microsoft made were to the EDM. You can see in Figure 7-7 that the properties page for the association has been modified. The information in the properties page isn't that different from EF 3.5, but you can see some property naming differences as well as a few additions. You now have End1 and End2 differentiation, and you still have the Multiplicity and Role for each end. New to EF 4.0 on this page is the OnDelete property for each end, which specifies the action to be taken when an entity on this specified end is deleted. Your options for the OnDelete property are None and Cascade.

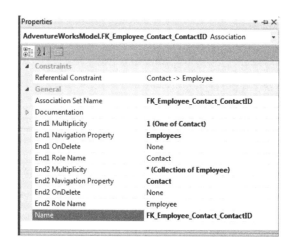

Figure 7-7. *EF 4.0 association properties*

Microsoft also added a couple of new visual items to the UI to help define and manage relationships between entities. These items and features are discussed in the following sections.

Defining Referential Constraints

Back in the EDM Designer, double-click the association between the two entities. In EF 4.0, a new Referential Constraint dialog opens, showing the foreign key properties for the relationship (see Figure 7-8).

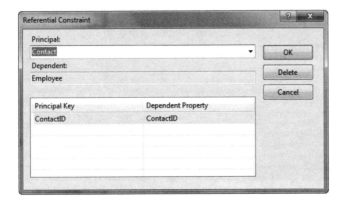

Figure 7-8. *Referential Contstraint Dialog*

The Referential Constraint dialog allows you to define the foreign key (FK) constraint between the source entity and the target entity. How do you know which is the target and which is the source? If it isn't obvious, click Cancel in the Referential Constraint dialog, and hold your mouse cursor over the association line between the two entities. As you hover your mouse over the association line, a small pop-up window displays, showing you which entity is the source and which entity is the target.

Double-click the association line again to display the Referential Constraint dialog. This dialog contains FK information. The Principle field displays the source entity and is a drop-down listing the entities defined in the relationship. By default, it lists the source entity in the relationship.

The Dependent field shows the source entity. This field isn't editable. The Principle Key and Dependent Property fields show the two fields that are used in the FK relationship.

Adding an Association

In your EDM Designer, drag a new entity from the toolbox, and drop it onto the designer surface. Next, right-click the new entity, and select Add ➤ Association from the context menu. Doing so displays the Add Association dialog box, shown in Figure 7-9. This dialog isn't new to the EF, but Microsoft did make some changes to it, the biggest being the "Add foreign key properties to the entityname Entity" check box.

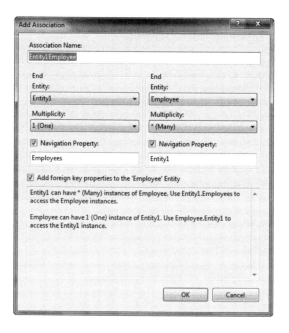

Figure 7-9. Add Association in EF 4.0

When you create an association, this check box lets you specify this association as a FK association. Can you specify a typical (non-FK) association? Absolutely: uncheck the "Add foreign key properties to the entityname Entity" check box. What does this do? I know I've been saying this for a few pages now, but bear with me—I'll explain shortly.

Also new in the Add Association dialog are the Navigation Property check boxes.

Looking at XML Differences

Before I get into the "I'll get to that shortly" topics, I want to cover the XML differences between EF 3.5 and 4.0. Close the EDM Designer, right-click the EDM, and select Open With from the context menu. In the Open With dialog, select XML Editor, and click OK.

Let's first look at the conceptual schema definition language (CSDL) XML for your EF 3.5 project. The XML fragment for the independent association looks like this:

```
<Association Name="FK_Employee_Contact_ContactID">
  <End Role="Contact" Type="AdventureWorksModel.Contact" Multiplicity="1" />
  <End Role="Employee" Type="AdventureWorksModel.Employee" Multiplicity="*" />
</Association>
<Association Name="FK_Employee_Employee_ManagerID">
  <End Role="Employee" Type="AdventureWorksModel.Employee" Multiplicity="0..1" />
  <End Role="Employee1" Type="AdventureWorksModel.Employee" Multiplicity="*" />
</Association>
```

The mapping for the association tells the EF how to negotiate the relationship. In EF 3.5 MSL, that mapping looks as follows:

```
<AssociationSetMapping Name="FK_Employee_Contact_ContactID" TypeName=↵
"AdventureWorksModel.FK_Employee_Contact_ContactID" StoreEntitySet="Employee">
  <EndProperty Name="Contact">
    <ScalarProperty Name="ContactID" ColumnName="ContactID" />
  </EndProperty>
  <EndProperty Name="Employee">
    <ScalarProperty Name="EmployeeID" ColumnName="EmployeeID" />
  </EndProperty>
</AssociationSetMapping>
<AssociationSetMapping Name="FK_Employee_Employee_ManagerID" TypeName=↵
"AdventureWorksModel.FK_Employee_Employee_ManagerID" StoreEntitySet="Employee">
  <EndProperty Name="Employee">
    <ScalarProperty Name="EmployeeID" ColumnName="ManagerID" />
  </EndProperty>
  <EndProperty Name="Employee1">
    <ScalarProperty Name="EmployeeID" ColumnName="EmployeeID" />
  </EndProperty>
  <Condition ColumnName="ManagerID" IsNull="false" />
</AssociationSetMapping>
```

Now, let's look at the EF 4.0 XML. The CSDL XML has two sections. The top of the CSDL contains the AssociationSet element:

```
<EntityContainer Name="AdventureWorksEntities3" annotation:LazyLoadingEnabled="true">
  <EntitySet Name="Employees" EntityType="AdventureWorksModel.Employee" />
  <EntitySet Name="Contacts" EntityType="AdventureWorksModel.Contact" />
  <AssociationSet Name="FK_Employee_Contact_ContactID" Association=↵
"AdventureWorksModel.FK_Employee_Contact_ContactID">
    <End Role="Contact" EntitySet="Contacts" />
    <End Role="Employee" EntitySet="Employees" />
  </AssociationSet>
  <AssociationSet Name="FK_Employee_Employee_ManagerID" Association=↵
"AdventureWorksModel.FK_Employee_Employee_ManagerID">
    <End Role="Employee" EntitySet="Employees" />
    <End Role="Employee1" EntitySet="Employees" />
  </AssociationSet>
</EntityContainer>
```

At the end of the CSDL is the following XML fragment, which contains the ReferentialConstraint element. The contents of this element define the FK. In other words, the data within the ReferentialConstraint element defines functionality that is similar to a database constraint. Notice that the element contains the entities and associated properties that make up the FK:

```
<Association Name="FK_Employee_Contact_ContactID">
  <End Role="Contact" Type="AdventureWorksModel.Contact" Multiplicity="1" />
  <End Role="Employee" Type="AdventureWorksModel.Employee" Multiplicity="*" />
  <ReferentialConstraint>
    <Principal Role="Contact">
      <PropertyRef Name="ContactID" />
    </Principal>
    <Dependent Role="Employee">
      <PropertyRef Name="ContactID" />
    </Dependent>
```

```
      </ReferentialConstraint>
    </Association>
    <Association Name="FK_Employee_Employee_ManagerID">
      <End Role="Employee" Type="AdventureWorksModel.Employee" Multiplicity="0..1" />
      <End Role="Employee1" Type="AdventureWorksModel.Employee" Multiplicity="*" />
      <ReferentialConstraint>
        <Principal Role="Employee">
          <PropertyRef Name="EmployeeID" />
        </Principal>
        <Dependent Role="Employee1">
          <PropertyRef Name="ManagerID" />
        </Dependent>
      </ReferentialConstraint>
    </Association>
```

Keep in mind that ReferentialConstraint also existed in EF 3.5, but the behavior was different. In EF 3.5, the ReferentialConstraint element was used in the conceptual model (CSDL) to specify the principle role and dependent role of an association.

Let's look at the mapping specification language (MSL) for a minute. Notice that no XML fragment maps the relationship. This is because all the important and pertinent information is contained in the CSDL.

Understanding Approaches to Foreign Keys in EF 4.0

I mentioned earlier that associations in EF 3.5 were considered first-class citizens, and I explained the reasoning for this. It's because the EF treats associations at the same level as entities and other objects. Microsoft wanted to know whether putting foreign keys in a conceptual and object model was necessary. So, Microsoft asked, and the company learned that some people thought it was a great idea and some thought it would muddy the waters.

The solution Microsoft came up with was to support both approaches. Although While Microsoft put FK support in the EDM, it also kept support for EF 3.5–style associations. The key to remember is that the old-style EF 3.5 associations are now called *independent associations*. They can still be used in EF 4.0.

Independent associations are those whose lifetime and representation are independent of any entity instances. An association relates two entities, as you've learned; but looking at it from a conceptual point of view, an association has a life of its own in a conceptual model. For example, let's consider the database perspective. An association in terms of the database most likely takes the form of a FK that exists on one of the two tables (entities)—but how do you tell which entity it belongs to by looking at the conceptual model?

On the other hand, a FK association in the conceptual model is represented by a FK that is part of one of the entities. This is important because it means the association has the same lifetime as the entity, is always retrieved when the entity is retrieved, and has the same concurrency-control mechanism as the entity. Independent associations are just that: independent. They have their own lifetime and their own concurrency control, and they aren't necessarily automatically returned when you retrieve an entity.

This information should answer the questions regarding why and how to use FK associations. Microsoft is convinced that when people start using FK associations, this will be the default choice going forward, because FK associations simplify key coding patterns considerably. Many of the things that were difficult to accomplish via independent associations are much easier using FK associations, including data binding, N-Tier, concurrency, and dynamic data.

Looking at the previous examples, you should be able to tell that the EF handles the two association types differently. You'll see that a little more in the next section as you look at some code examples using the EF 4.0 project you've created.

Using FK Associations in Code

The next few pages go through examples of how to code using FK associations. Each example takes a different approach and looks at how you can utilize FK associations to enhance your code. I introduce each example, show you the code, and then explain how the example uses the foreign keys.

Adding Dependent Objects

For this first example, add a button to the form, and add the following code behind the button. I'll explain the code shortly:

```
using (AdventureWorksEntities context = new AdventureWorksEntities())
{
    try
    {
        DateTime Birthdt = new DateTime(1965, 9, 26);
        DateTime Hiredt = new DateTime(2010, 1, 1);

        Contact con = new Contact { Title = "Geek", FirstName = "Scott", LastName = "Klein",
            EmailAddress = "ScottKlein@SqlXml.com", EmailPromotion = 0, Phone =↩
"555-55-5555",
            PasswordHash = "", PasswordSalt = "", rowguid = System.Guid.NewGuid(),
            ModifiedDate = DateTime.Now };

        Employee emp = new Employee { NationalIDNumber = "1234567890", LoginID = "sklein",
            ManagerID = 1, Title = "Geek", BirthDate = Birthdt, MaritalStatus = "M",
            Gender = "M", HireDate = Hiredt, SalariedFlag = true, VacationHours = 80,
            SickLeaveHours = 40, CurrentFlag = true, rowguid = System.Guid.NewGuid(),
            ModifiedDate = DateTime.Now };

        con.Employees.Add(emp);
        context.Contacts.AddObject(con);
        context.SaveChanges();

        Messagebox.Show("Items saved");
    }
    catch (Exception ex)
    {
        MessageBox.Show(ex.Message);
    }
}
```

This code does several things. In addition to opening a connection to the database and creating a few datetime variables, it does the following:

1. Creates a Contact object

2. Creates an Employee object

3. Adds the Employee object to the Contacts object's Employee collection

4. Adds the new Contact object to the context

5. Saves the changes

You may notice that this process doesn't use the FK association, and that is correct. This example illustrates that it's possible to work without using FK associations and that it's the recommended method when you're adding new dependent objects together (the key word being *new*). You can use the navigation properties when the Employee object is added to the Employee collection of the Contact object, allowing you to navigate between the Contact and Employee objects.

When you run the project and click the button, two records are saved; you can see that by querying the two tables. Figure 7-10 shows the two records added to the Contact table (top) and the Employee table (bottom).

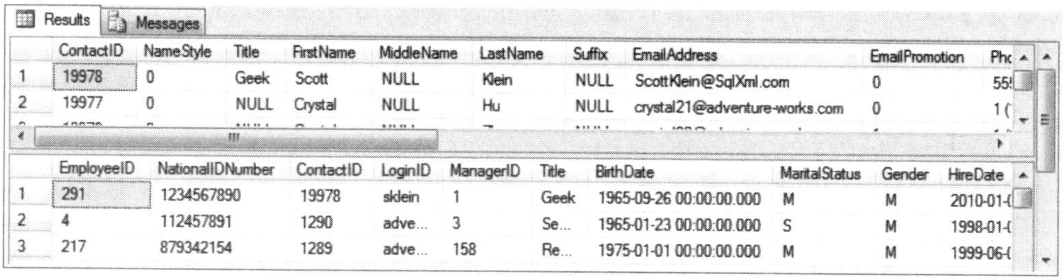

	ContactID	NameStyle	Title	FirstName	MiddleName	LastName	Suffix	EmailAddress		EmailPromotion	Ph
1	19978	0	Geek	Scott	NULL	Klein	NULL	ScottKlein@SqlXml.com		0	55!
2	19977	0	NULL	Crystal	NULL	Hu	NULL	crystal21@adventure-works.com		0	1(

	EmployeeID	NationalIDNumber	ContactID	LoginID	ManagerID	Title	BirthDate		MaritalStatus	Gender	HireDate
1	291	1234567890	19978	sklein	1	Geek	1965-09-26 00:00:00.000		M	M	2010-01-(
2	4	112457891	1290	adve...	3	Se...	1965-01-23 00:00:00.000		S	M	1998-01-(
3	217	879342154	1289	adve...	158	Re...	1975-01-01 00:00:00.000		M	M	1999-06-(

Figure 7-10. Example 1 results

Manually Setting the Foreign Key Property

The next two examples use FK associations and illustrate how to set the FK property manually. Add another button to the form, and behind it add the following code:

```
using (AdventureWorksEntities context = new AdventureWorksEntities())
{
    try
    {
        DateTime Birthdt = new DateTime(1965, 9, 26);
        DateTime Hiredt = new DateTime(2010, 1, 1);

        Contact con = new Contact { Title = "Geek", FirstName = "Scott", LastName = "Klein",
            EmailAddress = "ScottKlein@SqlXml.com", EmailPromotion = 0, Phone =↵
"555-55-5555",
            PasswordHash = "", PasswordSalt = "", rowguid = System.Guid.NewGuid(),
            ModifiedDate = DateTime.Now };

        Employee emp = new Employee { ContactID = 19983, NationalIDNumber = "12345678901",
            LoginID = "sklein1", ManagerID = 1, Title = "Geek", BirthDate = Birthdt,
            MaritalStatus = "M", Gender = "M", HireDate = Hiredt, SalariedFlag = true,
            VacationHours = 80, SickLeaveHours = 40, CurrentFlag = true,
            rowguid = System.Guid.NewGuid(), ModifiedDate = DateTime.Now };

        context.Employees.AddObject(emp);
        context.Contacts.AddObject(con);
        context.SaveChanges();

        Messagebox.Show("Items saved");
```

```
    }
    catch (Exception ex)
    {
        MessageBox.Show(ex.Message);
    }
}
```

This code looks similar to the first example, but here you manually set the `ContactID` FK property instead of adding it to the `Contact Employees` collection. You also change a few values so that no check constraints are violated.

This example also differs from the first in another significant way: because the context doesn't know about the parent object yet, the navigation properties on the two objects aren't mapped to each other until after `SaveChanges()` is called. This is because you add each object to the context, whereas in the first example you added the `Employee` object to the `Contacts` object's `Employee` collection.

When you run the project and click button2, two records are again saved; you can see that by querying the two tables. Figure 7-11 shows the two records added to the Contact table (top, top row) and Employee table (bottom, top row).

	ContactID	NameStyle	Title	FirstName	MiddleName	LastName	Suffix	EmailAddress	EmailPromotion	Pho
1	19983	0	Geek	Scott	NULL	Klein	NULL	ScottKlein@SqlXml.com	0	555
2	19978	0	Geek	Scott	NULL	Klein	NULL	ScottKlein@SqlXml.com	0	555
3	19977	0	NULL	Crystal	NULL	Hu	NULL	crystal21@adventure-works.com	0	1 (

	EmployeeID	NationalIDNumber	ContactID	LoginID	ManagerID	Title	BirthDate	MaritalStatus	Gender	HireDate
1	295	12345678901	19983	sklein1	1	Geek	1965-09-26 00:00:00.000	M	M	2010-01-0
2	291	1234567890	19978	sklein	1	Geek	1965-09-26 00:00:00.000	M	M	2010-01-0
3	4	112457891	1290	adve...	3	Se...	1965-01-23 00:00:00.000	S	M	1998-01-0
4	217	879342154	1289	adve...	158	Re...	1975-01-01 00:00:00.000	M	M	1999-06-0
5	140	184188301	1288	adve...	109	Chi...	1966-02-06 00:00:00.000	M	F	1999-03-0

Figure 7-11. Example 2 results

Setting the Foreign Key Automatically

A last example for this section illustrates how the FK is applied automatically. Add a third button to the form, and, in the button's Click event, add the following code:

```
using (AdventureWorksEntities context = new AdventureWorksEntities())
{
    try
    {
        DateTime Birthdt = new DateTime(1965, 9, 26);
        DateTime Hiredt = new DateTime(2010, 1, 1);

        Employee emp = new Employee { ContactID = 19983, NationalIDNumber = "12345678902",
            LoginID = "sklein2", ManagerID = 1, Title = "Geek", BirthDate = Birthdt,
            MaritalStatus = "M", Gender = "M", HireDate = Hiredt, SalariedFlag = true,
            VacationHours = 80, SickLeaveHours = 40, CurrentFlag = true,
            rowguid = System.Guid.NewGuid(), ModifiedDate = DateTime.Now };
```

```
            context.Employees.AddObject(emp);
            context.SaveChanges();

            Messagebox.Show("Items saved");
        }
        catch (Exception ex)
        {
            MessageBox.Show(ex.Message);
        }
    }
}
```

In this example, you never load the contact into memory. You know that ContactID is a valid ID, and you can set the ContactID property for the Employee object directly. Because the Contact object already exists in the context, your Employee.Contact navigation property becomes effective the second the FK property is set. Very nice.

Querying the Employee table again, you see the addition of the third record shown in Figure 7-12 (second row).

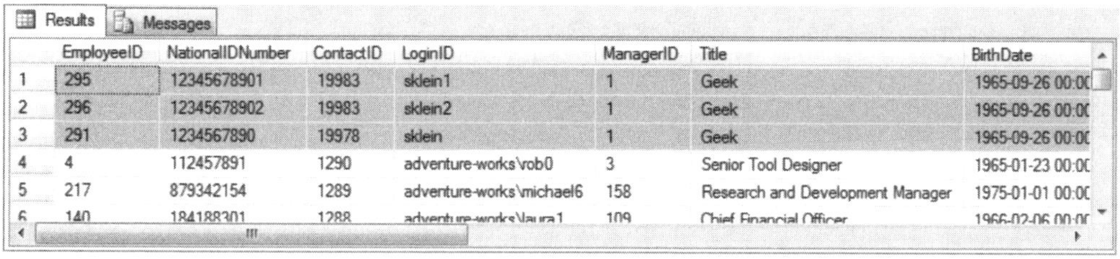

	EmployeeID	NationalIDNumber	ContactID	LoginID	ManagerID	Title	BirthDate
1	295	12345678901	19983	sklein1	1	Geek	1965-09-26 00:00
2	296	12345678902	19983	sklein2	1	Geek	1965-09-26 00:00
3	291	1234567890	19978	sklein	1	Geek	1965-09-26 00:00
4	4	112457891	1290	adventure-works\rob0	3	Senior Tool Designer	1965-01-23 00:00
5	217	879342154	1289	adventure-works\michael6	158	Research and Development Manager	1975-01-01 00:00
6	140	184188301	1288	adventure-works\laura1	109	Chief Financial Officer	1966-02-06 00:00

Figure 7-12. Example 3 results

This type of FK associations come in handy in data binding: in situations where you have data-bound grids and you have the new value of the FK in the grid but don't have the related object. Because you have the FK value, you don't have to bear the burden of getting the parent (principle) object.

You can also use the FK property to change relationships between objects—for example, changing the Employee ContactID to point to another contact. You also don't incur the overhead of getting the parent object.

The key takeaway from these examples is that the EF takes on the responsibility of keeping related references and FKs in sync and thus removes this burden from you.

Building the Sample Project

The last thing you do in this chapter is build a sample project that will be used in the remaining chapters of the book. You can also work with this data project on your own.

The downloads for this book include a SQL Server script called EF40CreationScript.sql. This script creates a database called EF40 and all the necessary objects that this project uses. Open the script in SQL Server Management Studio, and run it. This script assumes that you have the AdventureWorks database, so be sure to download that database prior to running the script.

Next, create a new Visual Studio Class Library project, and name it EF40Data (see Figure 7-13).

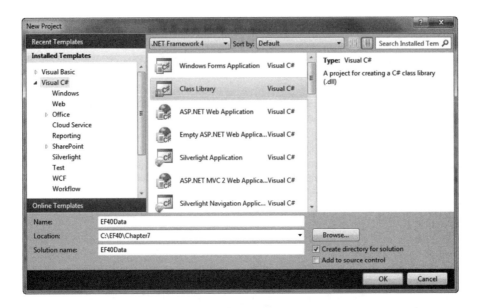

Figure 7-13. *New EF40Data project*

Delete the Class1.cs file (or Class1.vb if you choose to do this in Visual Basic.NET). Add a new ADO.NET EDM to the project, and name it EF40Model. Select Generate from Database in the Choose Model Contents dialog, and select all the tables and stored procedures in the Choose Your Database Objects dialog, as shown in Figure 7-14.

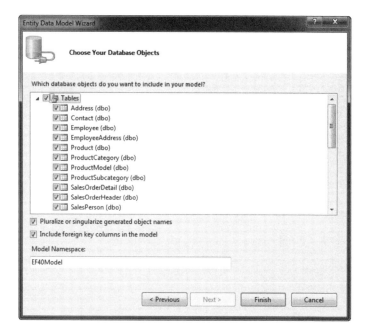

Figure 7-14. Selecting the tables for the project

Make sure you keep the "Pluralize or singularize generated object names" and "Include foreign key columns in the model" options checked. Click Finish. When your model is built, it should look like Figure 7-15.

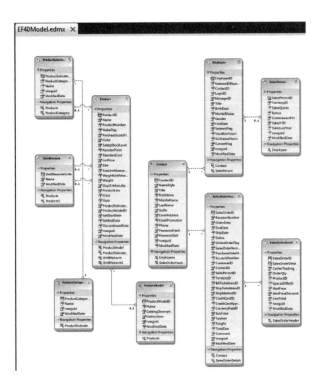

Figure 7-15. *The finished model*

You use many of the objects in the model in future chapters. In addition, you can see from Figure 7-15 that the model has plenty of tables and relationships around which you can design a nice application to start experimenting with the new FK associations.

Summary

In this chapter, you learned about the new ADO.NET Entity Framework 4.0 FK associations. You began by creating a simple example using EF 3.5 in order to provide a foundation for the discussion of EF 4.0. You then built the same example using EF 4.0, to illustrate the improvements and changes Microsoft has made. Significant changes were made to the UI alone to allow for better handling and support for FK associations without giving up EF 3.5 functionality by independent associations.

I spent the remainder of the chapter discussing how the new FK associations affect your queries and navigation between objects and how these changes simplify many things used in projects, such as data binding and concurrency.

CHAPTER 8

■ ■ ■

T4 Code Generation

Up until now, this book has focused primarily on enhancements to the ADO.NET 4.0 Entity Framework (EF), including improved stored procedure support (such as those that return unknown types), complex types, using ObjectSet versus ObjectQuery, and more. Some of the new features were discussed in previous chapters, such as complex types and stored procedure improvements. But Microsoft also spent a lot of time adding many great new features to the EF. Although V1 of the EF was groundbreaking, it lacked enough fundamental features that developers complained quite loudly. Microsoft listened, and EF4 is the result.

Starting with this chapter, the remainder of this book focuses on the new features that have been added to version 4 of the EF and that require chapters of their own. These topics include Text Template Transformation Toolkit (T4) support, model-first design, Plain Old Class Objects (POCO) support, and others. This chapter begins with T4 support and how it's utilized within the EF.

T4 Template Overview

T4 templates are a means of creating a code-generation artifact with the goal of saving developers a lot of time. T4 has been around since Visual Studio 2005. Even though you've had it for almost half a decade, it's one of those technologies that most developers still don't know exists. When told about it, the response is generally, "Really? What is it? Not that Microsoft has intentionally been keeping T4 secret since VS 2005; but many of the latest technologies, such as LINQ to SQL, MVC, and now EF, use T4 as their foundation and framework for code generation.

Adding a Template Using Visual Studio 2008

I hope you have VS 2008. Fire up an instance, and create a new C# console application. This example is to help you understand a little about how T4 templates work, so I didn't change the project name. Feel free to give your project a better name than ConsoleApplication1.

Add a new item to the project. When the Add New Item dialog appears, select the Text File template type. Looking through the list of templates, notice that there is no T4 template item. The trick to utilize T4 templates is to select the Text File template type but change the extension. The default name for the text file is TextFile1.txt; but in order to use the T4 template functionality, change the extension from .txt to .tt. In this example, change the name to TextTemplate.tt, as shown in Figure 8-1.

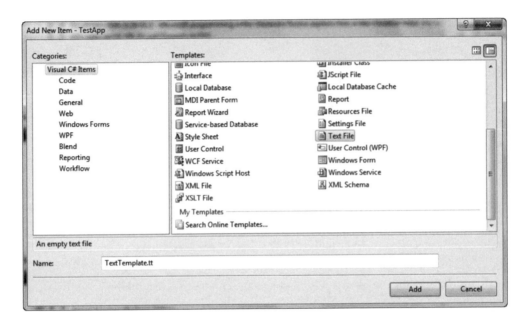

Figure 8-1. Adding a new template

Click Add in the Add New Item dialog. Looking in Solution Explorer, your T4 template is added to your solution along with its associated code file, as shown in Figure 8-2.

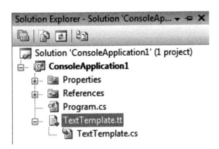

Figure 8-2. T4 template in Solution Explorer

Installing a T4 Editor
When you clicked Add in the Add New Item dialog, the TextTemplate.tt file as also opened in the Visual Studio IDE. It's just a blank text file, so you can do some text editing. The problem is, unless you know how to write T4 code, it's easy to get lost. If you've seen T4 code prior to now, you know that it looks a lot like ASP classic syntax with the brackets. But where do you begin? Luckily, the people at Clarius created a nifty utility called Visual T4 to alleviate some of the guesswork and pain. Visual T4 provides T4

IntelliSense and template editing. You can download this nifty tool from the following site:
www.visualt4.com.

On the website, click the Downloads link in the upper-right corner. On the Downloads page are
multiple versions. At the time of this writing, there isn't a version for VS 2010, which is why you're doing
this example in VS 2008. Download the Visual T4 Editor Community Edition for VS 2008. The file you
download is called T4EditorForVS2008-Community.msi. Just to be safe, close all instances of Visual Studio
prior to installing this utility.

With the T4 editor installed, open Visual Studio 2008 again as well as the TextTemplate.tt file. To get
an idea of how IntelliSense works, type a less-than sign (<). Immediately you see a list of directives, as
shown in Figure 8-3.

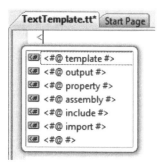

Figure 8-3. *T4 IntelliSense with listed directives*

These directives are essentially instructions to the T4 generator. There are more than are shown in
Figure 8-3, as you see shortly. This chapter isn't a tutorial on T4 syntax; you can find books or articles to
help with that. However, you use some of these directives in the following examples, and when you do, I
explain what they mean.

Writing Some T4 Code

The first two T4 directives you use are template and output. The template directive allows you to specify
instructions regarding this specific template. Notice as you type that this directive has several attributes,
such as language, debug, and inherits. For this example, you use the language attribute, which specifies
that you're creating your template using C# and that the generator must use the C# compiler.

The next directive you use is output. This directive has only one attribute: extension. This directive
and its associated attribute specify the type of output your template will generate. For example, you can
specify that you'll use the C# language in your template but that you want the resulting output to be
Visual Basic:

```
<#@ template language="C#" #>
<#@ output extension=".vb" #>
```

When you save the template, notice that the extension of the associated source code file in Solution
Explorer has changed from .cs to .vb. Looking at the properties of the file shows that the extension has
changed on the actual file, as shown in Figure 8-4.

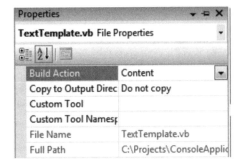

Figure 8-4. Output file properties

This example is simple and keeps everything C#. Add the `language` and `extension` directives to the top of the file. Also add a little code to the template, as follows:

```
<#@ template language="C#" #>
<#@ output extension=".cs" #>
namespace ConsoleApplication1
{
        public class CountStuff
        {
                public void DoCounter()
                {
                        //
                }
        }
}
```

The act of saving the template initiates the T4 code-generation engine, which generates the output source code. Looking at the `.cs` file, you can see that the code has been generated:

```
namespace ConsoleApplication1
{
        public class CountStuff
        {
                public void DoCounter()
                {
                        //
                }
        }
}
```

As is, this code doesn't do you much good. You need to add more T4 code; and again, this is where the T4 editor IntelliSense comes in very handy. Going back to the template, delete the two forward slashes, and type the less-than sign again. This time, notice that you get three entirely different directives, as shown in Figure 8-5.

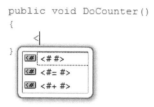

Figure 8-5. Inline code directives

These three directives apply solely to inline code. The first directive applies to inline code that is executed directly within the template. The second directive lets you write out results as is. The third directive allows you to create additional source, such as functions and methods that are called from another location. You use the first two directives in this example.

Use the top directive to add a for loop, as shown in the code that follows. Add a second line that uses the Console.WriteLine method to write the value to the console window. This example loops five times and writes the counter out to the console:

```
<#@ template language="C#" #>
<#@ output extension=".cs" #>
namespace ConsoleApplication1
{
        public class CountStuff
        {
                public void DoCounter()
                {
                        <# for (int i = 1; i < 6; i++)  #>
                        System.Console.WriteLine(i.ToString());
                }
        }
}
```

Save the template, and look at the generated code. No, the code you're looking at here isn't a copy/paste error. This layout is how it shows up in your .cs file:

```
namespace ConsoleApplication1
{
        public class CountStuff
        {
                public void DoCounter()
                {
                                                System.Console.WriteLine(i.ToString());
                }
        }
}
                System.Console.WriteLine(i.ToString());
                }
        }
}
                System.Console.WriteLine(i.ToString());
                }
        }
}
                System.Console.WriteLine(i.ToString());
                }
```

```
                }
        }                         System.Console.WriteLine(i.ToString());
                        }
                }
        }
```

Everything below the for loop was executed for each iteration—meaning WriteLine and the three closing braces (}) were executed each time. This example shows that you need to clearly understand the scope of your code and how the inline code directives can help you.

Scoping Your Code

The fix to the scoping problem is simple: you need to tell the code generator the scope of your code. You can do that by using the first derivative again. You need to include an open bracket ({) in your first line and then add the closing braces (}) within the first derivative, as shown here:

```
<# for (int i = 1; i < 6; i++) { #>
System.Console.WriteLine(i.ToString());
<# } #>
```

Save the template, and look at the code again. It still isn't quite correct, because you should see a handful of build errors stating that the name i doesn't exist; but you're getting closer. The format is still off, as well. But in this example, you can see how the derivatives are used to define the scope of the code appropriately:

```
namespace ConsoleApplication1
{
        public class CountStuff
        {
                public void DoCounter()
                {
                                                System.Console.WriteLine(i.ToString());
                                                System.Console.WriteLine(i.ToString());
                                                System.Console.WriteLine(i.ToString());
                                                System.Console.WriteLine(i.ToString());
                                                System.Console.WriteLine(i.ToString());
                }
        }
}
```

You're not finished: you need the WriteLine code to show the write information. For this, you use the second directive, as shown here:

```
System.Console.WriteLine(<#= i.ToString() #>);
```

Now, when you save the file and look at the output code again, the format is still off but your code is correct (you look at fixing the format in a bit):

```
namespace ConsoleApplication1
{
        public class CountStuff
        {
```

```
        public void DoCounter()
        {
                                        System.Console.WriteLine(1);
                                        System.Console.WriteLine(2);
                                        System.Console.WriteLine(3);
                                        System.Console.WriteLine(4);
                                        System.Console.WriteLine(5);
                }
    }
}
```

Example 1: Running the Project

Let's write some code that uses your generated code, with the end goal being to create a project that you can execute. Your console project automatically includes a Program.cs file. Open Program.cs, and add the following code to the Main method:

```
CountStuff count = new CountStuff();
count.DoCounter();
Console.ReadLine();
```

Your Program.cs should now look like the following:

```
using System;
using System.Collections.Generic;
using System.Linq;
using System.Text;

namespace ConsoleApplication1
{
    class Program
    {
        static void Main(string[] args)
        {
            CountStuff count = new CountStuff();
            count.DoCounter();
            Console.ReadLine();
        }
    }
}
```

The code in your Main method simply creates an instance of the T4-generated CounterStuff class and then calls the DoCounter method. This last line executes a ReadLine so the console window stays open until you press the Enter key.

Run the project by pressing F5. When the console window appears, it writes the numbers 1 through 5 to the window, exactly as you wanted. Press the Enter key to terminate the program. You can see the result of the execution in Figure 8-6.

Figure 8-6. Console output

Although this example isn't terribly exciting, it gives you an idea of how T4 templates work and a brief introduction to the T4 template syntax.

Example 2: Returning Your Computer's Processes

Let's work through two more examples that are more useful. In this example, you modify your template to use .NET classes that return all the processes on your computer. This illustrates how easy it is to use T-4 templates integrated with .NET code. Modify the template file to look like the following:

```
<#@ template language="C#" #>
<#@ output extension=".cs" #>
using System.Diagnostics;
namespace ConsoleApplication1
{
        public class CountStuff
        {
                public void DoCounter()
                {
                        Process[] procs = Process.GetProcesses();
                        foreach (Process proc in procs)
                                System.Console.WriteLine(proc.ProcessName);
                }
        }
}
```

This code is a little different from the first example. Here you use straight inline code, so you don't need the second derivative. The output, shown here, matches the template exactly:

```
using System.Diagnostics;
namespace ConsoleApplication1
{
        public class CountStuff
        {
```

```
        public void DoCounter()
        {
                Process[] procs = Process.GetProcesses();
                foreach (Process proc in procs)
                        System.Console.WriteLine(proc.ProcessName);
        }
    }
}
```

When you run this, the output is a list of all the processes on the computer that is running the application (see Figure 8-7).

Figure 8-7. *Process output results*

Example 3: Listing Your SQL Databases

Here's a final example to illustrate T4. For this example, you need to add the following references to your project:

- Microsoft.SqlServer.ConnectionInfo

- Microsoft.SqlServer.Management.Sdk.Sfc

- Microsoft.SqlServer.Smo

Next, in your template, you need to reference these classes. In T4, you do this by using one of the directives shown in Figure 8-3: the assembly directive. This directive identifies an assembly to be referenced so that you can use types within that assembly from code in the text template. This is equivalent to using Add Reference in Visual Studio.

You also need to use the namespace directive, which allows you to refer to types in a text template without providing a fully qualified name.

Modify your template to look like the following (be sure to change the server name to your actual SQL server instance name):

```
<#@ template language="C#" #>
<#@ output extension=".cs" #>
<#@ assembly name="Microsoft.SqlServer.Smo, Version=10.0.0.0, Culture=neutral,↵
 PublicKeyToken=89845dcd8080cc91" #>
<#@ assembly name="Microsoft.SqlServer.Management.Sdk.Sfc, Version=10.0.0.0,↵
 Culture=neutral, PublicKeyToken=89845dcd8080cc91" #>
<#@ assembly name="Microsoft.SqlServer.ConnectionInfo, Version=10.0.0.0,↵
 Culture=neutral, PublicKeyToken=89845dcd8080cc91" #>
<#@ import namespace="System" #>
<#@ import namespace="Microsoft.SqlServer.Management.Smo" #>
<#@ import namespace="Microsoft.SqlServer" #>
using Microsoft.SqlServer.Management.Smo;
using Microsoft.SqlServer.Server;
namespace ConsoleApplication1
{
        public class CountStuff
        {
                public void DoCounter()
                {
                        Server srv = new Server("servername");
                        foreach (Database db in srv.Databases)
                                System.Console.WriteLine(db.Name);
                }
        }
}
```

This example references some new namespaces because you use some of the classes in the code. You then use Server Management Objects (SMO) to query for all the databases on that server.

When run, your results are output in the console window as shown in Figure 8-8.

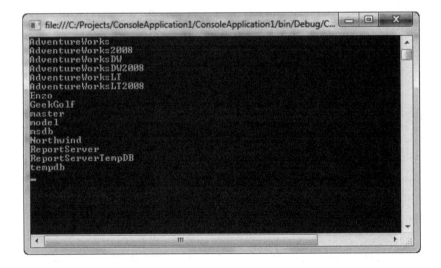

Figure 8-8. *Database output results*

That's enough of an introduction to T4. Let's get to the real reason for this chapter and discuss how T4 is used on the EF.

T4 Templates and the Entity Framework

After all you learned in the previous 10 pages, the question becomes, how are T4 templates used in the EF? Just as important is how you can use T4 to customize the classes from your EDM.

Let's start from the beginning and look at what the EF uses to build the classes from the entities defined in the model. Realistically, you could do the same thing you did in the first example at the beginning of the chapter: you could add a .tt file to the project and start from scratch. VS 2010 has a template for adding T4 templates, called the ADO.NET EntityObject Generator, shown in Figure 8-9. Adding a T4 template this way requires you to know where to find it in the list of templates and items.

Figure 8-9. ADO.NET EntityObject Generator item

But simply adding a blank text template doesn't gain you anything. Again, you're faced with a blank page, waiting for you to type something in. Why do that when the EF can do much of the work for you?

Open the EF40Data project for Chapter 8, and open the EDM. Open the properties for the EDM and locate the Custom Tool property, shown in Figure 8-10.

Figure 8-10. *EntityModelCodeGenerator*

The EntityModelCodeGenerator is the built-in tool that automatically generates an object layer based on your conceptual schema definition language (CSDL) in the .edmx file.

You don't want to delete the value of this property directly. Let's let EF do it properly for you. To do that, open the EDM; on the EDM surface, right-click, and select Add Code Generation Item from the context menu as shown in Figure 8-10. Selecting this menu option opens the all-too-familiar Add New Item dialog, shown in Figure 8-12.

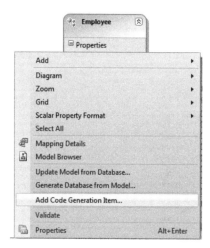

Figure 8-11. *Add Code Generation Item menu option*

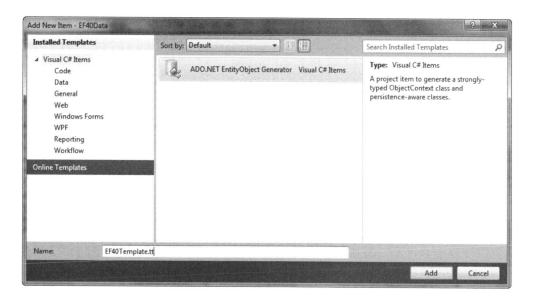

Figure 8-12. *Add New Item dialog*

The difference this time is that the Add New Item dialog knows exactly what you're looking for and presents you with the single item you want. Give it a good name, and click Add.

You now see the warning shown in Figure 8-13. It's a short, simple, but glaring message stating that if you continue, significant changes will be made to your model with a probability that something may break if you aren't careful. Go ahead and click OK, because the changes it makes are detailed next.

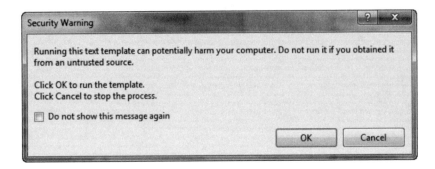

Figure 8-13. *T4 Template security warning*

By clicking OK, you telling the EF that you want to control the code generation from now on: "Thanks, Entity Framework, for all your hard work, but I'll take it from here." I know you're wondering if there is a way to tell the EF that you made a mistake and want it to take back control of the code generation. Absolutely. To do so, set the Custom Tool property back to the value EntityModelCodeGenerator, and you're back in business.

The only caveat is if you make custom changes that don't compile. The EF will tell you that you need to fix those errors prior to handing back control. You should understand this: it's like inheriting buggy code from a co-worker. The EF doesn't want to inherit buggy code. Get your code working before you hand it back.

By taking control of the code generation, the EF does a couple of things. First, the Custom Tool property value is automatically deleted. This means no code file (EF40Model.Designer.cs) is attached to the .edmx file.

Second, the new template is added to Solution Explorer. Figure 8-14 shows both the addition of the text template and the removal of the Custom Tool. The template is now responsible for generating the classes, so the class file is attached to the template. You saw this in the first section of this chapter and learned how the two work in harmony.

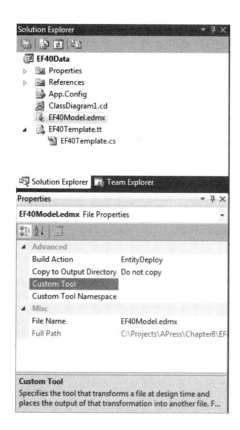

Figure 8-14. Custom Tool removed

The good thing is that the EF keeps everything intact. You may at first think that the text template the EF creates is empty. No way. The EF takes everything it uses for code generation and places it in your new text template. Double-click the .tt file to open it in the Visual Studio IDE.

If you have line numbers enabled, you see that the file is more than 1,250 lines long. At the top of the file, as shown here, are some nice instructions for modifying the template along with some URLs to provide further information. Not too shabby:

```
<#
// You can use this text template to customize object layer code generation for
// applications that use the Entity Framework. The template generates code based
 on an .edmx file.
// Before using this template, note the following:
//
//   *The name of the text template file will determine the name of the code file
 it generates.
//   For example, if the text template is named TextTemplate.tt, the generated
 file will be named
//   TextTemplate.vb or TextTemplate.cs.
//   *The Custom Tool property of the targeted .edmx file must be empty. For more
```

```
     information,
     //  see .edmx File Properties (http://go.microsoft.com/fwlink/?LinkId=139299).
     //  *The SourceCsdlPath initialization below must be set to one of the following:
     //  1) the path of the targeted .edmx or .csdl file
     //  2) the path of the targeted .edmx or .csdl file relative to the template path
     //
     //  For more detailed information about using this template, see
     //  How to: Customize Object Layer Code Generation↵
      (http://go.microsoft.com/fwlink/?LinkId=139297).
     //  For general information about text templates, see
     //  Generating Artifacts by Using Text Templates↵
      (http://go.microsoft.com/fwlink/?LinkId=139298)
     #>
     <#@ template language="C#" debug="false" hostspecific="true"#>
     <#@ include file="EF.Utility.CS.ttinclude"#>
     <#@ output extension=".cs"#>
     <#

UserSettings userSettings =
        new UserSettings
        {
             SourceCsdlPath = @"EF40Model.edmx",
             ReferenceCsdlPaths = new string[] {},
             FullyQualifySystemTypes = true,
             CreateContextAddToMethods = true,
             CamelCaseFields = false,
        };

ApplyUserSettings(userSettings);
if(Errors.HasErrors)
{
    return String.Empty;
}
```

With that background, let's look at an example of how you can use the new template to create custom classes.

T4 Customization Example

This section walks you through an example of customizing code generation. Let's begin by adding a new class called IValidator. It's a simple validation class. To do so, add a new class to the project, call it IValidator.cs, and click OK. In the class, add the following code:

```
using System;
using System.Collections.Generic;
using System.Linq;
using System.Text;

namespace EF40Data
{
    public interface IValidator
    {
        void Validate();
```

```
        }
}
```

Next, open the text template `EF40Template.tt`. Scroll down to line 316, and add the bold code to the end of that line. The bold code includes the comma before IValidator:

```
<#=Accessibility.ForType(entity)#> <#=code.SpaceAfter(code.AbstractOption(entity))#>↵
partial class <#=code.Escape(entity)#> : <#=BaseTypeName(entity, code)#>, IValidator
```

Next, just below the opening bracket on line 317, add the following code:

```
void IValidator.Validate()
{
        OnValidate();
}

partial void OnValidate();
```

Save the text template. Open the associated class, and scroll down to the entities section. Notice now that every entity inherits from the IValidator class:

```
#region Entities

/// <summary>
/// No Metadata Documentation available.
/// </summary>
 [EdmEntityTypeAttribute(NamespaceName="EF40Model", Name="Contact")]
 [Serializable()]
 [DataContractAttribute(IsReference=true)]
public partial class Contact : EntityObject, IValidator
{
    void IValidator.Validate()
    {
        OnValidate();
    }

 partial void OnValidate()
```

As you can see, T4 templates provide a nice way to customize your entity classes. The reason for implementing and using T4 for code generation is simply to make it easy to customize the way your entities are generated.

CHAPTER 9

■■■

Model-First Development

In the last chapter we focused on how to use text templates to customize the generation of the EDM. T4 has been incorporated in many facets in EF 4.0, and this chapter will build on that. One of the things requested by EF developers was the ability to generate a database based on the EDM. In the previous version of EF you could build an EDM starting with an empty model, but you couldn't do anything with it after that. More specifically, you could not build or create your database based on your EDM.

EF 4.0 fixes that problem, and not only lets you build your database based on your EDM, but also lets you customize the DDL that is generated. This chapter will focus on two aspects of model-first design, the first being the ability to build an EDM and to then create the database based on your EDM. The second part of the chapter will utilize the information you gained in the previous chapter by using T4 templates and Windows Workflow to customize the output of the DDL.

Model-First Design

One of the most glaring and almost agonizing exclusions from the first release of the Entity Framework was a complete model-first solution. With EF V1, you could create a model from scratch, but you could not really do much with mapping and database creation. Anyone who spent any time on the MSDN Entity Framework forums knows that creating the model first was one of the most requested pieces of functionality.

Microsoft listened, and, with Version 4.0 of the Entity Framework, they delivered. With version 4.0 of the Entity Framework, you now have a true "model-first" solution. Once you have your conceptual model created, you can now derive the storage model, mappings, and database from your conceptual model, all from a single menu item on the Designer context menu. From this menu you can generate a database schema directly from your model as well as the appropriate mappings.

Microsoft also provides the ability to customize the database creation process through T4 templates, giving developers much-needed flexibility and control over how the mappings and the schema are generated. I'm getting goose bumps.

This section will walk you through the entire process, from creating the conceptual model to the creation of the database and mappings.

Creating a Conceptual Model

Let's begin our model-first design by creating a somewhat simple model. Create a new Class Library project and name the project ModelFirst. We are not going to add any user interface components, so we don't need to create a Windows Forms application for this example.

Our model, and subsequent database, is going to track motocross teams, their riders, and the class in which each rider races. In the sport of motocross, a rider can actually race in multiple classes, but we don't want anything that complicated for this example. For the sake of this example, a rider will race a single class. Unlike other sports, in the sport of motocross a rider rarely changes, or "gets traded" to, another team during the year. So we won't worry about a rider changing teams either.

In this example we will create an EDM and then use a new feature to generate a database based on our model. Figure 9-1 shows the New Project creation screen—nothing new here. Pick the project type, enter the project name and click OK.

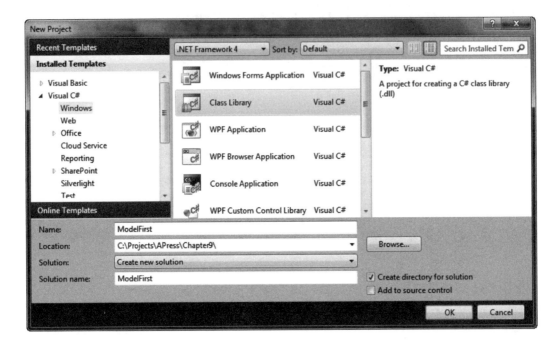

Figure 9-1. Project creation

Once the project has been created, add a new ADO.NET Entity Data Model item to the project. Name the model `Motocross.edmx` and click Add. What you're doing here is really no different than in previous examples, in previous chapters.

One difference with this example is that we will not be generating our model from a database, as we have done in previous examples. When we generate from a database, our mappings and model are already created for us. In this example, we want to start with an empty model from which to design our conceptual model. Create a new Windows Forms project, and once the project is created add a new ADO.NET Entity Data Model to your project, shown in Figure 9-2.

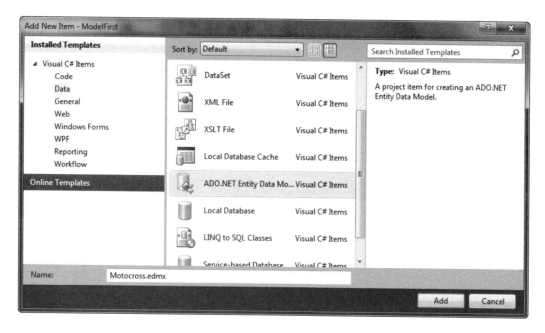

Figure 9-2. Adding an Entity Data Model

When the Entity Data Model Wizard begins, select the Empty Model option, shown in Figure 9-3, and click Finish. Visual Studio creates an empty EDM, an empty canvas, so to speak, in which to start designing your conceptual model.

The designer, when empty, contains a simple message, which states that to create new entities you need to drag them from the Toolbox. Just like normal Visual Studio development, the items you want to place on your designer are found in the Toolbox. The Toolbox contains, besides the Pointer, three controls, or items, from which to design your conceptual Entity Data Model. Those three items are the following:

- *Entity*: Used to define, or "model" a top-level concept.

- *Association*: Defines a relationship between two entity types.

- *Inheritance*: Authorizes a derived type to extend the features of another type.

We won't discuss inheritance in this chapter, but we will be using the Entity item and the Association item to build our conceptual model.

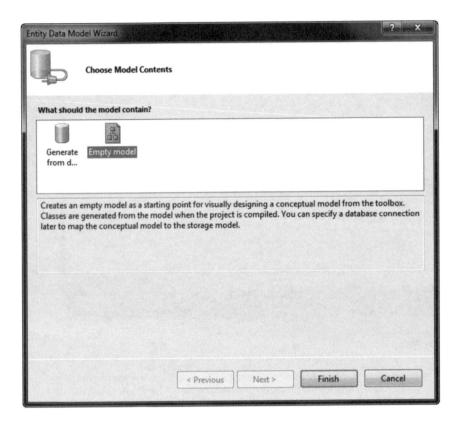

Figure 9-3. Selecting an empty model template

Creating Entities in the Empty Model

To appropriately track the information needed for our motocross application, we will need to create four entities:

- *Team*: This entity will contain the individual motocross teams.
- *Rider*: This entity will track the individual riders and the team each rides for, via an association to the Team entity.
- *Class*: This is the class the rider races in, 250 or 450.
- *Brand*: This is the brand of each team (Yamaha, Honda, etc.).

Begin by dropping four entities onto the designer from the Toolbox. Tables 9-1 through 9-4 show the properties that need to be added to each entity and their related data type. Let's begin with the Team table. To add properties to the entity, simply right-click on the entity and select Add ➤ Scalar Property from the context menu.

Table 9-1. *The Team Table*

Column Name	Data Type	Description
TeamID	Int32	Unique identifier
TeamName	String	The name of each team
IsSupportTeam	Boolean	Is this a factory team or a factory sponsored team?
BrandID	Int32	The FK to the Brand entity to associate the team with a bike brand the team uses

Table 9-2. *The Brand Table*

Column Name	Data Type	Description
BrandID	Int32	Unique identifier
BrandName	String	The brand name of the bike

Table 9-3. *The Rider Table*

Column Name	Data Type	Description
RiderID	Int32	Unique identifier
FirstName	String	The rider's first name
MiddleName	String	The rider's middle name
LastName	String	The rider's last name
Age	Int16	The rider's age
ClassID	Int32	The FK to the Brand entity to associate the team with a bike brand the team uses
TeamID	Int32	The FK to the Brand entity to associate the team with a bike brand the team uses

Table 9-4. The Class Table

Column Name	Data Type	Description
ClassID	Int32	Unique identifier
ClassName	String	The name of the class

You should have noticed that each time you added an entity to the designer it automatically added an ID column. The designer will have set the data type of that column to Int32. That's a good thing.

What the designer did not do was to set a property called StoreGeneratedPattern. For each entity, we want the IDs to be auto-generated primary keys. To achieve that goal, we need to set the StoreGeneratedPattern property. Select the TeamID property in Team entity and in the Properties window set the StoreGeneratedPattern to Identity. Figure 9-4 shows this being done for one of the entities. Do the same thing for the other three entities for the properties identified as Unique Identifiers.

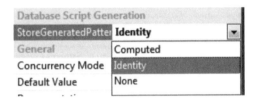

Figure 9-4. Setting the StoreGeneratedPattern property

Creating Associations and Navigation Properties

We are almost done, but we are missing our Associations and Navigation properties. Three associations need to be created, along with their respective navigation properties.

Table 9-5 details the three associations to be created between the entities and the column in each entity on which the associations need to be joined.

Table 9-5. Associations for the Motocross Model

Parent Entity	Child Entity	Property
Brand	Team	BrandID
Team	Rider	TeamID
Class	Rider	ClassID

Once you've created the associations in Table 9-5, your model should look something like Figure 9-5.

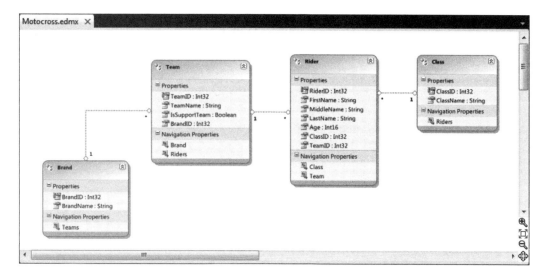

Figure 9-5. Completed model

Saving the Model

The model is finished, but when you open the model you should be presented with the warnings shown in Figure 9-6.

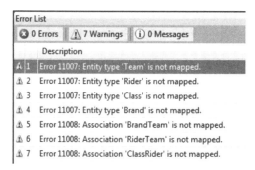

Figure 9-6. Mapping warnings

These warnings are completely valid, and the information is absolutely correct. These warnings are letting us know that the items in the designer are not mapped to anything. The project will save and compile as-is, since these are warnings, but beyond having our conceptual model we really don't have anything substantial.

Verifying Compilation

We can verify that our project will compile by closing our EDM, right-clicking on the Motocross.edmx in Solution Explorer, and selecting Open With from the context menu. In the Open With dialog, select XML Editor from the list of programs, then click OK.

Figure 9-7 shows the C-S Mapping Content section. You have seen this previously, but notice here the lack of content. The entire file itself is only 118 lines long. The mapping section is only ten lines long.

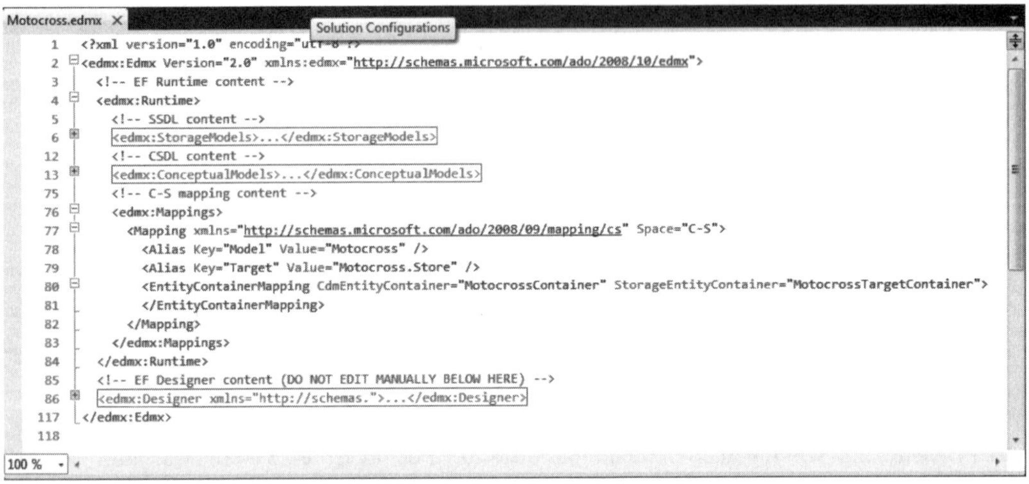

Figure 9-7. Model mapping content

Creating the Mappings and Database

We could spend a lot of time defining our mappings by hand, but that won't work simply because we don't have anything to map the entity types or associations to. Plus, I don't feel like writing, and debugging, a ton of XML, and I'm sure you don't either.

But this is where the model-first functionality of version 4.0 of the Entity Framework kicks in. We don't have to write any code, or do anything special, because the new model-first features take care of that for us. Let's put that great new technology to work and create our mapping and database.

Close the XML window and reopen the EDM. With the EDM open, right-click anywhere on the surface of the designer. A familiar context menu will appear, but you'll notice a new menu item in the menu, called Generate Database from Model. You can see this menu item in Figure 9-8.

Selecting this menu starts a very simple wizard, the Create Database Wizard. The first step in the wizard is the familiar Choose Your Data Connection dialog. This dialog lets you select or create a new database connection. This is the exact same dialog you see when you generate your model from a database and walk through that wizard. It is the dialog that lets you specify the data source, connection options, and database that you will use to run the generated script against.

While the name of the wizard leads you to believe it will create the physical database for you, the Generate Database Wizard does not actually create the physical target database. What the wizard really does is to generate and optionally execute the schema-creation script, which creates tables and other objects that you may need. You'll have to have already created an empty database. For the example in this chapter, I used the default, AdventureWorks database.

Figure 9-8. *Generate database from model*

Once you have specified the connection information, click Next. The next screen in the wizard is the Summary and Settings screen, shown in Figure 9-9. This step in the wizard shows the DDL that was generated from the conceptual model. Take a few minutes to scroll through the DDL, examining the statements that were generated. For your convenience, the entire DDL is shown as well. What should jump out at you are the DROP statements. This is vitally important to know, as the wizard does not UPDATE. This means that if you have an existing database, it does not go out to the schema and figure out the differences between your model and the database and create DDL that will modify or update your schema. It simply drops all the objects and recreates them.

This is important to know because any data you have, any schemas changes you made on the database side, will be lost if you run the generated DDL script. You will need to back up the current database to ensure no data or schema changes are lost. You will find out shortly that there is a second part of this as well, pertaining to the mapping.

If this is the first time you are running the DDL, then you have nothing to worry about. But if the opposite is true, meaning that you have previously generated DDL off of your model and created a database, then you need to take precautions to ensure that any database you want to keep does not get lost.

Click the Cancel button and the Summary and Settings form if you do not wish to execute the script. Clicking Cancel will terminate the wizard and take you back to the EDM. No mapping has taken place nor has any DDL been generated.

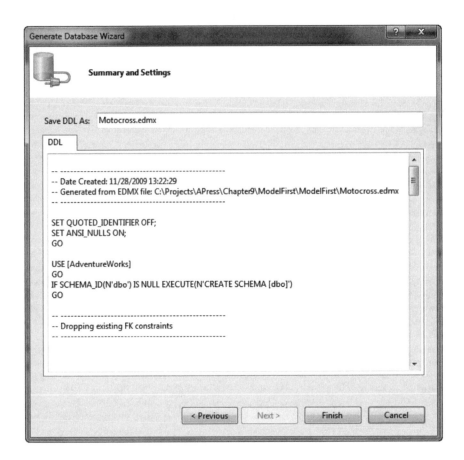

Figure 9-9. *Summary and settings*

Here is the entire DDL script from Figure 9-9:

```
-- --------------------------------------------------
-- Date Created: 12/05/2009 08:32:14
-- Generated from EDMX file: C:\Projects\APress\Chapter9\⏎
ModelFirst\ModelFirst\Motocross.edmx
-- --------------------------------------------------

SET QUOTED_IDENTIFIER OFF;
SET ANSI_NULLS ON;
GO

USE [AdventureWorks]
GO
IF SCHEMA_ID(N'dbo') IS NULL EXECUTE(N'CREATE SCHEMA [dbo]')
GO
```

```
-- ----------------------------------------------------
-- Dropping existing FK constraints
-- ----------------------------------------------------

IF OBJECT_ID(N'[dbo].[FK_BrandTeam]', 'F') IS NOT NULL
    ALTER TABLE [dbo].[Teams] DROP CONSTRAINT [FK_BrandTeam]
GO
IF OBJECT_ID(N'[dbo].[FK_RiderTeam]', 'F') IS NOT NULL
    ALTER TABLE [dbo].[Teams] DROP CONSTRAINT [FK_RiderTeam]
GO
IF OBJECT_ID(N'[dbo].[FK_ClassRider]', 'F') IS NOT NULL
    ALTER TABLE [dbo].[Riders] DROP CONSTRAINT [FK_ClassRider]
GO


-- ----------------------------------------------------
-- Dropping existing tables
-- ----------------------------------------------------

IF OBJECT_ID(N'[dbo].[Teams]', 'U') IS NOT NULL
    DROP TABLE [dbo].[Teams];
GO
IF OBJECT_ID(N'[dbo].[Riders]', 'U') IS NOT NULL
    DROP TABLE [dbo].[Riders];
GO
IF OBJECT_ID(N'[dbo].[Classes]', 'U') IS NOT NULL
    DROP TABLE [dbo].[Classes];
GO
IF OBJECT_ID(N'[dbo].[Brands]', 'U') IS NOT NULL
    DROP TABLE [dbo].[Brands];
GO


-- ----------------------------------------------------
-- Creating all tables
-- ----------------------------------------------------

-- Creating table 'Teams'
CREATE TABLE [dbo].[Teams] (
    [TeamID] int IDENTITY(1,1) NOT NULL,
    [TeamName] nvarchar(max)  NOT NULL,
    [IsSupportTeam] bit  NOT NULL,
    [BrandID] int  NOT NULL,
    [Brand_BrandID] int  NOT NULL
);
GO
-- Creating table 'Riders'
CREATE TABLE [dbo].[Riders] (
    [RiderID] int IDENTITY(1,1) NOT NULL,
    [FirstName] nvarchar(max)  NOT NULL,
    [MiddleName] nvarchar(max)  NULL,
    [LastName] nvarchar(max)  NOT NULL,
    [Age] smallint  NOT NULL,
    [ClassID] int  NOT NULL,
    [TeamID] int  NOT NULL,
    [Class_ClassID] int  NOT NULL,
```

```
    [Team_TeamID] int  NOT NULL
);
GO
-- Creating table 'Classes'
CREATE TABLE [dbo].[Classes] (
    [ClassID] int IDENTITY(1,1) NOT NULL,
    [ClassName] nvarchar(max)  NOT NULL
);
GO
-- Creating table 'Brands'
CREATE TABLE [dbo].[Brands] (
    [BrandID] int IDENTITY(1,1) NOT NULL,
    [BrandName] nvarchar(max)  NOT NULL
);
GO


-- --------------------------------------------------
-- Creating all Primary Key Constraints
-- --------------------------------------------------

-- Creating primary key on [TeamID] in table 'Teams'
ALTER TABLE [dbo].[Teams] WITH NOCHECK
ADD CONSTRAINT [PK_Teams]
    PRIMARY KEY CLUSTERED ([TeamID] ASC)
    ON [PRIMARY]
GO
-- Creating primary key on [RiderID] in table 'Riders'
ALTER TABLE [dbo].[Riders] WITH NOCHECK
ADD CONSTRAINT [PK_Riders]
    PRIMARY KEY CLUSTERED ([RiderID] ASC)
    ON [PRIMARY]
GO
-- Creating primary key on [ClassID] in table 'Classes'
ALTER TABLE [dbo].[Classes] WITH NOCHECK
ADD CONSTRAINT [PK_Classes]
    PRIMARY KEY CLUSTERED ([ClassID] ASC)
    ON [PRIMARY]
GO
-- Creating primary key on [BrandID] in table 'Brands'
ALTER TABLE [dbo].[Brands] WITH NOCHECK
ADD CONSTRAINT [PK_Brands]
    PRIMARY KEY CLUSTERED ([BrandID] ASC)
    ON [PRIMARY]
GO


-- --------------------------------------------------
-- Creating all Foreign Key Constraints
-- --------------------------------------------------

-- Creating foreign key on [Brand_BrandID] in table 'Teams'
ALTER TABLE [dbo].[Teams] WITH NOCHECK
ADD CONSTRAINT [FK_BrandTeam]
    FOREIGN KEY ([Brand_BrandID])
    REFERENCES [dbo].[Brands]
```

```
        ([BrandID])
    ON DELETE NO ACTION ON UPDATE NO ACTION
GO
-- Creating foreign key on [Class_ClassID] in table 'Riders'
ALTER TABLE [dbo].[Riders] WITH NOCHECK
ADD CONSTRAINT [FK_ClassRider]
    FOREIGN KEY ([Class_ClassID])
    REFERENCES [dbo].[Classes]
        ([ClassID])
    ON DELETE NO ACTION ON UPDATE NO ACTION
GO
-- Creating foreign key on [Team_TeamID] in table 'Riders'
ALTER TABLE [dbo].[Riders] WITH NOCHECK
ADD CONSTRAINT [FK_TeamRider]
    FOREIGN KEY ([Team_TeamID])
    REFERENCES [dbo].[Teams]
        ([TeamID])
    ON DELETE NO ACTION ON UPDATE NO ACTION
GO


-- --------------------------------------------------
-- Script has ended
-- --------------------------------------------------
```

As you can see by this DDL, the script is very thorough. It takes care of handling any existing relationships and keys so that the script will run successfully.

Click the Finish button in Figure 9-9 if you do wish to execute the script that you've generated. Clicking Finish on the Summary and Settings dialog closes the wizard, and then presents you with the warning shown in Figure 9-10.

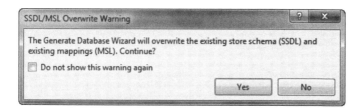

Figure 9-10. Overwrite warning

This warning is not to be taken lightly, as it is really telling you two things. First, if you haven't noticed the DROP statements in the DDL, it will be dropping and recreating the objects in your database (this was talked about earlier).

■ **Caution!** If you have existing objects to drop, you will lose any data in those objects. This goes without saying, but I'll say it anyway. If you have test or other data that is important to you, be sure to save it before you recreate your schema.

Second, the warning is telling you that any current mappings you have will be overwritten. This has significant meaning, in that if you have made any custom changes to the mapping, or have run this wizard before to generate the mapping, all of that will be lost. Just like the DDL, which deletes the objects and recreates them, the GDW (Generate Database Wizard) deletes all existing mapping and recreates them.

Go ahead and click Yes. This will open the DDL in a new tab in our Visual Studio environment, shown in Figure 9-11. This is quite handy because we can easily create a server connection in the Visual Studio Server Explorer window and connect our SQL window to execute the DDL. We don't have to copy the content and past it into a query window in SSMS (SQL Server Management Studio).

```
Motocross.edmx.sql - not connected   Motocross.edmx*
  1
  2   -- ----------------------------------------------
  3   -- Date Created: 11/28/2009 13:27:47
  4   -- Generated from EDMX file: C:\Projects\APress\Chapter9\ModelFirst\ModelFirst\Motocross.edmx
  5   -- ----------------------------------------------
  6
  7   SET QUOTED_IDENTIFIER OFF;
  8   SET ANSI_NULLS ON;
  9   GO
 10
 11   USE [AdventureWorks]
 12   GO
 13   IF SCHEMA_ID(N'dbo') IS NULL EXECUTE(N'CREATE SCHEMA [dbo]')
 14   GO
 15
 16   -- ----------------------------------------------
 17   -- Dropping existing FK constraints
 18   -- ----------------------------------------------
 19
 20   IF OBJECT_ID(N'[dbo].[FK_BrandTeam]', 'F') IS NOT NULL
 21       ALTER TABLE [dbo].[Entity1Set] DROP CONSTRAINT [FK_BrandTeam]
 22   GO
 23   IF OBJECT_ID(N'[dbo].[FK_RiderTeam]', 'F') IS NOT NULL
 24       ALTER TABLE [dbo].[Entity1Set] DROP CONSTRAINT [FK_RiderTeam]

100 %
Disconnected.
```

Figure 9-11. DDL not connected

Before we move on, take a good look at Figure 9-11. Besides the fact that the .sql window is not connected, you should notice one other important thing. Notice that the .edmx file has been modified, as you can see by the * on the tab. That is because the wizard did three things behind the scenes:

- Generated the store schema (SSDL) and the mapping specification (MSL) that provides the CSDL.

- Generated the DDL to be executed. This file was then saved as a .sql file in the project.

- Connection string information was added to the App.config/Web.config file.

Save and close the EDM and open it again using the XML Editor (just like you did earlier in this chapter). Looking again at the XML will show you that the .edmx file has been updated with the generated SSDL and MSL and related CSDL mapping information. You can see this in Figure 9-12.

```
Motocross.edmx  X
  1   k?xml version="1.0" encoding="utf-8"?>
  2  ⊟<edmx:Edmx Version="2.0" xmlns:edmx="http://schemas.microsoft.com/ado/2008/10/edmx">
  3      <!-- EF Runtime content -->
  4  ⊟  <edmx:Runtime>
  5        <!-- SSDL content -->
  6  ⊞      <edmx:StorageModels>...</edmx:StorageModels>
101        <!-- CSDL content -->
102  ⊞      <edmx:ConceptualModels>...</edmx:ConceptualModels>
164        <!-- C-S mapping content -->
165        <edmx:Mappings>
166  ⊟      <Mapping Space="C-S" xmlns="http://schemas.microsoft.com/ado/2008/09/mapping/cs">
167  ⊟      <EntityContainerMapping StorageEntityContainer="MotocrossStoreContainer" CdmEntityContainer="MotocrossContainer">
168  ⊟        <EntitySetMapping Name="Teams">
169  ⊟          <EntityTypeMapping TypeName="IsTypeOf(Motocross.Team)">
170  ⊟            <MappingFragment StoreEntitySet="Teams">
171                <ScalarProperty Name="TeamID" ColumnName="TeamID" />
172                <ScalarProperty Name="TeamName" ColumnName="TeamName" />
173                <ScalarProperty Name="IsSupportTeam" ColumnName="IsSupportTeam" />
174                <ScalarProperty Name="BrandID" ColumnName="BrandID" />
175                <ScalarProperty Name="RiderID" ColumnName="RiderID" />
176              </MappingFragment>
177            </EntityTypeMapping>
178          </EntitySetMapping>
179  ⊟        <EntitySetMapping Name="Riders">
180  ⊟          <EntityTypeMapping TypeName="IsTypeOf(Motocross.Rider)">
181  ⊟            <MappingFragment StoreEntitySet="Riders">
182                <ScalarProperty Name="RiderID" ColumnName="RiderID" />
183                <ScalarProperty Name="FirstName" ColumnName="FirstName" />
100 %  ▾
```

Figure 9-12. Updated mapping

Also, take a look at the content of the Solution Explorer window. As already stated, you will notice the addition of a new .sql file that contains the generated DDL. This file will be overwritten each time you run the Generate Database Wizard.

You have now walked through an example of how model-first design works, but let's take a quick look at some of the rules that the wizard follows.

Database Generation Rules

As you have learned, the Database Generation Wizard creates a schema from a conceptual model. This section will discuss the rules that the wizard follows to generate the schema and mapping.

Tables

Tables are generated by using a table-per-type mapping strategy, which means a separate table in the storage schema is used to maintain data from each type (EntityType) in the model. In other words, there is one database table for one entity type. Tables are based on entity types, using one set of rules for non-derived types, and another set for derived types.

Following are the rules for non-derived types:

- *Table name*: The element name of the type's EntitySet

- *Primary key*: Column or columns corresponding to the entity key property (or properties)

- *Columns*: One column for each scalar property. This also includes each scalar property used in complex type property.

And next are the rules for derived types:

- *Table name*: The base type's EntitySet element name and the type name are combined together.

- *Primary Key*: Column or columns corresponding to the inherited entity key property or properties

- *Columns*: One column for each non-inherited scalar property as well as each inherited key property. This also includes each scalar property used in a complex type property.

The example in the beginning of this chapter is a good example of type-per-type generation from non-derived types. In that example, the table names are taken from the EntitySet element name, each column maps to a specific scalar property, and the primary key is generated from the entity key of each entity.

Associations

Associations also follow some rules, regardless of the type. These are as follows:

- *One-to-zero / One-to-many*: Columns are added to the table that corresponds to the entity type of the one or many end of the association. Each added column has a foreign key constraint that references the primary key of the table that corresponds to the entity type on the other end of the association. The name of each added column in the association is the combination of the navigation property name and the key property name.

- *One-to-one*: In a one-to-one scenario where this is no primary key–to–primary key and no constraint, it is possible to select either end to hold the foreign key. Thus, one of the ends is arbitrarily selected to hold the foreign key. The added columns have foreign key constraints that reference the primary key of the table that corresponds to the entity type on the other end of the association. The name of each added column in the association is the combination of the navigation property name and the key property name.

- *Many-to-many*: A join table is created with the name of the AssociatedSet element name. The primary key of this table is a compound key consisting of all the columns in the table. A column is added to the table for each key property in each entity type, and these columns have foreign key constraints referencing the primary keys in the entity types on the other end of the association.

If a referential constraint exists on a one-to-zero, one-to-many, or one-to-one association in the conceptual model, foreign key constraints are created instead of adding the specific columns to the database. The result is a constraint in the database that matches the constraint in the conceptual model.

The example from earlier in this chapter shows how the foreign keys were generated using the rules just listed. The entities in our example used one-to-many association types, and, based on those associations, the appropriate DDL was generated following the rules listed previously.

For example, the following code shows the DDL generated for the association between the Team and Rider entities, and by looking at the DDL generated for the Rider table you can see that a column was added to the table following the rules specified.

```
ALTER TABLE [dbo].[Riders] WITH NOCHECK
ADD CONSTRAINT [FK_ClassRider]
    FOREIGN KEY ([Class_ClassID])
    REFERENCES [dbo].[Classes]
```

```
    ([ClassID])
  ON DELETE NO ACTION ON UPDATE NO ACTION
GO
```

Handling of Complex Types

Let's look at an example of how complex types are handled when generating a database from a model. Let's begin by creating a complex type that we can use in our model. For this example, add a new empty data model to the project. Once that is added, right-click anywhere on the surface of the designer and, from the context menu, select Add ➤ Complex Type. The complex type will be added to the Model Browser window underneath the Complex Types node with a default name of ComplexType1. For this example, rename the complex type to ContactInfo.

Next, right-click on the new complex type and select Add ➤ Scalar Property ➤ String from the context menu. Name the new scalar property CellPhone. Create three more string scalar properties named EmailAddress, Fax, and HomePhone. Figure 9-13 shows what the completed complex type will look like in the Model Browser window.

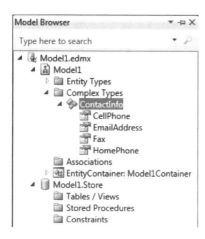

Figure 9-13. ContactInfo complex property

With the complex property created, let's add that to an entity. From the Toolbox window, drag an entity to the designer and name it Customer. Rename the Id field to CustomerId, and add four more string scalar properties called Firstname, Lastname, Address, and City.

Next, add the complex type property to the entity but, right-clicking the entity, select Add ➤ Complex Property from the context menu. Rename the complex property to AdditionalContactInfo. The completed entity will look like Figure 9-14.

Figure 9-14. Customer entity

Use the same steps you used earlier in the chapter to generate the DDL. Notice that a column for each scalar property of the complex type is added to the table that is created based on the entity type. Each column name in the complex type is the combination of the complex type property name along with an underscore character ("_") and the name of the corresponding complex type scalar property name.

```
-- --------------------------------------------------
-- Date Created: 11/28/2009 12:05:34
-- Generated from EDMX file: C:\Projects\APress\Chapter9\ModelFirst\ModelFirst\Model1.edmx
-- --------------------------------------------------


-- --------------------------------------------------
-- Creating all tables
-- --------------------------------------------------

-- Creating table 'Customers'
CREATE TABLE [dbo].[Customers] (
    [CustomerId] int  NOT NULL,
    [Firstname] nvarchar(max)  NOT NULL,
    [Lastname] nvarchar(max)  NOT NULL,
    [Address] nvarchar(max)  NOT NULL,
    [City] nvarchar(max)  NOT NULL,
    [AdditionalContactInfo_HomePhone] real  NOT NULL,
    [AdditionalContactInfo_CellPhone] nvarchar(max)  NOT NULL,
    [AdditionalContactInfo_Fax] nvarchar(max)  NOT NULL,
    [AdditionalContactInfo_EmailAddress] nvarchar(max)  NOT NULL
);
GO


-- --------------------------------------------------
-- Script has ended
-- --------------------------------------------------
```

DB Generation Script Customization

You saw earlier how to generate a database from your model. This section is going to show you how that is done and provide you with the information needed to customize the output of the DDL as well as the mapping information.

Open the Motocross EDM and then right-click anywhere on the designer surface and select Properties from the context menu. In the Properties window you will see a section called Database Script Generation, which has three properties:

- Database Generation Workflow

- Database Schema Name

- DDL Generation Template

You can see these in Figure 9-15. These three properties are used in the generation of the DDL when you run the Database Generation Wizard.

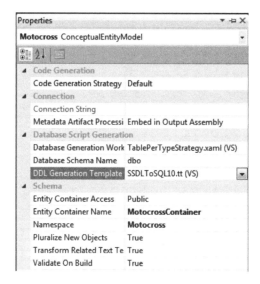

Figure 9-15. Database script generation

Two of the properties point to actual files located on your hard drive. The location of these two files is the following:

```
C:\Program Files\Microsoft Visual Studio 10.0\Common7\IDE\Extensions\Microsoft\Entity↵
  Framework Tools\DBGen
```

These two files, shown in Figure 9-16, make up the functionality that generates the DDL. One is a simple .tt (T4 Template) file, which you learned all about in Chapter 8. The other file is a Windows Workflow Markup .xaml file.

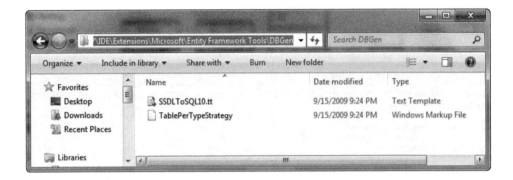

Figure 9-16. Script generation file location

I have opened up the .tt file and scrolled to the location in the template where it generated the DROP TABLE statements followed by the CREATE TABLE statements. You can see that location in Figure 9-17. In each instance the template is looping through the EntitySets and generating the appropriate DDL statements.

```
    }
#>

-- ------------------------------------------------
-- Dropping existing tables
<#  if (this.IsSQLCE)
    {
#>
-- NOTE: if the table does not exist, an ignorable error will be reported.
<#  } #>
-- ------------------------------------------------

<#
    foreach (EntitySet entitySet in ExistingStore.GetAllEntitySets())
    {
        string schemaName = Id(entitySet.GetSchemaName());
        string tableName = Id(entitySet.GetTableName());

        if (!this.IsSQLCE)
        {
#>
IF OBJECT_ID(N'[<#=Lit(schemaName)#>].[<#=Lit(tableName)#>]', 'U') IS NOT NULL
<#      } #>
    DROP TABLE <# if (!IsSQLCE) {#>[<#=schemaName#>].<#}#>[<#=tableName#>];
GO
<#
    }
#>

-- ------------------------------------------------
-- Creating all tables
-- ------------------------------------------------

<#
    foreach (EntitySet entitySet in Store.GetAllEntitySets())
    {
        string schemaName = Id(entitySet.GetSchemaName());
        string tableName = Id(entitySet.GetTableName());
#>
-- Creating table '<#=tableName#>'
CREATE TABLE <# if (!IsSQLCE) {#>[<#=schemaName#>].<#}#>[<#=tableName#>] (
```

Figure 9-17. SSDLToSQL10.tt

The question remains, however, what is the `.xaml` file and how is it used? Unlike the `.tt` file, you can't simply just open it up. This is, however, a `.xaml` file and it can be viewed. Fire up a new instance of Visual Studio and create a new project. The type of project you want to create is a Workflow type. In the list of Installed Templates, select Workflow (either C# or Visual Basic) and then select Workflow Console Application from the list of template types.

When the project loads, open the Solution Explorer window and right-click the project. Select Add ➤ Existing Item from the context menu and browse to the location previously listed. Select the `TablePerTypeStrategy.xaml` file and click Add. The `.xaml` file will be added to the project.

Double-click the `TablePerTypeStrategy.xaml` in Solution Explorer. When it opens you will see a GenerateDatabaseScriptWorkflow item, which is shown in Figure 9-18. If you are not familiar with Windows Workflow, you are looking at it. The `TablePerTypeStrategy.xaml` is a Windows Workflow that contains a Sequence Control Workflow and two activities. However, if you browse the components and activities in the Toolbox window, you won't find those two activities. This is because these activities are found in a unique class. Select one of the activities in the Sequence container and then open the properties window. You will notice that the activity comes from the following location:

```
Microsoft.Data.Entity.Design.DatabaseGeneration.Activities.CsdlToSsdlAndMslActivity
```

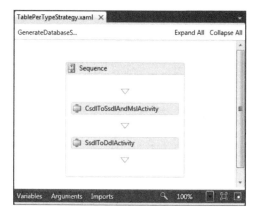

Figure 9-18. Generate database workflow

If you want look at this, add a reference to the `Microsoft.Data.Entity.Design.DatabaseGeneration` namespace. Then go to the Toolbox window, right-click anywhere in the Toolbox window and select Choose Items from the context menu. In the Choose Toolbox Items dialog, select the System.Activities.Components tab and select the CsdlToSsdlAndMslActivity then click OK. This activity should now be added to the Toolbox window.

Out of the box, Microsoft has made it fairly easy to customize many aspects of the Entity Framework, including how your DDL scripts are generated. T-4 templates are a great example of this. Yet it can be quite cumbersome if you are trying to learn T-4 and all the ins and outs of the T-4 language and how best to implement your customization.

While there is much room for improvement, they have not left developers out in the cold. One of the external tools Microsoft is working on is a tool called the Entity Designer Database Generation Power Pack. This is a free tool, currently in Community Technology Preview, which provides an enhanced user-interface to help manage database generation strategies. It also includes six new workflow options for generating your database. Since this tool is fairly new at the time of this writing, it was hard to put it into this book. However, by the time this book reaches your hands there will be several blog posts and articles on my blog and web site on how to use this great tool in your application to customize your database generation scripts.

http://visualstudiogallery.msdn.microsoft.com/en-us/df3541c3-d833-4b65-b942-989e7ec74c87

CHAPTER 10

■■■

Code-Only Development

When Microsoft set about to make the Entity Framework more flexible, their goal was to provide developers with an environment in which they could create their model from one of their approaches. The first approach, which has existed since the initial release of EF, is the ability to generate your model from a database. Many of the chapters in this book have covered the new features and concepts that are tied to this approach.

Chapter 9 covered the second approach, model-first, which lets developers start with a conceptual model and generate their database based on that conceptual model. This approach also lets developers customize DDL generation through T4 templates and Windows Workflow, giving them the utmost flexibility and control over the creation and generation of the DDL. This is truly a "model-first" solution. This ability to customize is a giant step over EF 3.5, in which you could define your conceptual model in EF but not do anything beyond that, such as generate your database.

This chapter will cover the third approach, the code-only approach, which provides developers the ability to use the Entity Framework using POCO entities and without an EDMX file. This approach lets developers view code as their model. There is a lot of discussion around the code-only approach, such as whether code-only will contain much of the functionality found in a standard EDM model approach. The goal from the outset was to ensure that most, if not all, of the functionality found in the other two approaches (model-first, database-first) is found in the code-only approach. This includes topics such as deferred/lazy loading, change tracking, and complex types. And let's not forget new foreign key association support. This is included as well.

In this chapter we will cover the code-only approach and discuss many aspects of building an EF project using code-only. We will build a simple example, and we will also discuss some of the other aspects that you can add to your code-only project, including deferred/lazy loading, complex types, and change tracking.

Let's get started.

Getting Started with Code-Only

The first thing you need to do is download a feature preview from the Microsoft website. In your favorite browser, go to the following URL:

```
http://www.microsoft.com/downloads/details.aspx?familyid↵
=13FDFCE4-7F92-438F-8058-B5B4041D0F01&displaylang=en
```

The ADO.NET Entity Framework Feature CTP is a set of features that adds additional features and components to EF 4.0. From this website, click the Download button, which downloads a file called EF4FeatureCTP2.exe. The ADO.NET Entity Framework Feature CTP installs the following components:

- Templates for self-tracking entities (used for N-Tier support...we'll use this in Chapter 11)

- Code-only programming model used with the Entity Data Model

Make sure Visual Studio is not open when you run the installation. When the installation is complete, we are ready to begin.

Creating the Data Project

In Visual Studio 2010, create a new Class Library project. I called mine CodeOnlyData, as you can see in Figure 10-1. The CodeOnlyData project is the data project that will contain the POCO classes that will mimic the EDM.

Figure 10-1. Create class library project

Once the project has been created, delete the Class1.cs class and add two additional classes:

- Contact.cs

- Employee.cs

We are ready to add code. The Contact and Employee classes are our POCO classes and are essentially called POCO entities. Let's work with the Contact class first. Open the Contact class and replace everything in that class with the following:

```
using System;
using System.Data;
using System.Collections.Generic;
using System.Linq;
using System.Text;
```

```
namespace CodeOnlyData
{
    public class Contact
    {
        public Contact() { }
        public int ContactID { get; set; }
        public bool NameStyle { get; set; }
        public string Title { get; set; }
        public string FirstName { get; set; }
        public string MiddleName { get; set; }
        public string LastName { get; set; }
        public string Suffix { get; set; }
        public string EmailAddress { get; set; }
        public int EmailPromotion { get; set; }
        public string Phone { get; set; }
        public string PasswordHash { get; set; }
        public string PasswordSalt { get; set; }
        public Guid rowguid { get; set; }
        public DateTime ModifiedDate { get; set; }
        public ICollection<Employee> Employees { get; set; }
    }
}
```

This code is our POCO class for Contact. If you were to look at an EDM generated from the AdventureWorks database for the same table, you would see that this nearly matches the CSDL entity type with many of the properties. It's as simple as that.

Now for the Employee class. Open Employee.cs and replace the code in that class with the following:

```
using System;
using System.Collections.Generic;
using System.Linq;
using System.Text;

namespace CodeOnlyData
{
    public class Employee
    {
        public Employee() { }
        public int EmployeeID { get; set; }
        public string NationalIDNumber { get; set; }
        public string LoginID { get; set; }
        public Nullable<int> ManagerID { get; set; }
        public string Title { get; set; }
        public DateTime BirthDate { get; set; }
        public string MaritalStatus { get; set; }
        public string Gender { get; set; }
        public DateTime HireDate { get; set; }
        public bool SalariedFlag { get; set; }
        public short VacationHours { get; set; }
        public short SickLeaveHours { get; set; }
        public bool CurrentFlag { get; set; }
        public Guid rowguid { get; set; }
```

```
        public DateTime ModifiedDate { get; set; }
        public Contact Contact { get; set; }
        //public int ContactID { get; set; }


    }
}
```

This creates our POCO class for the employee. At this point we are pretty much done with our data project. We haven't defined any relationships or configuration items, but we will do that shortly in a second project, and I'll explain why we do it there when we get to that point. So, let's build our UI project.

Adding the User-Interface Project

We need a UI project that will consume our data project, so let's add that. From the file menu, select Add ➤ New Project. When the Add New Project dialog opens, select Windows from the list of installed templates, then select Windows Forms Application from the list of templates. Name this project CodeOnlyUI and click OK.

You might be asking why we created a separate project for our POCO classes. The answer is simply because we want several things. First, this allows us to compile our classes into a separate and distinct assembly from the UI project. Second, and most important, is that this allows us to keep the data assembly persistence-ignorant.

Adding References

Here is where the ADO.NET Entity Framework Feature CTP comes in to play. We need to add a few references to our UI project. Right-click on the references node in Solution Explorer for the CodeOnlyUI project. When the references dialog displays, we need to add two references to this project. They are the following:

- System.Data.Entity

- Microsoft.Data.Entity.Ctp

Figure 10-2 shows the Microsoft.Data.Entity.Ctp component selected in the Add Reference dialog. This is the Code-Only Programming Model component. Select these two components and then click OK.

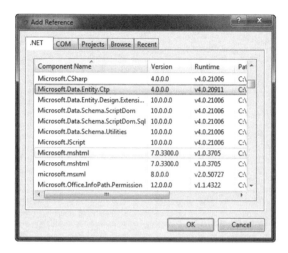

Figure 10-2. *Adding feature reference*

Why do we need a reference to the Code-Only Programming Model component? If you look at the properties of either the System.Data or Microsoft.Data.Entity.Ctp assemblies you will notice that they point to a location that is different from the System.Data assembly in your data project. Your System.Data component in your data project (CodeOnlyData) points to the following location:

```
C:\Program Files(x86)\Reference Assemblies\Microsoft\Framework\.NetFramework\v4.0
```

The System.Data and Microsoft.Data.Entity.Ctp assemblies in your UI project (CodeOnlyUI) are located here:

```
C:\Program Files(x86)\Reference Assemblies\Microsoft\Framework\.NetFramework\v4.0\↵
Profile\Client
```

The client profile target framework allows you to create an assembly that only needs the smaller subset of .NET 4.0 assemblies, which is in the client profile. If all of the assemblies in your application target the client profile target framework then this will allow you to install your application on a client computer with a very small footprint, and download and install only the smaller components.

We also need to add a reference to our data project within our UI project. Right-click on the references node again in Solution Explorer for the UI project, and select Add Reference. When the Add References dialog opens, select the Projects tab and select the CodeOnlyData project, shown in Figure 10-3. Click OK.

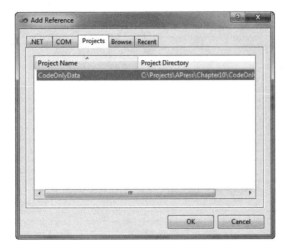

Figure 10-3. Adding project reference

Adding Context and Connections

At this point we have a simple code-only "model" via our POCO classes, and the beginnings of our UI application. What we don't have yet is our context and connections or any configuration components that define relationships and associations, so let's add those now.

Add the following three classes to the UI project:

- AWModel.cs

- ContactConfiguration.cs

- EmployeeConfiguration.cs

When we are all finished adding everything, our Solution Explorer should now look like Figure 10-4.

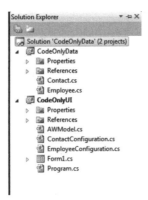

Figure 10-4. Solution Explorer

Coding the User Interface

It is time to start adding code to our UI project. Open `AWModel.cs` and replace the code that is there with the following:

```
using System;
using System.Collections.Generic;
using System.Linq;
using System.Text;
using System.Data.Objects;
using System.Data.EntityClient;
using CodeOnlyData;

namespace CodeOnlyUI
{
    public class AWModel : ObjectContext
    {
        public AWModel(EntityConnection connection)
            : base(connection)
        {
            DefaultContainerName = "AWModel";
        }

        public IObjectSet<Contact> Contact
        {
            get { return base.CreateObjectSet<Contact>(); }
        }

        public IObjectSet<Employee> Employee
        {
            get { return base.CreateObjectSet<Employee>(); }
        }
    }
}
```

This class is our context and extends the `ObjectContext`. It represents the shape of our model and is the entry and tunnel to the database. We added a single constructor, which accepts an EntityConnection. This is simply a wrapper around the true database connection and the EF metadata. This connection information is passed to the constructor when a new instance of the AWModel is instantiated.

We also declare two typed entities using the IObjectSet interface, which allow us to perform create, read, update, and delete operations. Since the `ObjectSet` class derives from `ObjectQuery`, it can also work as a query object.

Creating Configuration Classes

The next step is to create our configuration classes and methods, one for Contact and one for Employee. Open `ContactConfiguration.cs` and replace the code in that class with the following:

```
using System;
using System.Collections.Generic;
using System.Linq;
using System.Text;
```

```
using Microsoft.Data.Objects;
using CodeOnlyData;

namespace CodeOnlyUI
{
    class ContactConfiguration : EntityConfiguration<Contact>
    {
        public ContactConfiguration()
        {
            Property(c => c.ContactID).IsIdentity();
            Property(c => c.Title).HasMaxLength(8);
            Property(c => c.FirstName).HasMaxLength(50);
            Property(c => c.FirstName).IsRequired();
            Property(c => c.MiddleName).HasMaxLength(50);
            Property(c => c.LastName).HasMaxLength(50);
            Property(c => c.LastName).IsRequired();
            Property(c => c.Suffix).HasMaxLength(10);
            Property(c => c.EmailAddress).HasMaxLength(50);
            Property(c => c.Phone).HasMaxLength(25);

            Property(c => c.PasswordHash).HasMaxLength(128).IsRequired();
            Property(c => c.PasswordSalt).HasMaxLength(10).IsRequired;
        }
    }
}
```

This class holds the entire configuration for the Contact class. In this class we define the property that is the primary key by using the IsIdentity() property. We also specify other property facets such as MaxLength and IsRequired. Notice that this example also illustrates that you can combine the properties on a single line instead of two separate statements. The PasswordHash and PasswordSalt properties show this.

Let's do the Employee next. Open EmployeeConfiguration.cs and replace all the code that is there with the following:

```
using System;
using System.Collections.Generic;
using System.Linq;
using System.Text;
using Microsoft.Data.Objects;
using CodeOnlyData;

namespace CodeOnlyUI
{
    class EmployeeConfiguration : EntityConfiguration<Employee>
    {
        public EmployeeConfiguration()
        {
            Property(e => e.EmployeeID).IsIdentity();
            Property(e => e.NationalIDNumber).HasMaxLength(15).IsRequired();
            Property(e => e.LoginID).HasMaxLength(256).IsRequired();
            Property(e => e.Title).HasMaxLength(50).IsRequired();
            Property(e => e.MaritalStatus).HasMaxLength(1).IsRequired();
            Property(e => e.Gender).HasMaxLength(1).IsRequired();
```

```
        Relationship(e => e.Contact).IsRequired();

        Relationship(e => e.Contact).FromProperty(c => c.Employee);
    }
  }
}
```

In this code, we define the identity for the Employee and set the MaxLength and IsRequired properties as we did with the Contact class. However, we also did a couple of other things. First, we define the relationship between Contact and Employee, and second, we set the relationship as required. Thus, we have just defined the PK association.

Testing the Code-Only Model

Let's put this code to good use and test our code-only model. Open Form1 in design view and drop a list box onto the form. In the code behind the form, replace the code with the following:

```
using System;
using System.Collections.Generic;
using System.ComponentModel;
using System.Data;
using System.Drawing;
using System.Linq;
using System.Text;
using System.Windows.Forms;
using System.Data.SqlClient;
using Microsoft.Data.Objects;

namespace CodeOnlyUI
{
    public partial class Form1 : Form
    {
        public Form1()
        {
            InitializeComponent();
        }

        private void Form1_Load(object sender, EventArgs e)
        {
            try
            {

                SqlConnection conn = new SqlConnection("Data Source=servername;Initial↵
    Catalog=EF40;User ID=sa;PWD=password;MultipleActiveResultSets=True;");

                var builder = new ContextBuilder<AWModel>();
                Registerconfig(builder);
                var context = builder.Create(conn);

                var query = from c in context.Contact
                            select c;

                foreach (var con in query)
```

```
                    {
                          listBox1.Items.Add(con.FirstName);
                    }

                }
                catch (Exception ex)
                {
                     MessageBox.Show(ex.InnerException.Message);
                }
            }
            static void Registerconfig(ContextBuilder<AWModel> builder)
            {
                 builder.Configurations.Add(new ContactConfiguration());
                 builder.Configurations.Add(new EmployeeConfiguration());
            }
        }
    }
}
```

In this code we simply create an SQLConnection that defines our connection information. We then instantiate a new ContextBuilder. Our goal is to construct the context (of the AWModel) by passing in the EntityConnection to the constructor. The following is the relevant line of code from the example:

```
var context = builder.Create(conn)
```

Where did the ContextBuilder come from? It was installed as part of the ADO.NET Entity Framework Feature CTP and exists in the Microsoft.Data.Objects.ContextBuilder class. This class infers the Conceptual Model, Storage Model, and Mapping, using the metadata and the SqlConnection to create an EntityConnection.

Building the Project

Build the project to ensure there are no errors, then run the project by pressing F5. When the form displays, the list box will populate with the first name of all the contacts, shown in Figure 10-5. The form isn't very effective, but the purpose of this example isn't form functionality here. We'll make modifications shortly to add more functionality. Also, feel free to modify the query to experiment with this example.

Figure 10-5. *List of contact first names*

This example isn't very efficient because we are not filtering on anything, so we are returning a lot of records (nearly 20,000 to be exact). The form may take several seconds to load. Again, we aren't going after prettiness, but functionality of code-only.

Loading Some Rows

Let's continue this example by adding some code that will use the Employee entity. Stop the application and open the form in design view, and place a DataGridView on the form below the list box.

The first thing we need to do is modify the code so that it is more usable throughout the form. To do that, add the following three lines in the declaration section. The first line simply defines a variable so that we know whether the form is loading. The second line defines an SqlConnection variable, and the last line defines a ContextBuilder variable based on the model we are using.

```
bool isLoaded = false;
SqlConnection conn;
ContextBuilder<AWModel> builder
```

Next, we need to modify the code in the Load event of the form so that it is not loading all 20,000 rows—we just want a specific subset of that. Therefore, modify your code in the Load event to look like the following:

```
try
{

    conn = new SqlConnection("Data Source=SCOTT-LAPTOP;Initial Catalog=EF40;User↩
ID=sa;PWD=InsertYourPasswordHere;MultipleActiveResultSets=True;");

    builder = new ContextBuilder<AWModel>();
    Registerconfig(builder);
    var context = builder.Create(conn);
```

```
        context.ContextOptions.LazyLoadingEnabled = true;

        var query = from c in context.Contact
                    where c.LastName.StartsWith("G")
                    orderby c.FirstName
                    select new { c.ContactID, c.FirstName, c.LastName };

        isLoaded = false;
        listBox1.DataSource = query;
        listBox1.DisplayMember = "FirstName";
        listBox1.ValueMember = "ContactID";
        isLoaded = true;

}
catch (Exception ex)
{
    MessageBox.Show(ex.Message);
    if (ex.InnerException != null)
    {
        MessageBox.Show(ex.InnerException.Message);
    }
}
```

This code is much like our previous example, but with a few changes. We changed our query to return only those contacts whose last name starts with the letter G. We then load the list box a bit differently. Instead of looping through each row to load the list box, we bind the query to the list box itself by setting the DataSource property to the query, and then set the DisplayMember and ValueMember properties. The DisplayMember property identifies which value in the query to display in the list box. The ValueMember sets the property to use as the actual value of the items in the list box.

Connecting the DataGridView Control

Our next step is to wire up the DataGridView control. We do this by adding the following code to the SelectedIndexChanged event of the list box.

```
try
{
    if (isLoaded == true)
    {
        var context = builder.Create(conn);
        context.ContextOptions.LazyLoadingEnabled = true;

        int id = (int)listBox1.SelectedValue;
        label1.Text = id.ToString();

        var query = from emp in context.Employee
                    where emp.Contact.ContactID == id
                    select emp;

        dataGridView1.DataSource = query;
    }
}
catch (Exception ex)
```

```
{
    MessageBox.Show(ex.Message);
    if (ex.InnerException != null)
    {
        MessageBox.Show(ex.InnerException.Message);
    }
}
```

As we click on different names in the list box, the SelectedIndexChanged event gets called, executing the previous code. This code first creates our context, then gets the ID of the contact we just selected in the list box by using the SelectedValue property. We then use that value in a LINQ query to get the related Employee data; then, like we did earlier, we bind the query to the DataSource property of the DataGridView control.

Running the Application

Once you have added the code, run the application. When the form displays, it will list the first name of everyone from the Contact table, in alphabetical order, whose last name begins with the letter G. Scroll down in the list until you see those contacts whose first name is Scott. Select the second Scott. This contact's Employee information will then display in the grid, as seen in Figure 10-6.

You will notice that I have added a label on my form that displays the ContactID of the selected contact. You'll also notice that as you select other names in the list box that their associated Employee information does not display in the grid. That is because they don't have any Employee information. Our query in the Load event doesn't look for contacts who have related Employee information. We can fix that by joining the Contact table to Employee table as follows:

```
var query = from c in context.Contact
            join emp in context.Employee on c.ContactID equals emp.Contact.ContactID
            where c.LastName.StartsWith("G")
            orderby c.FirstName
            select new { c.ContactID, c.FirstName, c.LastName };
```

This query will return only eight rows because we are still looking for contacts whose last name begins with the letter G. Comment the where clause out in the query to remove the query filter.

Figure 10-6. *Contact and Related Employee Information*

Through these examples you can see how easy and flexible the code-only approach is compared to database-first and model-first.

Overcoming Restrictions in EF 3.5

When dealing with entity classes with EF 3.5, developers were faced with some restrictions that made it fairly difficult for developers to implement EF-friendly technology. These constraints included the following:

- Developers needed to implement IPOCO interfaces such as IEntityWithKey, IEntityWithChangeTracker, and IEntityWithRelationships.

- Entity classes needed to be sub-classes of EntityObject.

These restrictions made it difficult for developers to build domain classes that were persistence-ignorant, requiring developers to inherit and implement interfaces and base classes that were needed for persistence.

EF 4.0 overcomes this by utilizing the Entity Framework to query these instance types simply by using POCO, getting all of the regular EF functionality such as change tracking, FK associations, lazy loading, and complex-type support automatically.

The next section will talk about these features in detail and how to implement this functionality using POCO.

Additional POCO Information

Microsoft put a lot of effort into supporting POCO in the Entity Framework. They wanted to ensure that your experience with POCO would be a good one, and, therefore, they made sure that much of the functionality you get with the other facets (model-first and database-first) are also found in code-first. This section will discuss using complex types, lazy loading, and change tracking.

Complex-Type Support

As you become familiar with the code-only approach you will soon learn that much of the functionality found in the other facets is just as available in code-only. Complex types are an example of that. They are supported in POCO just as they are with the normal EntityObject-based entities.

The process for using complex types is quite simple. Let's walk through a quick example. Add a new class to the CodeOnlyData project called AdditionalContactInfo. In the class, replace the code that is there with the following:

```
using System;
using System.Collections.Generic;
using System.Linq;
using System.Text;
using System.Data;

namespace CodeOnlyData
{
    public class AdditionalContactInfo
    {
        public string CellPhone { get; set; }
        public string WorkPhone { get; set; }
        public string Fax { get; set; }
        public string EmailAddress2 { get; set; }
    }
}
```

This code is fairly straightforward. We simply declare four properties. So how do we tie that to the Contact? We tie it to the Contact by adding the highlighted line of the following code to the Contact class.

```
public Guid rowguid { get; set; }
public DateTime ModifiedDate { get; set; }
public ICollection<Employee> Employees { get; set; }
public AdditionalContactInfo AddtlContInfo { get; set; }
```

We can then query it normally just like we did when working with complex types in the normal EntityObject-based entities, such as the following query. The following code queries the complex-type filtering on the EmailAddress2 property of the AdditionalContactInfo class.

```
var query = from c in context.Contact
            where c.AddtlContInfo.EmailAddress2 == "headgeek@hotmail.com"
            select c;
```

It's not too difficult, really. It's much different than in EF 3.5 where you had to add complex types manually to the CSDL. With EF 4.0 it is as simple as creating a class and defining properties. However, there are two points that need to be mentioned when working with POCO complex types:

- Complex types must be classes. You cannot use structs.

- Inheritance is not allowed with complex-type classes.
Other than that, you are off and running!

Lazy Loading

This simply means going back to the database to get data related to data your current query has already returned. An example of this would be a customer/orders scenario. You already have the customers loaded, but you want their orders. So now you go back to the database to get orders for a particular customer. Lazy loading means that this trip to the database to get the sales information has happened automatically.

You'll be pleased to know that POCO supports deferred/lazy loading. And it is really quite easy to implement. It is a two-step process. The first step is to enable it on the context by setting the DeferredLoadingEnabled property to true, as shown in the following code snippet:

```
context.ContextOptions.LazyLoadingEnabled = true;
```

The next step is to set the property that you would like lazily loaded as virtual. For example, we can set the Contacts to load lazily by setting the Contact property to virtual as shown by the following highlighted code.

```
public Guid rowguid { get; set; }
public DateTime ModifiedDate { get; set; }
public virtual Contact Contact { get; set; }
public int ContactID { get; set; }
```

Properties that can be tagged as virtual can be any collection that implements ICollection<T> or can be referenced in a 1/0..1 relationship.

■ **Note** You are probably asking why we need to tag specific properties as virtual. Marking collection properties and relationships as virtual allows the Entity Framework to runtime proxy instance for all POCO types. These proxy types are what perform the lazy loading automatically. Based on a typed derived from the POCO entity class, the proxy instance allows all the functionality provided by the class to be preserved, allowing you to write persistence-ignorant code even though you might be required to maintain deferred loading.

Change Tracking

You might think that implementing change tracking is difficult using POCO—au contraire! We spoke about proxy creation a second ago, and it applies equally here in that they are utilized for change tracking.

Since our objects are persistence-ignorant and proxy creation is enabled, these objects implement IEntityWithChangeTracker automatically at runtime. This runtime implementation enables any persistence-ignorant object to be tracked, automatically, the same way that normal EDM, code-generated objects track objects. However, to enable change-tracking functionality, our objects must meet the requirements outlined here:

- A custom data class must be declared with public access.

- A custom data class cannot be declared as a sealed class (NotInheritable in Visual Basic) or abstract class (MustInherit in Visual Basic).

- A custom data class cannot implement the IEntityWithChangeTracker or IEntityWithRelationships interfaces.

- Custom data classes must implement a default constructor with no parameters.

- Properties mapped to a conceptual model entity type property must be public.

- Navigation properties defined in the conceptual model must correspond to a navigation property in the custom data class. These properties must be declared as virtual (Overridable in Visual Basic) in order to support lazy loading.

- The "many" end of a relationship representing a navigation property must return an ICollection<T> type, where the *T* represents the object at the other end of the relationship.

- Complex properties in the conceptual model must be mapped to a property in the custom data class that returns a reference type.

- Mapped entity type properties must implement get and set accessors.

- The name of the entity type must be the same as the custom data class. Properties of the entity type must map to a public property in the custom data class. Type names and mapped property names must be equivalent.

- You must use the CreateObject method on the ObjectContext when creating a new object when creating a proxy type with your object.

You saw an example of many of these requirements in the previous example. For instance, all the data classes were declared as public, did not implement the IEntityWithChangeTracker or IEntityWithRelationships interfaces, and implemented a default constructor, such as the following:

```
public class Employee
{
    public Employee() { }
    public int EmployeeID { get; set; }
    public string NationalIDNumber { get; set; }
```

You also saw that ICollection<T> was used in several places representing relationship ends, as well as other requirements that were followed in order to utilize change tracking.

You can also disable proxy creation by utilizing the ProxyCreationEnabled property on the context, as follows:

```
Context.ContextOptions.ProxyCreationEnabled = false;
```

By default, this property is enabled. It is also recommended that you disable proxies before serializing your persistence-ignorant objects to another tier. The downside to disabling proxy classes is that you are not responsible for managing your own change tracking. Changes can be detected by comparing snapshots of current values against the values in the initial snapshot (when your objects are first loaded into the context).

Finishing the Example

The example we started this chapter with was quite simple and showed a simple one-to-many relationship. Let's add to it a bit more to show the other relationship types and how these can be accomplished using POCO.

In the Data project, add four more classes. Add the following two to the Data project:

- SalesPerson.cs

- SalesTerritory.cs

Next, add the following two to the UI project:

- SalesPersonConfiguration.cs

- SalesTerritoryConfiguration.cs

In SalesPerson.cs, replace the existing code with the following:

```
using System;
using System.Collections.Generic;
using System.Linq;
using System.Text;
using System.Data;

namespace CodeOnlyData
{
    public class SalesPerson
    {
        public SalesPerson() {}
        public int SalesPersonID { get; set; }
        public int TerritoryID { get; set; }
        public decimal SalesQuota { get; set; }
        public decimal Bonus { get; set; }
        public decimal CommissionPct { get; set; }
        public decimal SalesYTD { get; set; }
        public decimal SalesLastYear { get; set; }
        public Guid rowguid { get; set; }
        public DateTime ModifiedDate { get; set; }
        public virtual Employee Employee { get; set; }
        public virtual SalesTerritory SalesTerritory { get; set; }
    }
}
```

This code is not that different from the classes we defined for Contact and Employee. In this code we define the SalesPerson entity with the appropriate properties. Notice also that we define the Employee property and SalesTerritory property that will be used for our navigation properties.

Next comes the SalesTerritory.cs. Open that class and replace existing code with the following:

```
using System;
using System.Collections.Generic;
using System.Linq;
using System.Text;
using System.Data;

namespace CodeOnlyData
{
    public class SalesTerritory
    {
        public SalesTerritory() {}
        public int TerritoryID { get; set; }
        public string Name { get; set; }
        public string CountryRegionCode { get; set; }
        public string Group { get; set; }
```

```
        public decimal SalesYTD { get; set; }
        public decimal SalesLastYear { get; set; }
        public decimal CostYTD { get; set; }
        public decimal CostLastYear { get; set; }
        public Guid rowguid { get; set; }
        public DateTime ModifiedDate { get; set; }
        public virtual SalesPerson SalesPeople { get; set; }
    }
}
```

In this code we define the SalesTerritory entity with the appropriate properties. Notice also that we define the SalesPerson property that will be used for our navigation property.

The model we are going after is one like Figure 10-7, if we were to model this conceptually via the EDM. However, we are able to do this via POCO using the four classes we defined throughout this chapter.

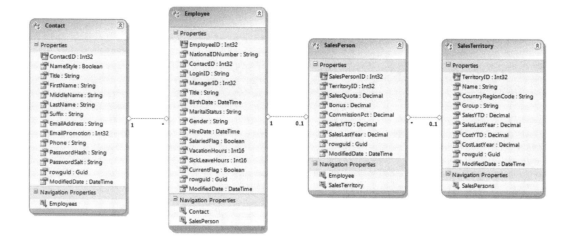

Figure 10-7. Desired model

The next thing to do is to define the configuration for these two class entities. In the SalesPersonConfiguration.cs class, replace what is there with the following:

```
using System;
using System.Collections.Generic;
using System.Linq;
using System.Text;
using Microsoft.Data.Objects;
using CodeOnlyData;

namespace CodeOnlyUI
{
    class SalesPersonConfiguration : EntityConfiguration<SalesPerson>
    {
        public SalesPersonConfiguration()
```

```
        {
            // add the appropriate items
        }
    }
}
```

Do the same with SalesTerritoryConfiguration.cs.

```
using System;
using System.Collections.Generic;
using System.Linq;
using System.Text;
using Microsoft.Data.Objects;
using CodeOnlyData;

namespace CodeOnlyUI
{
    class SalesTerritoryConfiguration : EntityConfiguration<SalesTerritory>
    {
        public SalesTerritoryConfiguration()
        {
            // add the appropriate items
        }
    }
}
```

The next task is to update the RegisterConfig method on the form. Add the following two lines to the RegisterConfig method:

```
builder.Configurations.Add(new SalesPersonConfiguration());
builder.Configurations.Add(new SalesTerritoryConfiguration());
```

You are not quite done. You are looking at these two configuration classes thinking that something is missing. You are correct. Your homework assignment is to fill in these two configuration classes with the appropriate properties and relationships. You can also modify the form to include the SalesPerson and SalesTerritory information. It is up to you how you want to add this information.
If you run into problems you can find finished solutions in the download for this book in the Chapter10 folder.

■ ■ ■

CHAPTER 11

N-tier Development
with WCF Data Services

We have spent the entire book so far walking through examples that illustrate how to work with data in a connected state, that is, making a direct connection to the database and working with data in a direct fashion. While this works in many cases, it is no secret or mystery that more and more business and applications require that they work in a disconnected, n-tier environment to support the ever-expanding SOA (service-oriented architecture) arena.

Microsoft seriously entered the fray with .NET Fx 3.0, releasing Windows Communication Foundation (WCF), which has been rapidly gaining acceptance as the .NET technology of choice to build rapid SOA applications that provide communication capabilities across the enterprise as well as the web.

Not far behind came .NET Rich Internet Application (RIA) Services, which provided a simplified approach to developing n-tier applications on ASP.NET and Silverlight platforms. .NET RIA Services is aimed at providing a simple pattern for developing middle-tier application logic focused on controlling data access by managing data access for queries, changes, and custom operations.

ADO.NET Data Services, on the heels of WCF and .NET RIA Services (and not to be forgotten), provides developers the ability to create and access data services for the web by exposing data as resource-addressable via URIs. ADO.NET Data Services also employs the use of the Entity Data Model and entity-relationship conventions to expose underlying sources as entities, thus allowing developers to work in the familiar entity concept.

Over the last few years Microsoft has realized that there is some commonality among these three technologies and has spent some serious time working to better support the types of applications that require hearty and flexible solutions. As such, Microsoft has made some name changes to better align these technologies. Thus, ADO.NET Data Services is now WCF Data Services and .NET RIA Services is now WCF RIA Services. That's right—Microsoft is building what they call a "one-stop shop" for architecting and deploying services and n-tier applications.

This chapter, therefore, will focus on WCF Data Services, beginning with a discussion on how to create and test a data service on top of a relational database using the Entity Framework. We will look at the WCF Data Service functionality and several examples of how you can use WCF Data Services to look at the underlying data.

We will then spend the remaining part of this chapter walking through an example that consumes the service, and then use that service to query the relational database using a WinForms front end to display the data.

Building the WCF Data Service

All of the examples in the book up to this point have primarily begun by creating a WinForms application in which to house the data model. As was mentioned earlier, this approach might work in some cases when the requirements of an application do not call for operating in a disconnected mode, i.e., in an n-tier environment. This chapter's example, however, is going to change direction a bit because it will allow us to look at how the WCF Data Service interacts with the EF. We'll also look at the functionality their interaction provides.

To begin, open Visual Studio 2010 and create a new ASP.NET Web Application project, as shown in Figure 11-1.

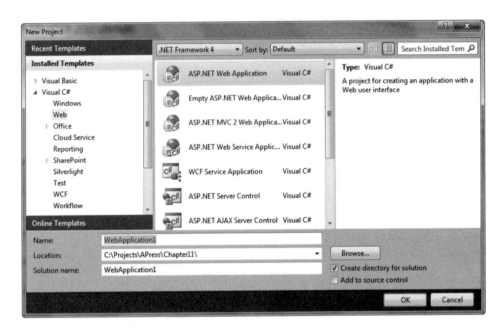

Figure 11-1. *Creating the ASP.NET web application*

I have kept the default project name in Figure 11-1, but you are free to change it. Click OK on the New Project dialog. Once the project is created, we now have an empty and non-functional web application. However, we are quickly going to make it functional with very little code.

As you have done many times before, add an ADO.NET Entity Data Model to the project. In the Add New Item dialog, shown in Figure 11-2, name the model AWModel and click Add. For this example we are going to generate our model of the AdventureWorks database.

Create a connection to the AdventureWorks database if you have not already done so, and continue through the wizard until you get to the step in the wizard in which you choose the database objects to include in your model. We are going to select only a few tables that will help demonstrate the WCF Data Services functionality.

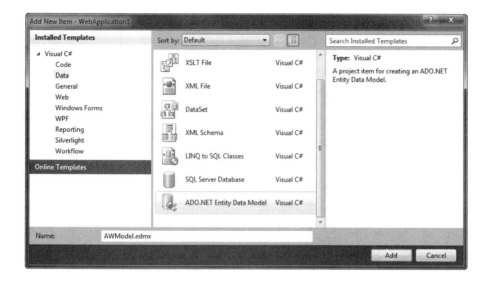

Figure 11-2. Adding the ADO.NET Entity Data Model

In the Choose Your Database Objects step of the wizard, select the following tables:

- HumanResources.Employee
- HumanResources.EmployeeAddress
- Person.Address
- Person.Contact
- Person.StateProvince
- Purchasing.PurchaseOrderHeader
- Sales.SalesPerson
- Sales.SalesTerritory

As shown in Figure 11-3, keep the pluralization and foreign key options checked, enter the value AdventureWorksModel for the model namespace, and then click Finish. We do not need any stored procedures or views for this example. At this point all we have is an ASP.NET Web Application containing an Entity Data Model. We really don't have anything functional yet, but we are at the point where we can introduce the WCF Data Services component, so let's do that.

■ **Note** The entity connection setting in the Choose Your Data Connection step of the wizard should default to AdventureWorksEntities. Change it to this value if it does not default properly, since the code examples in this chapter will state this value and it will be easier to follow along and debug your application if you keep to the same value.

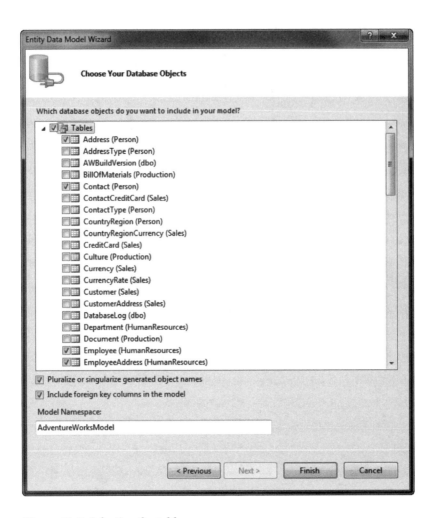

Figure 11-3. Selecting the tables

Right-click on the project in Solution Explorer and add a new item to the project. When the Add New Item dialog appears, select the Web option, then scroll down in the list of installed templates until you see ADO.NET Data Services template. Give this object the name of AWService.svc as shown in Figure 11-4, and then click Add.

Figure 11-4. Adding the ADO.NET Data Service to the project

Adding the ADO.NET Data Service to your project does several things. First, as you can see in Figure 11-5, it adds a number of namespace references to your project. Highlighted in Figure 11-5 is one of those, System.ServiceModel. That namespace contains all of the classes and interfaces necessary to build services and client applications in n-tier environments. Also added to the project by the ADO.NET Data Service template are the following references:

- System.Data.Services
- System.Data.Services.Web
- System.Data.Entity
- System.ServiceModel.Web

You are probably looking at this list thinking that the System.Data.Entity reference is added when you add an Entity Data Model to your project. That is true. However, if you add the Data Service to your project first (prior to adding the Entity Data Model), then the System.Data.Entity reference will also be added automatically.

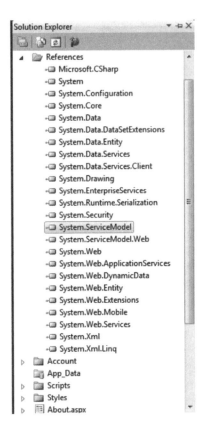

Figure 11-5. System.ServiceModel *namespace*

The second thing that was added by the ADO.NET Data Service template is, obviously, the service itself. Shown in Figure 11-6, the service is composed of AWService.svc and the supporting AWService.svc.cs file. You can't open and modify the .svc file directly. In fact, if you double-click the .svc file, the effect will be to open the underlying .cs file. However, if you right-click the .svc file, then select Open With, and then select XML Editor, you will see that the .svc file is simply an XML file consisting of a single line. Unlike the Entity Framework and the EDM where you can make changes to the underlying XML, Microsoft (and I, as well) highly recommend you don't modify the .svc file and its XML. This is simply because modifying the .svc file does not provide any benefits.

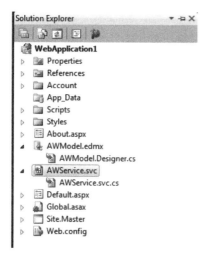

Figure 11-6. The AWService WCF Service

When the ADO.NET Data Service is added to our project, the associated .cs file will automatically be displayed in the IDE. Figure 11-7 shows that file, and what the ADO.NET Data Service template has generated for us. The result is basically the beginning of our data service.

```
AWService.svc.cs ×
WebApplication1.AWService                              InitializeService(DataServiceConfiguration config)
1   using System;
2   using System.Collections.Generic;
3   using System.Data.Services;
4   using System.Data.Services.Common;
5   using System.Linq;
6   using System.ServiceModel.Web;
7   using System.Web;
8
9   namespace WebApplication1
10  {
11      public class AWService : DataService< /* TODO: put your data source class name here */ >
12      {
13          // This method is called only once to initialize service-wide policies.
14          public static void InitializeService(DataServiceConfiguration config)
15          {
16              // TODO: set rules to indicate which entity sets and service operations are visible, updatable, etc.
17              // Examples:
18              // config.SetEntitySetAccessRule("MyEntityset", EntitySetRights.AllRead);
19              // config.SetServiceOperationAccessRule("MyServiceOperation", ServiceOperationRights.All);
20              config.DataServiceBehavior.MaxProtocolVersion = DataServiceProtocolVersion.V2;
21          }
22      }
23  }
100 %
```

Figure 11-7. Data Service shell

As you can see in Figure 11-7, the template also generates some instructions for us, which provide us some direction as to what we need to do next. The first thing we need to do is wire up our data service to our data model so that the service knows where to get its data. We know where to do this because, as you can see in the highlighted code in Figure 11-7, the code tells us where. Thus, replace the code comment with the name of the AdventureWorksEntities (see the note a few pages back regarding this value). When you have made the change, the public class line of code will look like the following:

```
public class AWService : DataService< AdventureWorksEntities >
```

Wiring up our data service to the model is as simple as that. Believe it or not, we are ready to test our service.

Testing the WCF Data Service

Testing our WCF Data Service provides us not only the chance to see if our little application works, but also the opportunity to explore some of the WCF Data Service functionality and the interaction between EF and the WCF Data Service. You will also see why we built this project in an ASP.NET Web Application.

Press Ctrl + F5 to compile and run the project. When the project runs, the web browser will open and display what you see in Figure 11-8.

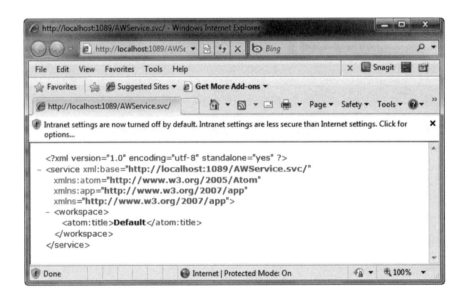

Figure 11-8. Initial test results

On the surface the results in Figure 11-8 really don't tell us much, except for the fact that we have a REST-based (REpresentational State Transfer) service running on top of our database using the Entity Framework. That's still very cool, though.

Yet, our output in the browser isn't showing us what we want. What we really want to see is data from the database. We don't see data because, by default, the WCF.NET Data Service is secured. The WCF Data Service needs to be told explicitly which data you want to see. The instructions in the code tell us this, as you can see in Figure 11-7, in the TODO comment. Some examples are even provided in the comments to help us out. But the comment is there as a reminder. We still have to do some work. Let's choose to not restrict anything in our example. Instead, we'll unlock all the entities. We do that by adding the highlighted code below to the InitializeService method:

```
public static void InitializeService(DataServiceConfiguration config)
{
    // TODO: set rules to indicate which entity sets and service operations are visible,↩
updatable, etc.
    // Examples:
    // config.SetEntitySetAccessRule("MyEntityset", EntitySetRights.AllRead);
    // config.SetServiceOperationAccessRule("MyServiceOperation",↩
 ServiceOperationRights.All);
    config.SetEntitySetAccessRule("*", EntitySetRights.All);
    config.DataServiceBehavior.MaxProtocolVersion = DataServiceProtocolVersion.V2;
}
```

The highlighted code sets the permissions for the specified entity sets in our model. The SetEntitySetAccessRule method takes two parameters. The first parameter is the entity we want to set permissions for, and the second parameter is the access rights to be granted to this resource (entity).

By specifying the value of * in the first parameter, we are specifying that we want to set permissions for all entity sets. The second parameter takes the EntitySetRights enumeration, which contains the following members:

- *None*: Denies all rights to data access

- *ReadSingle*: Authorizes read rights to single items

- *ReadMultiple*: Authorizes read rights to sets of data

- *WriteAppend*: Authorizes create rights on data items in data sets

- *WriteReplace*: Provides rights to replace data

- *WriteDelete*: Authorizes deletes on data items from data sets

- *WriteMerge*: Authorizes rights to merge data

- *AllRead*: Authorizes read data rights

- *AllWrite*: Authorizes write data rights

- *All*: Authorizes read, create, update, and delete rights on data

In our example we used the All enumeration to allow all rights to all entity sets. Run the application again, and when the web page appears you will see that you get back a list of all the entity sets in the underlying model, as shown in Figure 11-9.

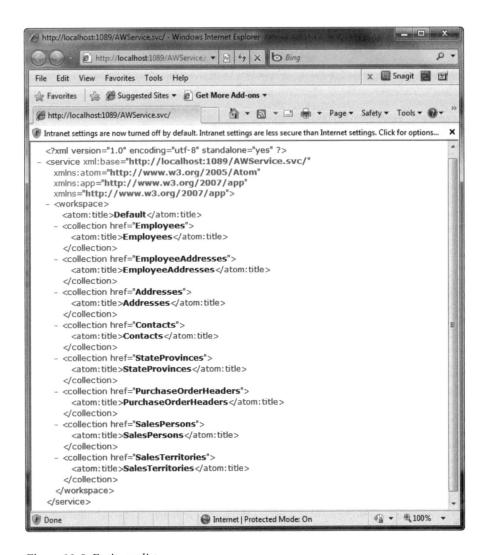

Figure 11-9. Entity set list

Earlier we mentioned that the WCF Data Service worked by exposing data as resource addressable via URIs, and to see the data we can use any of the URIs in Figure 11-9.

By utilizing the exposed URIs we can explore the data in the underlying model. For example, let's look at the SalesTerritory data by using the associated URI for that entity set and add it to the URI for this page. By using the appropriate URI, shown in Figure 11-10, we get a list of all the sales territories.

Figure 11-10. *Sales territories*

One of two things is going to happen when you try to browse the sales territories. You will either get a list of all the sales territories like you see in Figure 11-10, or you will get a page like that in Figure 11-11, indicating that we are receiving an RSS feed of sales territories.

Figure 11-11. RSS feed page

To fix the RSS feed issue we need to turn off the RSS Feed feature in Internet Explorer. With IE open, select Options from the Tools menu to open the Internet Options dialog. This dialog has a number of tabs along the top, which you might be familiar with. Select the Content tab and on that tab click the Settings button under Feeds and Web Slices.

Clicking the Settings button will display the Settings dialog, and on this dialog you need to uncheck the Turn on feed reading view checkbox, shown in Figure 11-12. Click OK on this dialog and the Internet Options dialog.

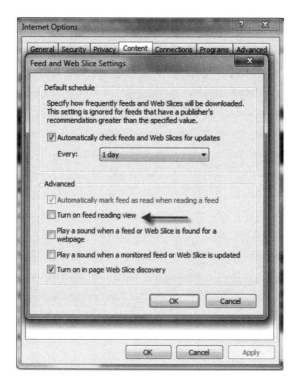

Figure 11-12. Turning off feed reading view

Back on our web page, press F5 to refresh the page. What you should get back now is a collection of sales territories like that shown earlier in Figure 11-10. The source for that list is a query against the underlying database for the sales territories.

We are not done exploring all of the service functionality yet—there is still so much more we can do here. For example, the page you are currently looking at displays all the sales territories, but what if we want to return a specific territory?

Looking at the data we can see that the each record contains the ID of the specific row, and we can use that to our advantage by including that in our URI. For this example, let's use Sales Territory ID 4. Modify the URI by appending the number four to the end of the URI enclosed in parentheses, as shown in Figure 11-13.

By loading the URI, which includes the ID of a specific record, I can now drill down further and return just the record I am looking for. This is just like applying a WHERE clause to a T-SQL query, in this case WHERE TerritoryID = 4. In this case I have queried the underlying store for a specific sales territory by simply passing the appropriate ID in the URI.

Figure 11-13. A specific sales territory

This is not all, however. Since our service is based on an Entity Framework EDM, we can easily navigate between entities to pull related data. For example, let's say we wanted to see all the sales people that are related to a specific sales territory. By simply appending the SalesPerson entity to the end of the URI we can navigate between entities. By taking a good look at the information in Figures 11-13 and 11-10 we can see some elements called link elements, which means that the current sales territory has a relationship to other items, such as StateProvince and SalesPerson. You can use these link items to navigate these relationships by first selecting the specific sales territory you want to work with and then including the specific link item in your URI.

Figure 11-14 illustrates how this is done. In this example we are still using SalesTerritory ID 4 and then we append the SalesPerson item to the end of our URI, which allows us to navigate the relationship between SalesTerritory and SalesPerson for the given TerritoryID.

Figure 11-14. Sales people for a selected sales territory

When refreshing the page we are presented with all the sales people associated to the selected sales territory, TerritoryID 4 in this case. You can probably guess that we can drill down even further, by adding properties to the end of the URI to bring back specific column data. After all of the examples we have done so far, I'll let you do that.

While all of this is interesting, let's take it to the next level and add a WinForms application to consume the service. This will also allow us to utilize the service and write LINQ queries using the service.

Consuming the WCF Data Service

In the last section we walked through how to create a WCF Data Service and then looked at the data using a REST-based interface. This section is going to walk you through how to consume the service built in the previous section and then use that service to query data from the underlying EF model.

The first thing we need to do is add a WinForms project to the solution. Within Solution Explorer, right-click on the solution and select Add ➤ New Project from the context menu. In the Add New Project dialog, select Windows Forms Application from the list of templates. Feel free to name the project whatever you want—I kept the default name. Click OK on the Add New Project dialog, then click OK. Your Solution Explorer should now look like Figure 11-15.

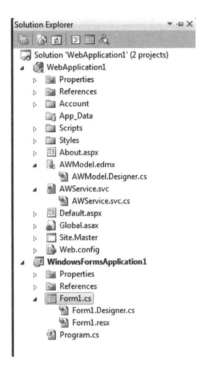

Figure 11-15. *Adding the WinForms project*

Our service at this point lives in the project we created at the beginning of that chapter, but we are working within the new WinForms project we just added. So we need something that can communicate to the service in the other project. What we need is a proxy object that we can add to our WinForms project that we can use to communicate with the service in the other project.

There are number of ways to do this, but we are going to use the easy way, which is simply by adding a service reference to our WinForms project.

Adding the Service Reference

In order to use the WCF Data Service in our new WinForms project, we need to add a proxy object that will be our communication gateway to the service in the other project. To add this proxy object, right-click on the References node in Solution Explorer for the WinForms project and select Add Service Reference, as seen in Figure 11-16.

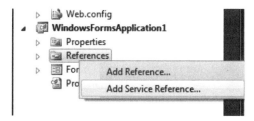

Figure 11-16. Adding the service reference

Selecting the Add Service Reference menu option, open the Add Service Reference dialog shown in Figure 11-17. This dialog allows us to find and discover services that exist in either our current solution or out on the web.

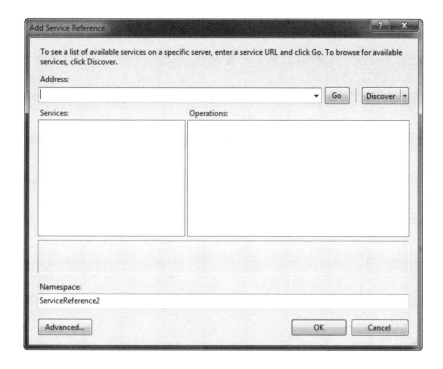

Figure 11-17. Service information

On the Add Service Reference dialog in Figure 11-17, you will see a Discover button. Later, we'll click it to find services within our solution. When we click the button, we'll select the Services in Solution option, as shown in Figure 11-18.

Figure 11-18. *Discovering the service within the solution*

You will also see a textbox in Figure 11-17 labeled "Address:". This allows us to type in a URI address to a service that exists out on the web and consume that service in our application. By typing in the URI and clicking the Go button, the application will interrogate the specified URI and look for the location of that service and any metadata for that service, and then create objects for that service.

Go ahead and click the Discover button and select Services in Solution. The application will then interrogate the solution and look for any services contained within our solution. You'll see those services displayed in the dialog shown in Figure 11-19. Click the service that we've created, named AWService.svc.

Figure 11-19. *The AWService and related types*

There is not much more to do on the Add Service Reference dialog other than providing a name for our service namespace. For the sake of this example, keep the default name. Before you click OK on the dialog, it would be wise to copy the URI displayed in the dialog, as it will come in handy shortly.

Go ahead and click OK on the dialog. Doing so will cause the Add Service Reference wizard to generate our client objects and add them to our WinForms solution.

Looking at our WinForms project now, we can see that the service proxy has been added to our solution. You can see that in Figure 11-20.

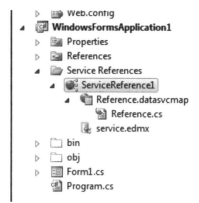

Figure 11-20. *The service in Solution Explorer*

If you haven't already done so, click on the Show All Files button in Solution Explorer, as there are files of the newly-added service that we should look at. Expand the ServiceReference1 node and you will see that some code was generated. Open the Reference.cs file and let's look at the code.

In the Reference.cs file we can see that a number of partial classes were created. The first class, called AdventureWorksEntities, represents the entire service and allows us to work at the service level. You'll also notice that a partial class was created for each entity in the remote service, allowing us to work with the entities individually. The following snippet shows such a partial class.

```
public partial class AdventureWorksEntities :
global::System.Data.Services.Client.DataServiceContext
{
    /// <summary>
    /// Initialize a new AdventureWorksEntities object.
    /// </summary>
    public AdventureWorksEntities(global::System.Uri serviceRoot) :
            base(serviceRoot)
    {
        this.ResolveName = new global::System.Func<global::System.Type,↵
string>(this.ResolveNameFromType);
        this.ResolveType = new global::System.Func<string,↵
global::System.Type>(this.ResolveTypeFromName);
        this.OnContextCreated();
    }
    partial void OnContextCreated();
    /// <summary>
    /// Since the namespace configured for this service reference
.
.
```

```
        .
        .
/// <summary>
/// There are no comments for AdventureWorksModel.Contact in the schema.
/// </summary>
/// <KeyProperties>
/// ContactID
/// </KeyProperties>
[global::System.Data.Services.Common.EntitySetAttribute("Contacts")]
[global::System.Data.Services.Common.DataServiceKeyAttribute("ContactID")]
public partial class Contact : global::System.ComponentModel.INotifyPropertyChanged
{
    /// <summary>
    /// Create a new Contact object.
```

The AdventureWorksEntities class is a logical representation of the service that we have consumed. It does not work with connections; it does not open, close, or manage any connection information. This class simply allows us to work with the service.

At this point we have consumed the WCF Data Service in our application. Now let's put that service to good use.

Utilizing the Service

Up to this point we have created our service and consumed that service within a WinForms application. Our next step is to write code to utilize the service to query the underlying data store. In the WinForms project, open the form in design view and add two buttons and a list box. Double-click the first button to view the code.

The first thing we need to do is add a using statement for the service proxy (the generated classes we just looked at), shown in the code here.

```
namespace WindowsFormsApplication1
{
    using ServiceReference1;
```

Now add the following code to the Click event of the first button.

```
try
{
    AdventureWorksEntities svc = new AdventureWorksEntities(new
Uri("http://localhost:1089/AWService.svc"));

    foreach (Employee emp in svc.Employees)
    {
        listBox1.Items.Add(string.Format("{0} {1}", emp.ContactID, emp.Title));
    }
}
catch (Exception ex)
{
    MessageBox.Show(ex.Message);
}
```

The first line of this code instantiates the class that represents the service. As part of this instantiation we need to pass it the URI of the service that we want to talk to. Remember the information

I asked you to copy from the Add Service Reference dialog? This is where you add it, as a parameter to the constructor of this class.

When you selected to discover the services within the project, the discovery came back and said that it found a service at the location displayed on the dialog. In order for your application to use the service, you need to include this URI so that your application knows which service to talk to.

The next section of code loops through the collection of employees and writes the ContactID and Title to the list box on the form, using the generated Employee type in the class we looked at earlier.

Let's run the solution (make sure you set the WinForms project as the solution startup project) and when the form displays, click button1. The list box on the form should populate with the ContactID and the Title off everyone in the underlying Employee table, shown in Figure 11-21.

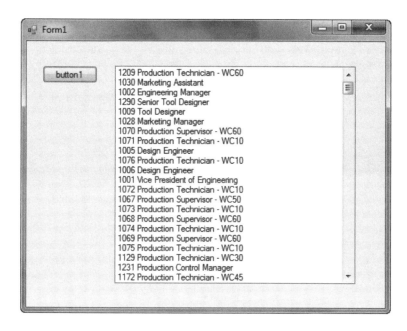

Figure 11-21. First query results

While this first example isn't very complicated, it does show how easy it is to utilize WCF Data Services in your applications. But let's build on this example a little bit because it does not illustrate any LINQ features. The next example will utilize LINQ to construct a query to pull contacts. What you should notice are the similarities between the classes created by the service proxy and the classes of an EDM. They look very similar. Additionally, because we are coding against objects, we have all the benefits of LINQ.

Let's take advantage of LINQ. Edit the Click event of the second button and add the following code:

```
try
{
    AdventureWorksEntities svc = new AdventureWorksEntities(new↵
Uri("http://localhost:1089/AWService.svc"));

    var query = from c in svc.Contacts
```

```
                where c.LastName.StartsWith("K")
                orderby c.LastName
                select c;

        foreach (var con in query)
        {
            listBox1.Items.Add(string.Format("{0} {1}", con.FirstName, con.LastName));
        }
    }
    catch (Exception ex)
    {
        MessageBox.Show(ex.Message);
    }
```

This code really isn't much different from the first example, except for the fact that we are using a LINQ to query for specific contacts. We still need to instantiate the class that represents the service and we still iterate over the results to display the information to the list box. However, the difference here is that we are using the generated classes of the service proxy to construct our query.

Run the solution and when the form displays, click button2. The list box will quickly fill with all contacts whose last name begins with the letter K, as shown in Figure 11-22.

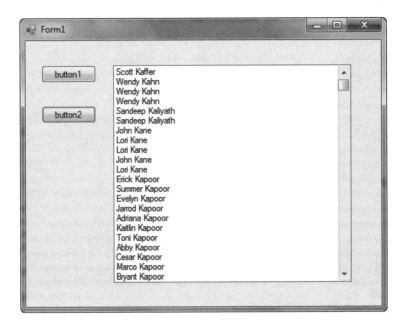

Figure 11-22. Query results using LINQ to Entities

The purpose of this chapter is to illustrate how to build n-tier applications using the Entity Framework and WCF Data Services. As you can see via the examples in this chapter, the two technologies work wonderfully together and provide a very flexible yet powerful multi-tier application solution. As you have been going through the examples in this chapter, specifically the last example, you will also notice that there really is no performance lost going through a WCF Data Service.

■ ■ ■

CHAPTER 12

Performance Tuning and Exception Handling

The majority of this book has focused primarily on the new features and enhancements to the Entity Framework, including the Entity Data Model, foreign keys, and querying concepts. For the most part we have used what the EF generated for us because Microsoft fixed and addressed a lot of issues that were apparent in EF 3.5, such as relationships and object naming. We have not covered the topic of how to handle EF specific errors within the code. Knowing how to deal with Entity Framework specific errors is half the battle, and if you know what to look and trap for, it will go a long way toward ensuring a smooth-flowing application.

This chapter will therefore focus on both of these aspects. First, we will look at how to tune your EDM by looking at object naming, relationships, and other performance aspects. Second, we will look at how to handle Entity Framework specific exceptions. By understanding the types of exceptions the EF can throw, you will know better how to approach your code.

For this chapter we will use the same project we created in Chapter 7 and that we have used since then, the EF40 project.

Updating the Model

For this chapter we need to add run an additional SQL script to add a few stored procedures that we will use later in the chapter. Open SQL Server Management Studio and open the file AddContactProcedures.sql that is found in the Chapter12 directory. This script will create three stored procedures that are used to insert, update, and delete from the Contact table. Go ahead and execute that SQL script. It will automatically select the appropriate database via the USE statement at the top of the script.

In Chapter 10 we added a few more tables to the EF40 database, but we have not yet added them to our EDM. We also need to add the three stored procedures to our model that we just added to the EF40 database. Open Visual Studio 2010 project and open the EDM. Right-click in the EDM Designer and select Update Model from Database from the context menu, shown in Figure 12-1.

We have seen this menu used in previous chapters, and it works very well. We simply want to update our model with the objects that we added to the database.

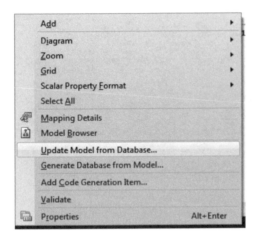

Figure 12-1. Update model from database menu item

In the Choose Your Database Objects dialog, shown in Figure 12-2, expand the Tables node and select the following tables:

- Address
- EmployeeAddress
- SalesTerritory

Expand the Stored Procedures Node and select the following:

- DeleteContact
- InsertContact
- UpdateContact

Keep the pluralization and FK checkboxes checked as shown in Figure 12-2, and click Finish. We'll use the stored procedures later in the chapter when we talk about performance tuning.

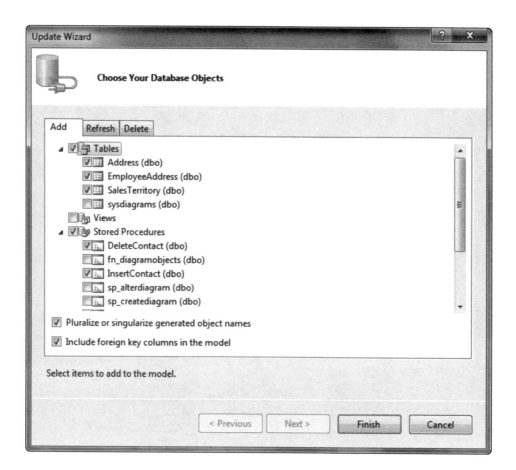

Figure 12-2. Choosing the tables

Your model should now look like Figure 12-3. Notice that our stored procedures are not added to the EDM designer, but they are definitely added to the EDM. You can see this by opening the Model Browser tab in Visual Studio and expanding the Stored Procedures node.

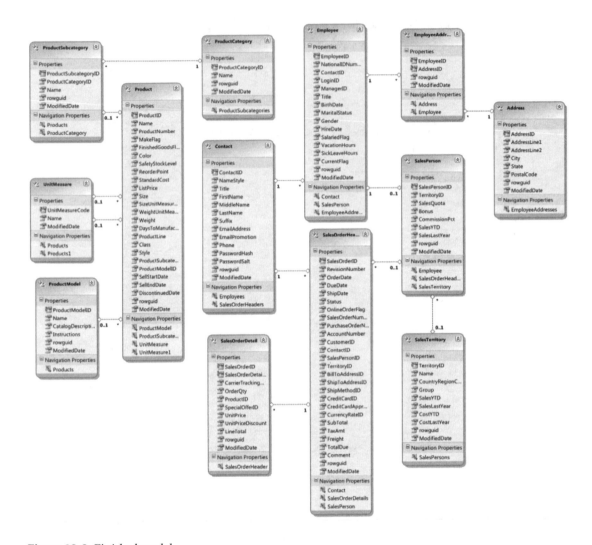

Figure 12-3. Finished model

For the most part, the Entity Framework was fairly accurate when deciding on the pluralization and singularization of the generated object names. If you recall from our discussion in Chapters 2 and 7, the "Pluralize or singularize generated object names" checkbox on the Choose Your Database Objects dialog does four things if you leave the checkbox checked:

- Makes all EntityType names singular
- Makes all EntitySet names plural
- Makes all Navigation properties singular that return at most one entity
- Makes all Navigation properties plural that return more than one entity

In our model, we left the checkbox checked, so it should do all of these things. However, as smart as the Entity Framework is, let's make sure it did its job correctly.

Checking the Model

We can now check to make sure the EntityType and EntitySet names are set correctly. Figure 12-4 shows the properties for the SalesTerritory entity. We can see that indeed the EntityType property is singular and the EntitySet name is plural. The EDM wizard is quite accurate when pluralizing names. Generally, the EDM takes anything that ends in "y" and changes it to "ies." For example, ProductCategory becomes ProductCategories, and SalesTerritory becomes SalesTerritories. For other names an "s" will be appended. For example, SalesOrderHeader becomes SalesOrderHeaders, UnitMeasure becomes UnitMeasures, and Product becomes Products. Not too complicated.

You are also free to change the Entity Set Name to something more meaningful if you like. I did not change any of the Entity Set Names simply because their pluralization names are sufficient. Changing their names would not gain anything.

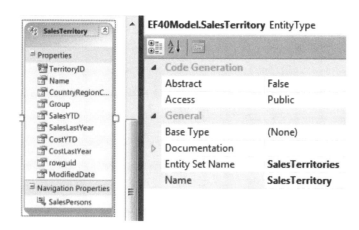

Figure 12-4. EntityType and EntitySet properties

We can also verify that the navigation properties were set properly as well, based on the previous pluralization and singularization rules. Figure 12-5 shows a section of the EDM containing five tables and three relationship types (one, many, and zero-or-one). Following the relationship rules, we can see the following:

- In the Employee entity, the EmployeeAddresses navigation property is plural because it is coming from a many side of a relationship, but the SalesPerson navigation property is coming from a zero-or-one side.

- In the EmployeeAddress entity, both the navigation properties are singular because they are both coming from a one side relationship, returning at most one entity.

- In the Address entity, the EmployeeAddresses property is plural because that property is returning more than one entity (coming from a many side of a relationship).

- In the SalesPerson entity, both the Employee and SalesTerritory navigation properties are singular because both will return at most one entity.

- In the SalesTerritory entity, the SalesPersons navigation property is plural because it returns more than one entity.

With this information, you can interrogate the rest of the navigation properties. Like most everything else, you are free to change the navigation property names. However, since they follow the rules outlined by the Designer, I have kept them the same.

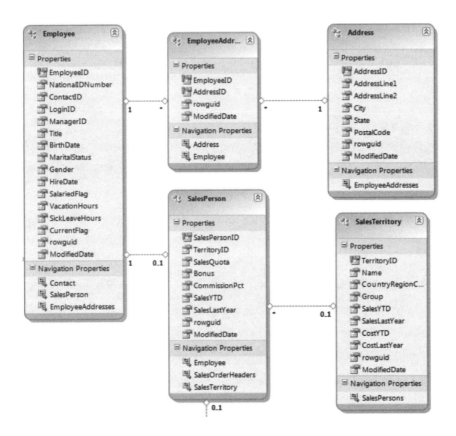

Figure 12-5. Navigation properties

If you change any names, whether it be entity, property, or EntitySet, you need to ensure that the names do not conflict with other names. For example, you can't have an entity called Contact that has a property called Contact. You can rename entities without needing to rename the underlying table. Remember, the MSL takes care of the mapping, so you can change any EDM object name and still be fine as long as you don't have name collision.

Also, be careful not to rename an object to the same name as a .NET reserved word. I'm sure this would be rare but it could happen if you're not careful.

Stored Procedure Mapping

Our model is good to go, but there is one more thing we can do to tune the EDM and improve performance. In Chapter 6 you learned about stored procedures. Using stored procedures is one of the best ways you can potentially improve performance and tune your EDM.

When we updated the model from the database, we included three stored procedures that are used to perform some CRUD (create, read, update, delete) operations on the Contact table. Let's map the insert procedure first. Select the Contact entity in the EDM and then open the Mapping Details window, then select Map Entity to Functions on the left. For the Insert Function, select InsertContact from the list.

For the Insert function there really isn't any work we have to do other than map the Result Column Bindings. This stored procedure returns the ContactID of the newly inserted row, so we need to map this value. Figure 12-6 shows what the mapping should look like.

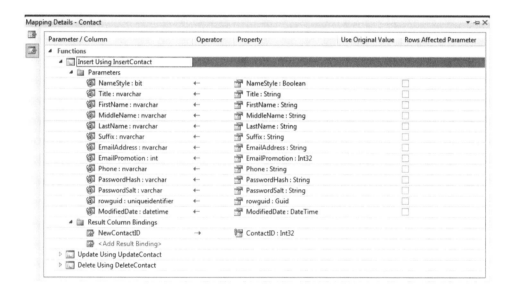

Figure 12-6. Mapping the insert procedure

Now let's map the update procedure. For the Update Function, select UpdateContact from the list. Since we are updating an existing contact, we are not returning anything, so there is no Result Column Binding. For this example we won't select the Use Original Value checkboxes, but you recall from Chapter 6 that this provides us a way to check concurrency in our application code. Figure 12-7 shows the mapping.

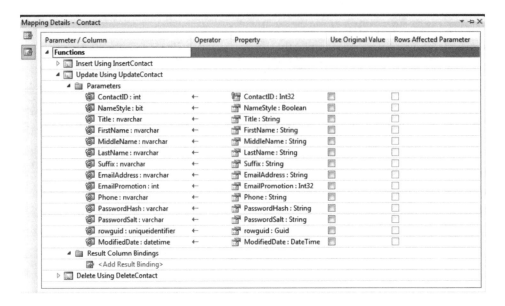

Figure 12-7. Mapping the update procedure

Lastly, let's map the Delete procedure. For the Delete Function, select DeleteContact from the list. Figure 12-8 shows what the delete mapping looks like. This stored procedure takes a single parameter, which is the ID of the contact we want to delete. Very simple.

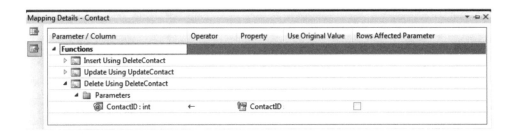

Figure 12-8. Mapping the delete procedure

At this point, you should now have an EDM that you can easily work with and normalize from a database perspective. From here let's talk about the project itself and the components a compiled project has and how to work with them.

Building an Entity Framework Project

Earlier in the book we mentioned, albeit briefly, what happens to the xml schema of the EDM (the EDMX) when the project containing the EDM is compiled. By default, the EDMX is separated into three distinct files and included as separate files within the project binary. We can see this by using a .NET reflector tool to browse the contents of the binary, as shown in Figure 12-9.

Figure 12-9. Individual schemas in the binary

When the schema files are included in the binary, the metadata portion of the connection string found in the app.config looks like this:

res://*/EF40Model.csdl|res://*/EF40Model.ssdl|res://*/EF40Model.msl

The * in the line means that schema files are included in the binary assembly. Can you change this? In other words, can you tell the assembly that you don't want to include the individual schema files in the binary assembly? Absolutely!

With the EDM open, open the Properties window. Or, right-click anywhere on the Designer window and select Properties from the context menu. In the Properties window of the EDM, shown in Figure 12-10, is a property called Metadata Artifact Processing. By default, this value is set to Embed in Output Assembly.

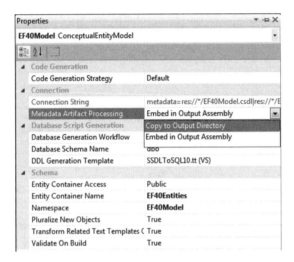

Figure 12-10. Metadata artifact processing

Changing this property to Copy to Output Directory as shown in Figure 12-10 will do two things. First, it will tell the compiler to not include the schemas in the binary assembly but to create three separate schema files in the build folder. Second, it will change the metadata string in the connection string.

Go ahead and change the Metadata Artifact Processing property value from Embed in Output Assembly to Copy to Output Directory, then save the EDM. From the Build menu in Visual Studio select Build Solution. Once the project has finished compiling, browse to the build folder, which is the bin\release folder for your project.

In this folder you will see the three schema files along with the binary assembly. These three files will have the extensions of .csdl (conceptual schema definition language), .msl (mapping schema language), and .ssdl (store schema definition language). You can see this in Figure 12-11.

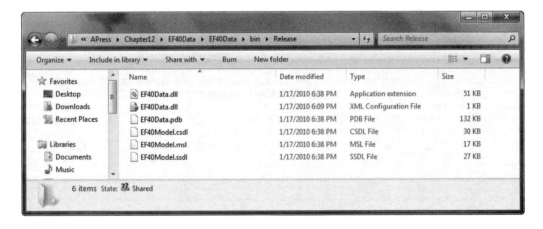

Figure 12-11. External schema files

Looking at the metadata section of the connection string of the `app.config`, you will notice that the metadata section has changed as well.

```
metadata=.\EF40Model.csdl|.\EF40Model.ssdl|.\EF40Model.msl;
```

However, you don't have to look at the `app.config` file to see the metadata changes. Whenever you change the Metadata Artifact Processing property value and then save the EDM, you can visually see the Connection String property (Figure 12-10) change accordingly. You can also copy the schema files wherever you want and specify the location in the metadata by specifying the location of the files.

```
metadata=C:\AW\EF40Model.csdl | C:\AW\EF40Model.ssdl | C:\AW\EF40Model.msl
```

So, the question is, why would you want to have the schema files outside of the binary assembly? The answer really boils down to how often you change the model after deployment. By separating the schema files from the binary assembly you provide a loosely coupled scenario. For example, non-breaking schema changes could be made on the database, such as adding a table, which allow you to modify the SSDL and MSL to reflect these changes while the CSDL could be left alone. Be careful with this. If you move these, and the `ObjectContext` cannot find them, an exception will be thrown.

Exception Handling

Let's talk about handling Entity Framework specific exceptions. Obviously we are not going to discuss all of them because that would take a really long time and be completely boring. However, we will talk about how to handle specific types of errors and the best way to approach your code to handle these exceptions.

Some of what I cover is standard .NET error handling standards, while the rest is particular to the Entity Framework. We'll begin by discussing some standard ways to trap and handle errors and then take a look at some specific EF exceptions and how the standard exception handling can help.

If you have been developing applications for any length of time you know that exceptions can be generated from the second you launch the application all the way until you close the application. The Entity Framework is no different. An exception can be generated from the moment you create your context (by instantiating an `ObjectContext`) all the way through to the point you call `SaveChanges`. We can efficiently and elegantly handle these exceptions by using `try/catch` blocks supplied by the .NET Framework.

Try/Catch Blocks

Try/Catch blocks can be the cure to many headaches when used effectively. I'm hoping all of you know how to use a `try/catch` block, but in case you are new to .NET, the basic `try/catch` block looks like this:

```
try
{
    // Do Something
}
catch (Exception ex)
{
    // handle the exception
}
```

In this example, the `try` block is where you perform any task such as instantiating an `ObjectContext` or performing some queries. When an exception is generated within the `try` block, the flow is routed to the catch block where you can obtain error information and handle it accordingly. When exceptions are generated, the program automatically looks for the catch statement block to handle the exception.

For example, the following code snippet uses the try block to instantiate an instance of the EF40Entities ObjectContext then creates a simple LINQ-to-Entities query. If an exception is generated, the flow is routed to the catch block and executes the throw statement. For those not familiar with the throw statement, it is a simple statement that is used to indicate an anomalous exception.

```
try
{
    EF40Entities context = new EF40Entities ();
    var query = from con in context.Contacts select con;
}
catch (Exception ex)
{
    throw;
}
```

More on the throw statement and how it can be used can be found here:

http://msdn.microsoft.com/en-us/library/aa664760(VS.71).aspx

Optionally, instead of using the throw statement, you could display the message using the MessageBox class (if you are within your user interface) to display the exception, such as

MessageBox.Show(ex.Message);

The following code includes a finally block, which can be included as part of the try/catch. The finally block is useful for cleaning up resources allocated in the try block as well as running and executing any code that needs to be run, despite whether there is an exception. In other words, execution control is always passed to the finally block regardless of what happens in the try block, even if no exception occurred and the catch block was not executed.

In this example, an instance of the ObjectContext is created in the try block. When program execution hits the finally block the instance is disposed of, freeing up memory, by setting the context to null (the context has been defined prior to the try block).

```
try
{
    context = new EF40Entities();
}
catch (Exception ex)
{
    throw;
}
finally
{
    context = null;
}
```

While the finally block is nice and comes in handy, there are other ways to dispose of objects, and make code a little cleaner and more efficient. The using statement provides this functionality.

The Using Statement

Instead of including a `finally` block and manually disposing of objects, the `using` statement provides a clean and convenient way of ensuring that objects are disposed of. The `using` statement automatically releases memory used to store objects that are no longer required. `using` statements can be exited automatically when the end of the `using` statement is reached or if an exception is thrown (at which point control leaves the statement block).

In the following code, the `using` statement is used to create an instance of the EF40Entities `ObjectContext`. At the end of the `using` block, all objects and resources controlled by the `using` block are automatically disposed of.

```
using (EF40Entities context = new EF40Entities())
{
    //peform a query
}
```

As such, disposing of the context manually by setting it to null is not required. The appropriate way to use the `using` block is to include it with a `try/catch` block, as follows:

```
try
{
    using (EF40Entities context = new EF40Entities())
    {
        //
    }
}
catch (Exception ex)
{
    throw;
}
```

As explained earlier, `using` statements are exited automatically when code execution reaches the end of the `using` statement or when an exception is thrown. Thus, in the previous code, the `catch` block will handle any and all exceptions thrown within the `using` statement.

Exception Class

The `Exception` class, found in the `System.Exception` namespace, is your best friend when working with exceptions. This is the class that represents errors that occur during application execution. You have seen throughout this book the use of the `Exception` class in the `catch` block to display errors. Effectively using the methods and properties of the `Exception` class can provide great insight into the error that caused the exception to be thrown.

Two of these properties are the Message property and InnerException property. The Message property should completely describe the error and explain how to correct it when possible. The value of the Message property is included in the information returned by ToString. For example, the following code will display the exception information in a message box that was thrown by the exception thrown in the `try` block.

```
try
{
    // Do Something Cool
}
catch (Exception ex)
```

```
{
    MessageBox.Show(ex.Message.ToString());
}
```

However, the keyword in the previous paragraph is the word *should*. This is where the InnerException comes in to play. The InnerException property is used to get the set of exceptions that led to the current exception. Sometimes, however, the Exception.Message property doesn't have a whole lot of information, and this is when you can find more detailed information in the InnerException. A lot of times the Message property is helpful and will tell you that you need to look in the InnerException.

```
"An error occurred while executing the command definition. See the inner exception↵
 for details."
```

Getting to the InnerException is easy, as it is a property of the Exception class. The following code illustrates how to use the InnerException property. This property also has a Message property, which contains the set of exceptions that led to the exception.

```
try
{
    // Do Something
}
catch (Exception ex)
{
    MessageBox.Show(ex.Message.ToString());
    if (ex.InnerException != null)
    {
        MessageBox.Show(ex.InnerException.Message.ToString());
    }
}
```

To see this at work, open up the code-only example of Chapter 10. Open up the Employee.cs class in the AWCodeOnlyData project and add the following line of code:

```
public int ContactID { get; set; }
```

Go to the AWCodeOnlyUI project and in the Load event of the form change the code to the following:

```
try
{
    SqlConnection conn = new SqlConnection("Data Source=SCOTT-LAPTOP;Initial
Catalog=EF40;User ID=userid;PWD=pwd");

    var builder = new ContextBuilder<AWModel>();
    Registerconfig(builder);
    var context = builder.Create(conn);

    var query = from emp in context.Employee
                select emp;

    foreach (var empl in query)
    {
```

```
            listBox1.Items.Add(empl.LoginID);
        }
}
catch (Exception ex)
{
    MessageBox.Show(ex.Message);
    If (ex.InnerException != null)
    {
        MessageBox.Show(ex.InnerException.Message.ToString());
    }
}
```

Now run the project. When the form loads you will see two errors. The first message box will tell you that you need to look at the InnerException for more information. Click OK on the first message box. The next message box now displays the real cause of the error.

OK, enough background. Let's take a look at some Entity Framework-specific errors.

Connection Exceptions

Connection issues can be cumbersome when working with the ObjectContext. The ObjectContext is created for you by default and out of the box creates three connection constructors. The following code shows the three constructors for the Chapter 12 project.

```
public partial class EF40Entities : ObjectContext
{
    #region Constructors

    /// <summary>
    /// Initializes a new EF40Entities object using the connection string found↩
 in the 'EF40Entities' section
        of the application configuration file.
    /// </summary>
    public EF40Entities() : base("name=EF40Entities", "EF40Entities")
    {
        this.ContextOptions.LazyLoadingEnabled = true;
        OnContextCreated();
    }

    /// <summary>
    /// Initialize a new EF40Entities object.
    /// </summary>
    public EF40Entities(string connectionString) : base(connectionString, "EF40Entities")
    {
        this.ContextOptions.LazyLoadingEnabled = true;
        OnContextCreated();
    }

    /// <summary>
    /// Initialize a new EF40Entities object.
    /// </summary>
    public EF40Entities(EntityConnection connection) : base(connection, "EF40Entities")
    {
        this.ContextOptions.LazyLoadingEnabled = true;
```

```
    OnContextCreated();
}
```

```
#endregion
```

The main thing to recognize here is that each constructor contains connection information relating to the entity connection string. This information maps the connection information found in the app.config file, in the <connectionStrings> section. For example,

```xml
<?xml version="1.0" encoding="utf-8"?>
<configuration>
  <connectionStrings>
    <add name="EF40Entities" connectionString="..." />
  </connectionStrings>
</configuration>
```

If the ObjectContext cannot find the corresponding name within the app.config, you will receive the following error:

```
The specified named connection is either not found in the configuration, not intended↩
 to be used with the EntityClient provider, or not valid.
```

To illustrate this, open the form in this project in design mode and add a button and a list box to the form. In the code behind the button, add the following:

```csharp
try
{
    EF40Entities context = new EF40Entities();
}
Catch (Exception ex)
{
    MessageBox.Show(ex.Message.ToString());
}
```

Next, modify the name attribute in your app.config as follows:

```xml
<?xml version="1.0" encoding="utf-8"?>
<configuration>
  <connectionStrings>
    <add name="EF40EntitiesNew" ... />
  </connectionStrings>
</configuration>
```

Run the project and click the button. You should get the same error mentioned previously.

Other connection problems could include invalid connection information. For example, in your app.config, set the connection name back to EF40Entities, and change the connection password, like the following:

```
provider connection string=&quot;Data Source=SCOTT-LAPTOP;Initial Catalog=EF40;User
ID=sa;Password=badpassword
```

Next, on the form, modify the code behind the button to look like the following:

```
try
{
    context = new EF40Entities();
    var query = from con in context.Contacts
                select con;

    foreach (var cont in query)
    {
        listBox1.Items.Add(cont.FirstName);
    }
}
catch (Exception ex)
{
    MessageBox.Show(ex.Message.ToString());
}
finally
{
    context = null;
}
```

Run the project and click the button. The error you get this time informs you that your login for the specified user is invalid.

There are several ways to handle errors such as these, but the most important thing is to gracefully handle the exceptions. For example, in your exception block you could trap for specific text in the error message returned by the exception.

```
catch (Exception ex)
{
    If (ex.Message.Contains("specified name connection"))
    {
        //log the error, inform the user, and exit gracefully
    }
}
```

We mentioned that you could compile the EDM with the schema files external to the assembly. Errors can be thrown in this case if the ObjectContext cannot find those files or the metadata tags can't be found. In cases such as these you can use the MetadataException class, as shown here:

```
catch (MetadataException ex)
{
    // throw back to calling application or handle here
}
```

The key here is that there are many errors ranging from the moment the application starts to the moment the application closes, and it all boils down to how you handle those errors.

Query Exceptions

One of the benefits of the LINQ query language is the IntelliSense and compile-time syntax checking. Thus, the opportunity for query expression errors drops dramatically to nearly non-existent. However, as good as the compiler is, while the majority of the syntax might pass the compiler check, some syntax will still fail at runtime.

Most of the offenders, i.e., runtime exceptions, are when you are dealing with dates. For example, the following compiles but shows errors during runtime:

```
var query = from emp in context.Employees
                select emp.HireDate.ToLongDateString();

foreach (var empl in query)
(
    //do something
)
```

The compiler has no problem with the previous code snippet. However, at runtime the minute you start to iterate through the returned collection you will receive an error stating that the ToLongDateString method cannot be translated into a store expression. You will also get the same exception if you use the ToShortDateString method.

As we discussed earlier, you can look to see if the InnerException property has any additional information, but in this case it does not.

However, dates are not the only culprit for this type of error. You can also receive the previous error if you are trying to convert a decimal to a string, as shown in the following code snippet.

```
var query = from prod in context.Products
                select prod.StandardCost.ToString();

foreach (var pro in query)
(
    //do something
)
```

This code compiles fine but returns the same "method cannot be translated to a store expression" exception. Now, granted, we should ask, how many times are you going to convert a decimal to a string? Probably not a lot, but the point is that there are times when query expressions won't get caught until runtime, and you need to handle them appropriately by using the try/catch block.

EntitySQL Exceptions

I prefer LINQ to Entities over EntitySQL, but if you are the opposite and prefer EntitySQL over LINQ to Entities, you will be spending a lot more of your time debugging your EntitySQL. EntitySQL exceptions generate EntitySQLException exceptions, and this typically happens when your EntitySQL expression is invalid or can't be processed by SQL.

The key to handling EntitySQL exceptions is to use the EntitySQLException class in your catch block, shown in the following code snippet. The EntitySQLException class handles exceptions due to invalid EntitySQL commands, such as when syntactic or semantic rules are violated.

```
catch (EntitySQLException ex)
{
    //handle the exception
}
```

The EntitySQLException class contains the same properties as the other exception classes discussed in this chapter, such as the Message property and InnerException property. The important takeaway is that you need to understand the type of exceptions you might be, or probably will be, dealing with and take the necessary steps to handle each type of exception appropriately, whether it is an EntityConnection or EntitySQLException exception.

There are several tools out there that assist in writing EntitySQL code. The query builder is one of them, but if you have used it at all you know that it is limited in the usable number of operators and functions. Another option is eSqlBlast, found here:

`http://code.msdn.microsoft.com/esql`

eSqlBlast is a useful tool that helps with testing EntitySQL queries and expressions prior to implementing your queries in your application code.

■ ■ ■

CHAPTER 13

Data Binding with the Entity Framework

The last few chapters have focused on new features in the ADO.NET 4.0 Entity Framework (EF), things that have been very needed and extremely beneficial to the EF. Chapter 12 focused specifically on how to use the EF in an N-Tier scenario. You can apply the knowledge and information you gained from Chapter 12 to what you learn in this chapter regarding the art of data binding with the EF.

This chapter focuses on the topic of data binding using Windows Forms and Windows Presentation Foundation (WPF). Although data binding isn't new to the EF, several enhancements have been made to the EF to make data binding much easier to work with. For example, the chapter discusses the INotifyPropertyChanged event, which is used to notify clients that a property value has changed.

You also learn about the data-binding features of Visual Studio when used with EF objects. If you're familiar with data binding with Datasets, then this shouldn't be too much of a stretch, due to some similarities; the examples you walk through in this chapter show how to bind EF query results directly to WinForms controls as well as WPF controls. The chapter also spends some time discussing binding best practices to help you get the most out of binding.

Windows Forms Data Binding

Let's get started with binding EF objects to a WinForms application. You begin by creating a project directory. Then, you create a form, add some controls to that form, and write some code to bind those controls to your data. Finally, you introduce add/delete/change functionality.

Creating a Project Directory

The first thing you need to do is create a new directory for your project. Create a new folder named Chapter 13 in the ApressSamples directory, and then copy the EF40Data project from the Chapter 7 folder into the Chapter 13 folder. Fire up Visual Studio, and open the EF40Data project from within the Chapter 13 folder.

Creating a New Form

When the project has loaded, you want to add a new WinForms project. From the File menu, select Add ➤ New Project. The New Project dialog opens, as shown in Figure 13-1.

Figure 13-1. New Project dialog

In the list of templates, select a Visual C# Windows Forms Application template, and give it the name WinFormsBinding. Make sure you set the directory for the new project to the correct location. Figure 13-1 shows the New Project dialog with the appropriate settings filled in.

When you've added the new Windows Forms Application project, you should have two projects in your solution: EF40Data and WinFormsBinding. You're not ready to start coding, because you need to do a little prep work to get the two projects in sync. First, expand the References node in the WinFormsBinding project. You need to add a reference to the EF40Data project. To do that, right-click the References node, and select Add Reference from the context menu. The Add Reference dialog opens, as shown in Figure 13-2. In this dialog, select the Projects tab, select the EF40Data project, and click OK.

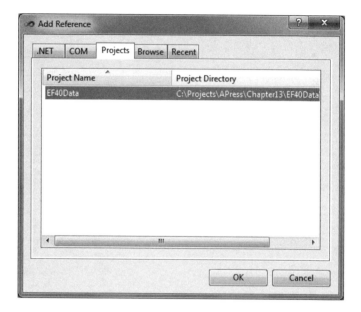

Figure 13-2. Adding a project reference

You also need to add a reference to the System.Data.Entity namespace. It contains all the EF runtime objects, so you need to be to access it from within your WinForms application. The EDM wizard automatically adds this reference for you when you add an Entity Data Model (EDM) to a project. Because your EDM is in another project (within the same solution), you must manually add that reference.

Add another reference. This time, when the Add Reference dialog appears, select the .NET tab, and scroll down in the list of components until you see the System.Data.Entity namespace. Select that, and click OK.

Next, you need to copy the app.config file from the EF40Data project to the WinFormsBinding project. To do so, right-click the app.config file in the EF40Data project, and select Copy from the context menu. Right-click the WinFormsBinding project, and select Paste from the context menu.

Your solution at this point should look like Figure 13-3, which shows the two solutions and the appropriate references to the EF40Data solution as well as to the System.Data.Entity namespace.

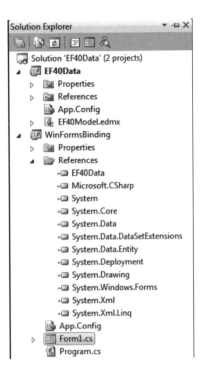

Figure 13-3. Solution Explorer

You could now start adding controls to your form—but those of you who have done data binding before know that in a binding solution, this would be fruitless, because you have nothing to bind to. Prior to adding controls to a form, you need to create data sources.

Creating Data Sources

Data sources aren't new to Visual Studio; they have been around since Visual Studio 2005 and provide an effective and efficient mechanism to bind data within your applications. A data source is, in essence, what links the data to the controls on your form.

Just as you'd use a data source to bind a Dataset or DataTable, you can equally bind entity classes. In the examples in this chapter, you see how easy it is to use the data-binding features of Visual Studio to bind dynamically generated entities.

Data binding allows you to retrieve data from a myriad of different data sources such as a service, SharePoint (new for Visual Studio 2010), directly from a database, or an object. These different data source types make data binding in Visual Studio flexible, powerful, and yet quite easy. In this example you bind to an object because you work with entity objects (object classes) with the EF.

Let's add the data source. Just like the Solution Explorer or Properties window, you should have a Data Sources window, which by default docks to the left side of the Visual Studio IDE. If you don't see the Data Sources window, you can open it by selecting Data ➤ Show Data Sources (see Figure 13-4).

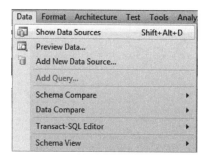

Figure 13-4. *Displaying the Data Sources window*

Figure 13-5 shows the Data Sources window.

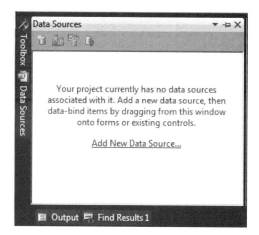

Figure 13-5. *Data Sources window*

Unless you've previously configured any data sources, the Data Sources window doesn't display any data sources and provides a link to add new data sources. Click the Add New Data Source link. Doing so starts the Data Sources Configuration Wizard.

The first page of the wizard—shown in Figure 13-6—is where you choose the data source type. You have four to choose from:

- *Database:* Binds to database objects, such as a table, though a database connection.

- *Service:* Binds and returns data through a connection to a service. Selecting this option opens the Add Service Reference dialog.

- *Object:* Provides data binding through objects, such as Datasets or entity classes.

- *SharePoint:* Provides binding to SharePoint objects through a connection to a SharePoint site.

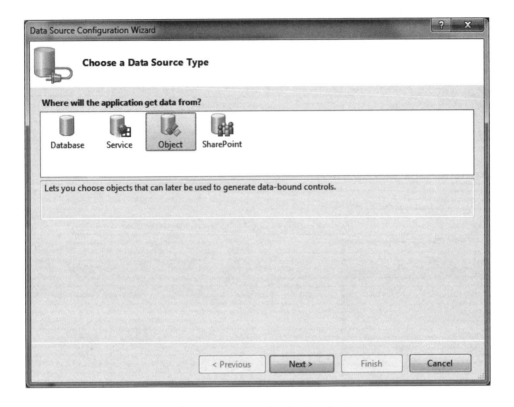

Figure 13-6. Data Source Configuration Wizard: selecting the data source type

You need to be sure you understand the differences in the way these types interact with data. Let's focus on the Database type and the Object type, which handle data binding a little differently from each other.

A Database binding source pulls data automatically when the form loads. This means no extra code has to be written to get the data and populate the binding source. Not so with an Object data source type. Although an Object data source provides class schemas to the controls and facilitates interaction with the controls, it doesn't trigger data pull. Additional code must be written to fetch the data and bind it to the binding source.

As mentioned previously, you want your form and controls to bind to entity objects; so, select the Object type, and click Next. Doing so takes you to the second step of the wizard, which displays a list of objects from which you can choose to use for data binding.

The second page of the wizard, shown in Figure 13-7, can cause a little confusion. If you don't see any objects listed, don't panic. Microsoft is keenly aware of what is going on and provides a hint: the text in the wizard informs you that you need to cancel the wizard, build/rebuild your project, and then restart the Data Source Configuration Wizard. When you get to the second page of the wizard, you see all the objects, as in Figure 13-7.

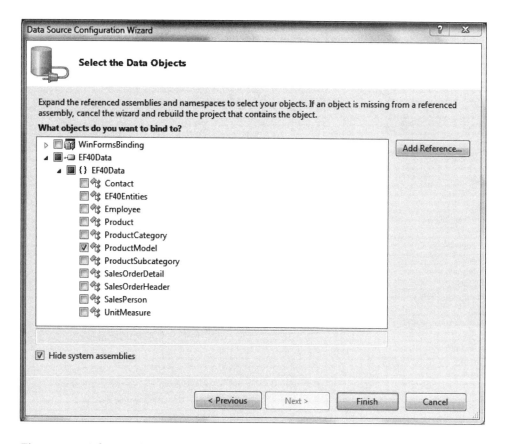

Figure 13-7. Selecting the data objects

Notice the Add Reference button. If the object you want to bind to isn't located in the immediate project, you need to add a reference to the object in order for it to appear in the wizard. Clicking the Add Reference button opens the standard and familiar Add Reference dialog, which allows you to browse to the project or .NET/COM assembly that contains the object.

Figure 13-7 shows what objects are available in your project to select for data binding. Prior to moving on, let's look at these objects. At the root node are the WinFormsBinding project and the EF40Data project. Expanding each of these nodes displays the available objects in each project that you can bind to. Because the WinFormsBinding project is brand new, there isn't anything for you to use. If you were to expand this node, you would see Form1 and Program, which represent the Program.cs file and the default Form1 that was created when the project was added.

The EF40Data node is where you want to concentrate your attention for this example. Expanding this node displays all of the entity classes that were added to your EDM, as shown in Figure 13-7.

Notice that an object is listed per entity. This is because Object data sources can't bind to a full EntityContainer. Remember that an EntityContainer is a logical grouping of entity and association sets. An Object data source can only bind to a single entity (a single class).

Again, because you're dealing with Object data sources, you need to take the extra step of actually querying the data that you then apply to the binding source at runtime. This is am important difference over the Database data source. The EF makes it easy and nearly flawless, although there are some best practices you should follow when doing data binding using the EF.

You're almost ready to start laying out your form and adding code. As shown in Figure 13-7, select the ProductModel class, and click Finish. Your Data Sources window should now look somewhat like Figure 13-8.

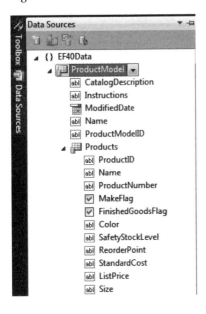

Figure 13-8. *Data Sources Window*

It's important to understand the use of the term *somewhat* in the preceding paragraph. Toward that end, let's pause and look at Figure 13-8. The ProductModel node is expanded. The Products node is also expanded under the ProductModel node.

As you can see, even though you only selected ProductModel, you also have access to the Products entity. And if you scroll down in the Data Sources window, you notice that through the Products entity, you have access to other entities as well, such as ProductSubCategory and UnitMeasure. This access is due to the associations (relationships) that are defined within the class. Through the defined navigation properties, you can easily navigate to other scalar properties in related entities. Thus, you don't need to select all the classes in the wizard; you simply select the appropriate class that you need to display on the form.

Each class (entity) also lists its available properties (columns), and you use these properties to create the form. In this example, you create a simple parent/child form in which the top portion of the form displays product model information and the lower portion displays product information related to the selected product model.

Adding Code to the Form

It's time to get to designing the form and writing some code. Open Form1 in design from the Data Sources window. From the ProductModel class, drag the ProductModelID and Name properties onto the form. Here you have the beginnings of a simple form. You notice that an extra control was placed on the form: this is the BindingNavigator, part of the System.Windows.Forms namespace, which is paired with a

BindingSource control (which appears below the form on the perimeter). You bind the results of your query the BindingSource control. The BindingNavigator provides navigation (forward, back) and manipulation (add, delete, save) for the controls on the form that the controls are bound to.

As you drag each property to the form, notice that the IDE selects the appropriate control to use on the form for each given property. In fact, you can even see this correlation between property and control in the Data Sources window (Figure 13-8); Visual Studio knows how to handle and present the appropriate control, whether the property is a string, a date, or a boolean.

Go ahead and run the project. When the form displays, no data is displayed. This is because you haven't written any code to query the data to bind to the BindingSource control. Even though you have a data source that is essentially bound to your ProductModel entity, you haven't populated the entity with any data.

In the code behind Form1, add the following bold code:

```
using System;
using System.Collections.Generic;
using System.ComponentModel;
using System.Data;
using System.Data.Objects;
using System.Drawing;
using System.Linq;
using System.Text;
using System.Windows.Forms;

namespace WinFormsBinding
{
    public partial class Form1 : Form
    {
        EF40Data.EF40Entities context;

        public Form1()
        {
            InitializeComponent();
        }

        private void Form1_Load(object sender, EventArgs e)
        {
            context = new EF40Data.EF40Entities();

            ObjectResult<EF40Data.ProductModel> pm =
                    context.ProductModels.Execute(MergeOption.AppendOnly);

            productModelBindingSource.DataSource = pm;

            grid.Rows[e.RowIndex].Cells[ProductModelName.Index].Value =
                prod.ProductModel.Name;
            grid.Rows[e.RowIndex].Cells[ProductSubCategoryName.Index].Value =
                prod.ProductSubcategory.Name;
        }
    }
}
```

This example, like the many others you've done, needs access to the context, so the first thing you do is define the context. You do this on a wider scope, not just in the Load event of the form, because you want access to the context at the form level so that you can save, delete, and delete.

In the form's Load event, you create an instance of the context, and then you use the ObjectResult class to return an object query. The ObjectResult class is the base class for the results of an object query. You're using a typed query, so you use ObjectResult<T>, which returns a typed object—in this case, the ProductModel object.

One of the important keys in this example is the use of ObjectResult for binding. Microsoft recommends binding to ObjectResult<T> to avoid repeated query executions. If you bind to an ObjectQuery<T>, you get repeated query executions during the binding process.

Rerun the application. When the form displays, you see data in the two fields on the form: Product Model ID and Name (see Figure 13-9). You can also navigate between records using the BindingNavigator control, which you see at the top of the form.

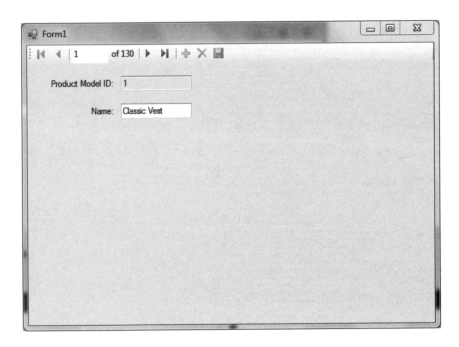

Figure 13-9. *WinForm binding step 1*

Adding a Grid Control

Your form so far is very simple, so let's spruce it up. With Form1 in design view, go back to the Data Sources window, and drag the entire Products class onto the form. When you do, Visual Studio is smart enough to realize that because you want to see all the scalar properties of the Products class, the appropriate control to use is the DataGrid. Very nice. Size the grid so that it fills the entire lower portion of the form.

Getting the Grid to Display Some Data

At this point, ask yourself whether the grid would display data if you ran the project right now. The answer to this question, or at least part of the answer, lies below the form, again in the perimeter. A new BindingSource has been added, called productsBindingSource.

Take a minute to look at the properties of the productsBindingSource control. The first thing to notice is that its DataSource property is the binding source of the product model, productModelBindingSource.

Let's answer the original question by running the application. When the form displays, you definitely see product data in the grid that is related to the selected product model. As you scroll through the records, the data in the grid changes to display the appropriate related data. This is data binding at its best. Figure 13-10 shows the form displaying the selected product model and related product information.

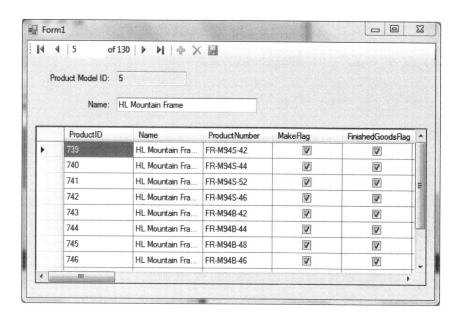

Figure 13-10. WinForm binding step 2

However, there is a problem. Scroll the grid all the way to the right, as shown in Figure 13-11. The last four columns in the grid aren't displaying the correct values, but instead are showing the type. That's not very useful. The reason is that the grid can't figure out the relation between ProductModel and Products. This is a limitation of the grid, not of the EF or binding.

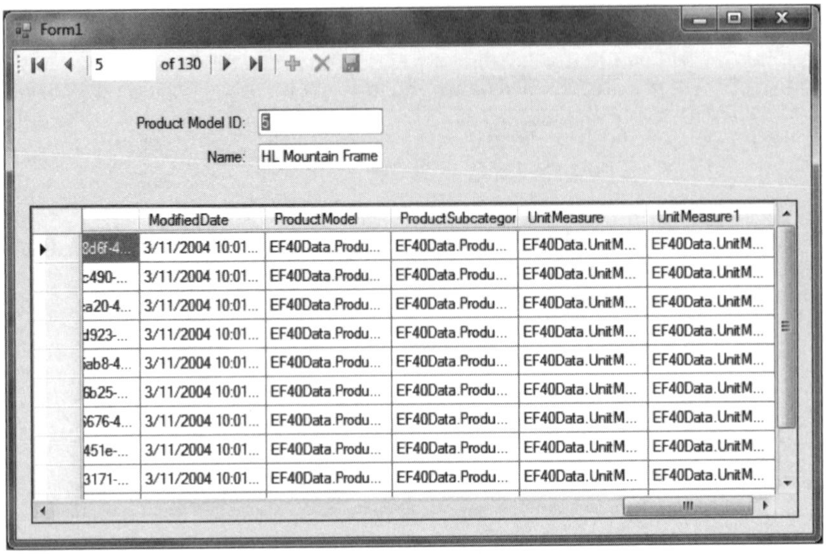

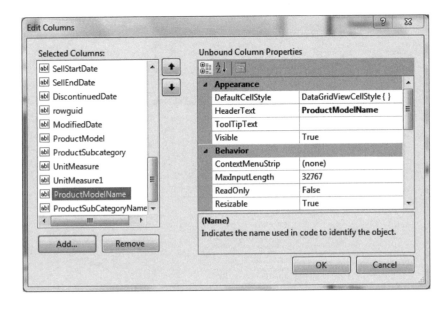

Figure 13-11. Unbound columns

The fix is simple. Stop the application, and open the form in design. Select the grid, and open its Properties window. Scroll down until you see the Columns property. Select the ellipse button for this property to open the Edit Columns dialog, shown in Figure 13-12.

Figure 13-12. Edit Columns dialog

In order to fix the columns that are displaying incorrect data, you need to add a couple of additional columns to the grid. Click the Add button, and add two additional columns: ProductModelName and ProductSubCategoryName. Then, click OK to save your changes.

You're probably thinking that based on the fact that the grid is bound to the productsBindingSource, you could have typed ProductModel.Name in the DataPropertyName property for the ProductModel column in the grid. Good guess, but unfortunately that doesn't work. The trick to addressing this issue is in the code. Let's look at that next.

Helping the Grid to Navigate the Relation

Select the grid while in design view. In the Properties window, click the Events button. In the list of events for the grid, scroll down until you see the RowPrePaint event, and double-click it. In the newly created RowPrePaint event, add the following code in bold:

```
private void productsDataGridView_RowPrePaint(object sender,
        DataGridViewRowPrePaintEventArgs e)
{
    var prod = (EF40Data.Product)(productsBindingSource[e.RowIndex]);

    var grid = productsDataGridView;

    grid.Rows[e.RowIndex].Cells[ProductModelName.Index].Value = prod.ProductModel.Name;
    grid.Rows[e.RowIndex].Cells[ProductSubCategoryName.Index].Value =
        prod.ProductSubcategory.Name;
}
```

The key here is that even though the grid is unable to figure out and navigate the relationships, you can still use the grid to fix the problem by superseding the functionality at the row and cell level. As the grid is being rendered and each row is being formatted, you can tell the appropriate cells what values to display based on the row index.

Telling the cells what values to display is exactly what the code is doing. For each row that is being painted, you grab the row index and then set each to the appropriate value by using the navigation properties.

Testing Your Final Grid Implementation

Let's test the changes by running the application again. This time, when the form displays, you should see the appropriate values when you scroll to the end of grid, as shown in Figure 13-13.

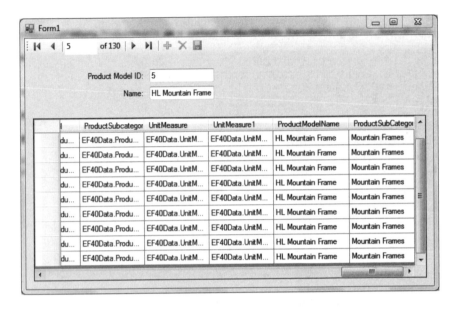

Figure 13-13. Correct values in the grid

The takeaway is the simple fact that you didn't need to write any additional code to populate the grid or any additional queries to display the correct values in the two columns you added. Nor did you have to write any additional binding logic or the grid.

Implementing Add, Delete, and Save Functionality

Before moving on to WPF, let's modify the form so that you can add and delete records. Thankfully, the modification is pretty simple. Notice in Figure 13-13 that the Add, Delete, and Save buttons are disabled. They're disabled by default; to enable them, you need to right-click each button and select Enabled from the context menu.

Having enabled the buttons, you need to write some code behind each one of them. Flip back a few pages, and look at the code in the form's Load event. Notice that you don't declare the context there, but at the form level, so the entire form has access to it. Remember that the context is what tracks changes to entities: by putting the context at the form level, you just need to add a single line of code behind each button to facilitate adding, deleting, and saving records.

Implementing Add Functionality

Adding data when working with data-bound controls takes a bit of thinking and planning but isn't too complicated. Adding new data requires the use of several methods on the form controls. When you dropped a data source for the ProductModel onto the form, a BindingSource control called productModelBindingSource was added to the form. This control has several events that allow you to properly implement adding operations for new records, as you see momentarily.

The first thing you need to do is add a few variables to the form's declaration section. The first variable declares the context you use to add new records, using the EF40Entities data model from the EF40Data project. The second variable defines the ProductModel entity to which you add a record. Last is a boolean variable that you use to determine when a new records is created. The following code snippet shows the variable declarations:

```
EF40Data.EF40Entities context;
EF40Data.ProductModel prodMods;
bool isNew;
```

The next step is to implement the isNew variable, which must be placed in the AddingNew event of the productModelBindingSource. This event is one of the events mentioned earlier. It's fired every time a new record is added to the productModel object. The following code shows the implementation of this event and the boolean variable:

```
private void productModelBindingSource_AddingNew(object sender, AddingNewEventArgs e)
{
    isNew = true;
}
```

Next, you implement the code that adds the new record. This is done via the Click event of the productModelBindingNavigationSaveItem button. In this event, you check to see if the isNew variable has the value true; if it does, you check the length of the product model name text box to ensure that the user has added a new product model. You then call the EndEdit method of the productModelBindingSource, which applies any pending changes to the underlying data source. You create a new instance of the ProductModel object, and add the new product model name to the Name property of the ProductModel object. You then add the ProductModel object to the context using the AddObject method, which adds the specified object (the ProductModel object, in this case) to the object context in the current entity set. Finally, you call the SaveChanges() method on the context and set the isNew variable to false:

```
private void productModelBindingNavigationSaveItem_Click(object sender, EventArgs e)
{
    if (isNew)
    {
        try
        {
            if (nameTextBox.Text.Length > 0)
            {
                productModelBindingSource.EndEdit();
                prodMods = new EF40Data.ProductModel();
                prodMods.Name = nameTextBox.Text;
                context.ProductModels.AddObject(prodMods);
                context.SaveChanges();
                isNew = false;
            }
        }
        catch (Exception ex)
        {
            if (ex.InnerException != null)
                MessageBox.Show(ex.InnerException.Message.ToString());
            else
                MessageBox.Show(ex.Message.ToString());
        }
    }
    else
```

```
    {
        productModelBindingSource.EndEdit();
        context.SaveChanges();
    }
}
```

Last, you implement the saving of the new record. As you've previously learned, this is accomplished via the SaveChanges method on the context. As you did in the previous code snippet, you first call the EndEdit method on the BindingSource, which applies pending changes to the underlying data source:

```
private void productModelBindingNavigatorSaveItem_Click(object sender, EventArgs e)

{
    productModelBindingSource.EndEdit();
    context.SaveChanges();
}
```

Press F5 to run the project. When the form appears, click the plus (+) button to add a new record. The Binding Navigator counter goes from 1 to 130. The Product Model ID displays a value of 0 because this is a new record: the ProductModelID column is autogenerated, and 0 is the default value for new records that haven't yet been saved to the underlying data store. Add a product model name, and click the Save button (you aren't worrying about related products yet). Clicking Save adds your new product model to the database. Querying the ProductModel table shows the new record added.

Implementing Delete Functionality

Deleting records is much easier than deleting records, fortunately. Not that adding records is extremely difficult, but deleting records is far easier. With the project running, navigate to the record you just added, click the Delete button on the Product Model Binding Navigator, and then click the Save button. Voila: the record is deleted. Clicking the Delete button removes the record from the ProductModel class within the context, and clicking the Save button calls the SaveChanges event of the context—which, as you've learned, tracks changes to entities and ushers those changes back to the database. No special code needs to be added to the underlying Click event of the Delete button because the object context handles the state of all entity objects.

Implementing Save Functionality

You've seen data being saved in several chapters, including Chapter 5, so you don't spend a lot of time on it here. Saving of records is accomplished via the context's SaveChanges method. As you learned in Chapter 5, the SaveChanges method persists all changes to the data source, whether those changes are updates, deletes, or inserts.

To wrap up this section, let's look at what you've done. You first created the data object from which the controls are bound. You then placed some controls on your form and added code that populates the controls. You made a few adjustments for those columns in the grid to address the relationship between ProductModel and Products so the appropriate foreign key values appear in the grid. You also added code to add new records.

Your homework assignment for this section is to fix the other two columns in the grid, UnitMeasure and UnitMeasure1. Both of these columns are foreign keys to the UnitMeasure table. You can use the previous example of how you fixed the columns earlier.

Let's move on to data binding with WPF.

WPF Data Binding

This section discusses binding with Windows Presentation Foundation (WPF). In this example, you focus on the sales side of things, pulling in SalesOrderHeader and SalesOrderDetail information to populate a simple WPF form.

If you've never developed an application with WPF before, don't fear. This example doesn't go deep into the intricacies of WPF (there are many great WPF books out there), but you get an idea of how to build a simple EF data binding application for WPF.

Creating a Project

Binding in WPF is quite different from a Windows form because WPF has no built-in binding controls. The first thing you need to do is create the project; in the existing solution that you've been using, choose File ➤ Add ➤ New Project. This opens the Add New Project dialog, show earlier in Figure 13-1. This time, however, you want to select the WPF Application template. Give it the name WPFBinding, and click OK.

Just like your WinFormsBinding project, add a reference to the EF40Data project to this WPFBinding project. Before you start adding code, drag a WPF list box onto the window. Again, you aren't going for a well-designed layout—you simply need a list box. In the code, I've renamed Window1 to MainWindow. You may want to do the same to avoid any confusion.

Adding Some Code

Let's add some code. Modify the code behind the MainWindow to look like the following. Notice the addition of some using statements (besides the default using statements), some variable declarations at the Window level, and some code in the Loaded event for the window:

```
using EF40Data;
using System;
using System.Collections.Generic;
using System.Linq;
using System.Text;
using System.Windows;
using System.Windows.Controls;
using System.Windows.Data;
using System.Data.Objects;
using System.Collections.ObjectModel;
using System.Windows.Documents;
using System.Windows.Input;
using System.Windows.Media;
using System.Windows.Media.Imaging;
using System.Windows.Navigation;
using System.Windows.Shapes;

namespace WPFBinding
{
    /// <summary>
    /// Interaction logic for MainWindow.xaml
    /// </summary>
    public partial class MainWindow : Window
    {
        private EF40Entities context;
        private List<SalesOrderHeader> soh;
```

```
        public MainWindow()
        {
            InitializeComponent();
        }

        private void Window_Loaded(object sender, RoutedEventArgs e)
        {
            context = new EF40Entities();

            soh = context.SalesOrderHeaders.OrderBy(o => o.AccountNumber).ToList();

            listBox1.ItemsSource = soh;
        }
    }
}
```

Running the Project

To run this project you need to set it as the default project. In Solution Explorer, right-click the WPFBinding project, and select Set as Default Project from the context menu. Press F5 to run the application. When the WPF form displays, you should immediately notice that the data in the list box doesn't look right, as shown in Figure 13-14.

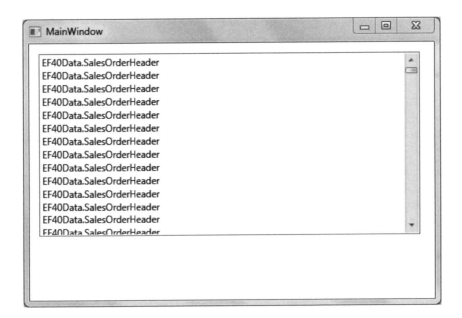

Figure 13-14. WPF main form

The problem in this example is much like the problem you had with the data grid in the previous example: the columns in the list box don't know where to get the data. Sure, you bound the list box control using the ItemsSource property, which is the method that WPF uses to bind controls. But you haven't defined the appropriate columns, nor have you defined how the columns get their data from the query results.

In essence, you haven't given the list box any specific instructions, so the list box by default calls the ToString method when trying to display objects. Thus, the list box displays the string representation of each source in the object. Displaying string representations of everything isn't very useful.

The fix to the problem of displaying string representations isn't in the code, but in the WPF XAML. Switch to design view for the window, and you should see some XML in the design window. This is where you need to make your changes.

Go to the window in design view and add the following code in bold in the form's XAML window. Your results should appear similar to those in Figure 13-15.

```
<ListBox Height="222" HorizontalAlignment="Left" Margin="12,12,0,0" Name="listBox1"
VerticalAlignment="Top" Width="599">
    <ListBox.ItemTemplate>
        <DataTemplate>
            <StackPanel Orientation="Horizontal">
                <TextBlock Width="200" Text="{Binding Path=AccountNumber}" />
                <TextBlock Text="{Binding Path=PurchaseOrderNumber}" />
            </StackPanel>
        </DataTemplate>
    </ListBox.ItemTemplate>
</ListBox>
```

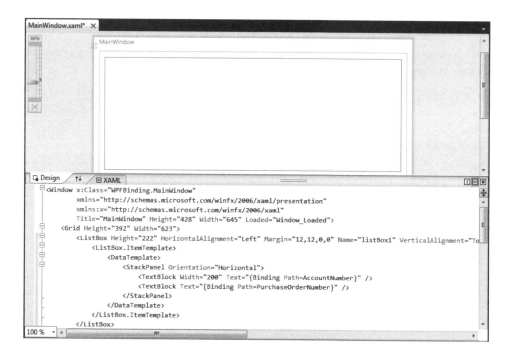

Figure 13-15. XAML window

Before you run this code to test it, let's look at what you're doing. You're adding to the list box control itself. First, you define the rows and what they look like, via the `ListBox.ItemTemplate`. The `ItemTemplate` is used to specify the visualization (visual structure) of the data objects.

Inside the `ItemTemplate`, you use a `DataTemplate`, because that is what helps you specify how each item appears in your next element, the `StackPanel`. The `StackPanel` arranges each child element into a single line that can be oriented either horizontally or vertically. In this example, you want the rows laid out horizontally.

You then use the `TextBlock` element to define your columns and display the data. However, this is just simple XAML. The key here is the `Text` property of each `TextBlock`, which allows you to specify your binding properties. The `Binding` property lets you specify where the `TextBlock` gets its data via binding. The `Path` property specifies the name of the entity property from which it's bound.

Now you're ready to run the project again. Press F5; when the form displays, you should a nice listbox with two columns that display the account number and the purchase order number, as shown in Figure 13-16.

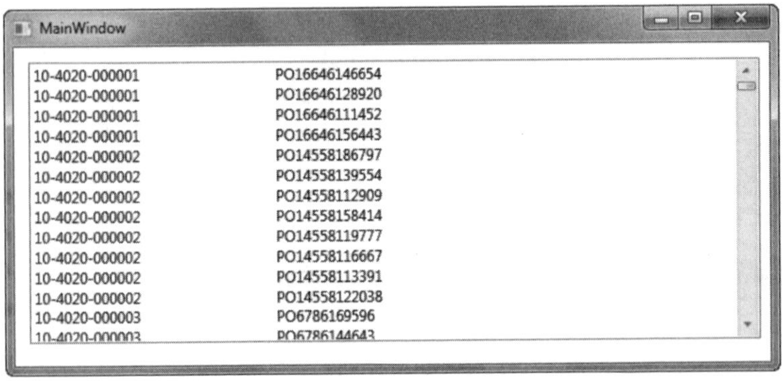

Figure 13-16. Displaying account numbers and purchase orders

The list box knows where it's getting the values because you defined that in the code. You had to define the list box columns and specify where the columns get their data.

Displaying Related Detail

As is, the form isn't very useful. It simply displays sales header information: account numbers and related purchase orders. Let's modify this window a bit to display related sales detail information. With the window in design mode, size the window so that there is extra space below the list box, and place eight labels, seven text boxes, and one combo box on the window. See Figure 13-17.

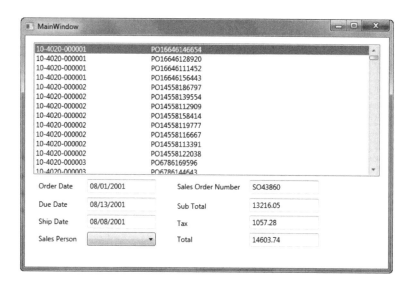

Figure 13-17. Completed form

You can modify the window so that as you select on a row within the list box, related sales order detail information is displayed in the new controls you placed in the window. Displaying the details isn't as difficult as you may imagine.

After you've placed and arranged the controls, binding them is simple. No extra code needs to be written—in fact, the only thing you need to do is modify the TextBox elements to include the binding details. The syntax from the form in the following code example shows two ways the controls can be bound.

The first method is to include a completely separate Binding child element of the TextBox element, shown in the first bold code. The second method is to include the binding within the Text property of the TextBox element, as shown in the second highlighted section of code:

```
<Label Content="Order Date" Height="25" HorizontalAlignment="Left" Margin="16,240,0,0"
        Name="label1" VerticalAlignment="Top" Width="74" Visibility="Visible" />
<Label Content="Due Date" Height="25" HorizontalAlignment="Left" Margin="16,271,0,0"
        Name="label2" VerticalAlignment="Top" Width="74" Visibility="Visible" />
<Label Content="Ship Date" Height="25" HorizontalAlignment="Left" Margin="16,300,0,0"
        Name="label3" VerticalAlignment="Top" Width="74" Visibility="Visible" />
<Label Content="Sales Order Number" Height="25" HorizontalAlignment="Left"↵
 Margin="257,240,0,0"
        Name="label4" VerticalAlignment="Top" Width="123" Visibility="Visible" />
<Label Content="Sub Total" Height="25" HorizontalAlignment="Left" Margin="257,273,0,0"
        Name="label5" VerticalAlignment="Top" Width="123" Visibility="Visible" />
<Label Content="Tax" Height="25" HorizontalAlignment="Left" Margin="257,302,0,0"↵
 Name="label6"
        VerticalAlignment="Top" Width="123" Visibility="Visible" />
<Label Content="Total" Height="25" HorizontalAlignment="Left" Margin="257,329,0,0"↵
 Name="label7"
        VerticalAlignment="Top" Width="123" Visibility="Visible" />
<Label Content="Sales Person" HorizontalAlignment="Left" Margin="16,329,0,38" Name="label8"
        Width="83" Visibility="Visible" />
```

```
<TextBox Height="23" HorizontalAlignment="Left" Margin="105,242,0,0" Name="textBox1"
        VerticalAlignment="Top" Width="120" Visibility="Visible">
    <Binding ElementName="listBox1" Path="SelectedItem.OrderDate"↵
 StringFormat="{}{0:MM/dd/yyyy}" />
</TextBox>
<TextBox Height="23" HorizontalAlignment="Left" Margin="105,273,0,0" Name="textBox2"
        Text="{Binding ElementName=listBox1, Path=SelectedItem.DueDate,
        StringFormat=\{0:MM/dd/yyyy\}}" VerticalAlignment="Top" Width="120"↵
 Visibility="Visible" />
<TextBox Height="23" HorizontalAlignment="Left" Margin="105,302,0,0" Name="textBox3"
        Text="{Binding ElementName=listBox1, Path=SelectedItem.ShipDate,
        StringFormat=\{0:MM/dd/yyyy\}}" VerticalAlignment="Top" Width="120"↵
 Visibility="Visible" />
<TextBox Height="23" HorizontalAlignment="Left" Margin="386,242,0,0" Name="textBox4"
        Text="{Binding ElementName=listBox1, Path=SelectedItem.SalesOrderNumber}"
        VerticalAlignment="Top" Width="120" Visibility="Visible" />
<TextBox Height="23" HorizontalAlignment="Left" Margin="386,273,0,0" Name="textBox5"
        Text="{Binding ElementName=listBox1, Path=SelectedItem.SubTotal,
        StringFormat=\{0:######.##\}}" VerticalAlignment="Top" Width="120"↵
 Visibility="Visible" />
<TextBox Height="23" HorizontalAlignment="Left" Margin="386,302,0,0" Name="textBox6"
        Text="{Binding ElementName=listBox1, Path=SelectedItem.TaxAmt,
        StringFormat=\{0:######.##\}}" VerticalAlignment="Top" Width="120"↵
 Visibility="Visible" />
<TextBox Height="23" HorizontalAlignment="Left" Margin="386,331,0,0" Name="textBox7"
        Text="{Binding ElementName=listBox1, Path=SelectedItem.TotalDue,
        StringFormat=\{0:######.##\}}" VerticalAlignment="Top" Width="120"↵
 Visibility="Visible" />
<ComboBox Height="23" HorizontalAlignment="Right" Margin="0,331,398,0" Name="comboBox1"
        VerticalAlignment="Top" Width="120" DisplayMemberPath="LastName"
        SelectedValuePath="ContactID" SelectedValue="{Binding ElementName=listBox1,
        Path=SelectedItem.SalesPersonID}" Visibility="Visible" />
```

Either method works—use whichever is more readable for you. The key here is the information that shows how the binding takes place. First, notice the ElementName property, which specifies the name of the binding source object. Next is the familiar Path property, which specifies the name of the entity property from which the element is bound. Last, notice that some text boxes have a StringFormat property, which specifies how to format the string when it's displayed in the text box.

Because you've already placed the controls (labels, text boxes, and a combo box) on the window, the only thing you need to be concerned about is the binding information. You're ready to test. Run the project again; and when the form displays, select the first record in the list box. The text boxes should display the related sales order detail information for the selected sales order header record in the list box.

You can test this form easily. Open the form in design view, and add a button to the form. Set the Content property to Save. In the Click event, add the following code:

```
context.SaveChanges();
```

Run the project again; and when the form displays, change the Tax value. (In my test, I changed the value from 1057.28 to 2057.28.) Watch the Total value when you click the Save button. It changes, doesn't it? The Total value is a calculated column in the database, so the fact that the field on the form updates when you change and save the Tax value shows that binding is working and that the values are being saved and updated in the database.

What you haven't done is hook up the combo box. Guess what your homework assignment is? Yep, you get to hook up the combo box. However, I won't leave you without a hint. You first need this declaration in the code behind the window:

```
private List<SalesPerson> sp;
```

Here is the code to put in the Window_Loaded event, underneath the code to get the sales order header data

```
sp = context.SalesPersons.OrderBy(s => s.SalesPersonID).ToList();
comboBox1.ItemsSource = sp;
```

Next, you need to modify the XAML code for the combo. The hint for this is that the SalesPerson information comes from the SalesOrderHeader, and you need to use the navigation properties to get to the contact info if you want to display the name of the sales person. Got it?

As you've probably gathered from this chapter, data binding with the EF is flexible and powerful regardless of the application type. There are certain nuances you need to be prepared to work with depending on the environment, as you've seen in this chapter, such as displaying relational data in grids or working with data sources in WPF. Yet regardless of what issues you may run in to, data binding with the EF makes for rapid application development with the flexibility of working with EF objects.

Index

You Need the Companion eBook

Your purchase of this book entitles you to buy the companion PDF-version eBook for only $10. Take the weightless companion with you anywhere.

We believe this Apress title will prove so indispensable that you'll want to carry it with you everywhere, which is why we are offering the companion eBook (in PDF format) for $10 to customers who purchase this book now. Convenient and fully searchable, the PDF version of any content-rich, page-heavy Apress book makes a valuable addition to your programming library. You can easily find and copy code—or perform examples by quickly toggling between instructions and the application. Even simultaneously tackling a donut, diet soda, and complex code becomes simplified with hands-free eBooks!

Once you purchase your book, getting the $10 companion eBook is simple:

❶ Visit **www.apress.com/promo/tendollars/**.

❷ Complete a basic registration form to receive a randomly generated question about this title.

❸ Answer the question correctly in 60 seconds, and you will receive a promotional code to redeem for the $10.00 eBook.

THE EXPERT'S VOICE™

233 Spring Street, New York, NY 10013

Offer valid through 8/10.